The body of the sleeper is as one dead, but the soul lives on in the fullness of its power.

— Greek philosopher Posidonius, more than 2,000 years ago

You are about to embark on the most unusual and spiritually uplifting voyage you will ever undertake. You'll travel at the speed of light to a place where all past, present, and future events occur simultaneously. You might visit foreign countries, or journey countless miles above the Earth, setting off on your very own walk across the Moon. You can even travel backward or forward in time when you discover the absolute liberation of astral voyages. Free yourself from the limitations of the earth plane and the laws of space and time, and finally discover unwavering proof of reincarnation and our divine immortality.

We all experience astral travel, whether we are conscious of it or not. It takes place every night when we sleep, during physical or emotional trauma, and at times when we are intensely focused or preoccupied with something. Out-of-body experiences are as natural to our functioning as breathing. In *Astral Voyages,* Dr. Bruce Goldberg presents dozens of time-tested techniques that train you to safely leave your physical body and explore other dimensions, near and far. Freedom from physical, mental, emotional, psychic, and spiritual entanglements is yours at last through astral travel. Get ready for the trip of a lifetime!

About the Author

Dr. Bruce Goldberg holds a B.A. in Biology and Chemistry, is a Doctor of Dental Surgery, and has an M.S. in Counseling Psychology. He retired from dentistry in 1989, and has concentrated on his hypnotherapy practice in Los Angeles. Dr. Goldberg was trained by the American Society of Clinical Hypnosis in the techniques and clinical applications of hypnosis.

Dr. Goldberg has been interviewed on shows such as *Donahue, Oprah, Leeza, Joan Rivers, The Other Side, Regis and Kathie Lee, Tom Snyder, Jerry Springer, Jenny Jones,* and *Montel Williams*; by CNN, CBS News, and many others.

Through lectures, television and radio appearances, and newspaper articles, including interviews in *TIME,* the *Los Angeles Times,* and the *Washington Post,* Dr. Goldberg has conducted more than 33,000 past life regressions and future life progressions since 1974, helping thousands of patients empower themselves through these techniques. His cassette tapes teach people self-hypnosis, and guide them into past and future lives. He gives lectures and seminars on hypnosis, regression and progression therapy, and conscious dying; he is a also a consultant to corporations, attorneys, and local and network media. His first edition of *The Search for Grace* was made into a television movie by CBS. His third book, the award-winning *Soul Healing,* is a classic on alternative medicine and psychic empowerment.

Dr. Goldberg distributes cassette tapes to teach people self-hypnosis and to guide them into past and future lives. For information on self-hypnosis tapes, speaking engagements, or private sessions, Dr. Goldberg can be contacted directly by writing to:

Bruce Goldberg, D.D.S., M.S.
4300 Natoma Avenue
Woodland Hills, CA 91364
Telephone: (800) KARMA-4-U or (800) 527-6248
Fax: (818) 704-9189
email: karma4u@webtv.net
Web Site: www.drbrucegoldberg.com

Please include a self-addressed, stamped envelope with your letter.

DR. BRUCE GOLDBERG

Astral Voyages

MASTERING THE ART OF SOUL TRAVEL

1999
Llewellyn Publications
St. Paul, Minnesota 55164-0383, U.S.A.

FIRST EDITION
Second Printing, 1999

Cover design by Tom Grewe
Cover photo from Digital Stock
Illustrations on pages 30, 79, and 165 by Carrie Westfall
Editing and interior design by Connie Hill

Library of Congress Cataloging-in-Publication Data
Goldberg, Bruce, 1948–
    Astral voyages : mastering the art of soul travel / Bruce Goldberg.
    — 1st ed.
    p.   cm. --
    Includes bibliographical references and index.
    ISBN 1–56718–308–5 (pbk)
    1. Astral projection. I. Title.
BF1389.A7G64   1998
133.9'5—dc21   98-42217
                                                                      CIP

Llewellyn Worldwide does not participate in, endorse, or have any authority or responsibility concerning private business transactions between our authors and the public.

All mail addressed to the author is forwarded but the publisher cannot, unless specifically instructed by the author, give out an address or phone number.

Information on page 165 reprinted with permission from *Ecstatic Body Postures* by Belinda Gore, copyright 1995, Bear & Co., Santa Fe, NM.

Llewellyn Publications
A Division of Llewellyn Worldwide, Ltd.
P.O. Box 64383, Dept. K308–5
St. Paul, Minnesota 55164-0383, U.S.A.

 Printed in the United States of America on recycled paper

*Astral voyaging affords us
the opportunity to reach new levels
of awareness and perfect our souls.*

Other Books by Dr. Bruce Goldberg

Contents

Acknowledgments

I would first like to express my appreciation to Nancy J. Mostad, acquisitions and development manager for Llewellyn Publications. Secondly, my multi-dimensioned thanks goes to Carl Llewellyn Weschcke, president of Llewellyn Publications, for his continued support and personal interest in the art and science of astral voyaging. With your assistance Carl, it is my hope that this book will build a bridge to the other dimensions for all who wish to access them.

My editor, Connie Hill, deserves my undying and conscious dying appreciation for her professionalism and non-hypnotic suggestions. Finally, I am always amazed and in awe of the universe, with all of its dimensions and complexities, that invite astral voyaging as a way of unlocking its mysteries.

Notes to the Reader

This book is the result of the professional experiences accumulated by the author since 1974, working individually with over 11,000 patients. The material included herein is intended to complement, not replace, the advice of your own physician, psychotherapist, or other health care professional, whom you should always consult about your circumstances in reference to your own physical, psychological, and spiritual well-being.

Several self-hypnosis scripts are included in this book. You may find it convenient to tape-record them so that you do not need to hold the book while practicing the techniques.

Introduction

The absolute beauty of astral voyages, or astral projection, is one of freeing ourselves from the limitations of the earth plane and the laws of space and time. Astral voyages (to the astral plane and beyond) give tremendous credence to the concept of reincarnation and immortality.

Throughout civilization's history, many prominent men and women have voiced their acceptance of both the concept of reincarnation and of soul travel.

Without astral voyages as a mechanism, there could not be reincarnation or karma. You will find in this book documentation of these concepts, along with many easy-to-use techniques so that you can experience this form of astral bliss yourself.

Astral voyages may occur as one of four types: out-of-body experiences, during which the soul or subconscious mind leaves the physical body and travels for a time and finally returns; a near-death experience, characterized by the actual death of the physical body for a brief time and its subsequent return to life; a conscious out-of-body experience, which represents a merging of the soul with its Higher Self in preparation for ascension; and finally reincarnation, where the soul leaves its current dead physical body permanently and occupies a new body in a future life.

If you are doubtful whether you can successfully apply these time-tested and simple techniques, remember that the only prerequisites for success are motivation for an experience and practice.

We will discuss the well-publicized "silver cord" that attaches the astral body to the physical body. In Ecclesiastes 12:67, we find: "Remember him—before the silver cord is severed, or the golden bowl is broken…and the dust returns to the ground it came from, and the spirit returns to God who gave it."[1] As long as this pulsating silver cord remains intact, the astral voyager is safe. Upon death this cord is severed and the astral body permanently loses contact with its physical counterpart.

Some have described this out-of-body state as one of "disembodied consciousness." We will discuss the various degrees of altered states of consciousness exhibited by astral voyagers, and case histories will further describe just what it is like to leave one's body and travel to distant locations.

These excursions beyond the physical body are perfectly safe. As with all of the techniques I use in my Los Angeles hypnotherapy practice and depict in my books and cassette tapes, I have successfully and safely experienced these effects myself. In addition, I can state with absolute confidence and certainty that there is no danger whatsoever in becoming an astral voyager. Considering the number of soul travels that I have participated in, if this was in any way dangerous you would have to channel my spirit to receive this communication.

You will read how astral voyagers travel back and forward in time, in addition to great distances. My instructions will guide you in doing this yourself, as well as facilitate your own spiritual growth. You will also be shown how to investigate parallel universes and how to contact spirit guides.

We will present the ideal conditions that facilitate successful and informative astral voyages, and how you can simulate these yourself.

---

1 Holy Bible, Revised Standard Version

Other questions to be explored are:

- Why do some people leave their physical body while talking, walking, etc.?
- Why do others leave their body with other souls and travel back or forward through time together?
- How do you meet kindred souls on the astral plane?
- What type of entities do you keep away from when voyaging?
- How can you be completely spiritually protected during these astral and other trips?
- What happens to the physical body while the soul is voyaging?
- Why do some people see their astral or etheric body while still in the physical body?
- What is it like to be with your Masters and Guides and overview your karmic cycle on the soul plane?
- How can you find out your karmic purpose?
- How can you expand your consciousness?
- What is the difference between an out-of-body experience, a near-death experience, and a conscious out-of-body experience?
- What is lucid dreaming, and how can you experience this state?
- What other dimensions are out there, and how can we experience them?

In the classic book on astral voyaging, *The Phenomena of Astral Projection*, Hereward Carrington and Sylvan Muldoon quote a Tahitian missionary on the mechanism of death:

> *At death the soul was believed to be drawn out of the head, whence it was borne away, to be slowly and gradually united to the god from whom it had emanated…the Tahitians have concluded that a substance, taking human form, issued from the head of the corpse, because among the privileged few who have the blessed gift of clairvoyance, some affirm that, shortly after a human body ceases to breathe, a vapour arises from the head, hovering a little way above it, but attached by a vapoury cord.*

The substance, it is said, gradually increases in bulk and assumes the form of the inert body. When this has become quite cold, the connecting cord disappears and the disentangled soul-form floats away as if borne by invisible carriers.[2]

This book may very well change your life. Read on and practice these simple exercises so that you too may learn to leave your physical body and travel to other dimensions. Be prepared for the most dynamic voyage you will ever take in this incarnation. If this book eases the fears of only one reader concerning death, or gives solace to someone who has lost a loved one, then the energy and time expended in preparing this work will have been amply spent.

---

2   S. Muldoon and H. Carrington, quoting from *Metaphysical Magazine* (Oct. 1896), in *The Phenomena of Astral Projection* (London: Rider and Co., 1951), p. 23.

Astral Projection

I magine this scenario: your physical body becomes paralyzed and you enter into a hypnotic trance; you blackout for a few moments; a second body rises above your physical body in a horizontal direction and finally uprights itself; you now look back and observe your physical body on a chair or bed; a pulsating silver cord connects these two bodies; and finally you return to your physical body, reversing the above steps. This is called astral projection, and trips that this astral body undertakes are astral voyages.

The previous description is most commonly reported, but there are other possibilities. For example, the astral body may simply rotate out of the physical body in a spiral-like fashion, and return the same way. The voyager may experience a vibrating or rocking motion, accompanied by a feeling of weightlessness and a sensation of flying or falling. Suddenly, the astral body rises quickly, the physical body now feeling cataleptic and paralyzed.

This second body not only appears to be weightless, but it may radiate a glow that can illuminate a dark room. The astral body floats to the ceiling, glides around the room, or just appears to take a walk down the street. Trips encompassing great distances may also be experienced by this second body. You could travel to foreign countries, or end up hundreds of miles above the Earth during one of these voyages.

As we shall explore in this book, an astral voyage can lead you to an etheric or unreal environment characterized by shadowy figures moving through a fog-like mist. This environment may take the appearance of a heaven with vivid colors and a brilliant white or gold light. You may even travel back or forward in time.

Throughout history there have been many terms used to describe this phenomena—among them: astral projection, out-of-body experiences (OBE), remote viewing, soul travel, astral travel, near-death experience (NDE), and traveling clairvoyance.

The second body to which I alluded has been referred to with various terms: a double, the subtle body, the desire body, the soul body, the astral body, or the light body.

We will discuss these terms in greater detail in chapter 3. For now, let us assume it is certain that we have a second body that can safely leave and return to our physical body. While out of our physical body, it is quite possible for this second body to travel to other places, even other dimensions, and experience the most unusual and spiritually uplifting voyage we will ever undertake.

Many astral voyagers have described this phenomena as a "state of ecstasy." Ecstasy literally means to "stand outside one's self." Others have used such terms as "beside oneself with joy." Working with thousands of individuals in training them to leave their bodies, I can testify to the fact that most of my patients relate their experience as a fascinating, pleasant, and even joyful trip. The great majority of them want to do it again and again.

Those of you who are concerned about safety need not be fearful of an out-of-body experience. Not only have none of my 11,000 patients ever been harmed by this experience, there has never been a report by the metaphysical and scientific literature in this field of any injury. What they do report is a spiritually uplifting experience that can result in therapeutic growth of all kinds.

Characteristics of a typical astral voyage include:

- The physical body becomes immobile and rigid (this effect can be neutralized by white light protection and other techniques in my tapes). The voyager is unable to move his or her limbs. This response ends once the two bodies separate.

- A pulsating silver cord connects the astral body to the physical body. This cord appears to become thinner as the distance between the two bodies increases.

- The astral body is weightless, but possesses very acute perceptive abilities, especially toward sounds and bright and vivid colors.

- It is the physical body that now appears as an empty shell. The focal point of consciousness is from the astral body.

- Awareness of being out-of-body is usually due to the inability to move objects on the physical plane.

- We see some portion of the environment that could not possibly be perceived from where our physical body is known to be at the time.

- We know at the time that we are not dreaming or experiencing a fantasy. Although we may deduce that this cannot be happening, we are in possession of all of our critical functions and later can state with absolute certainty that the astral voyage was not a dream.

- Voyagers commonly describe a sensation of moving through a dark tunnel and entering a white light.

- The senses of perception are more acute in this new dimension.

- The soul commonly leaves the physical body at the solar plexus or stomach area for those individuals who are relative novices at astral voyaging. When you become more adept at leaving the body, other exit points are: the third eye region between the eyebrows, the back of the head, the heart chakra, and the 7th chakra, located at the top of the head (some studies report this as the most common exit point).

- When beyond the physical body, there are no physical laws as we know on the Earth plane. All time is simultaneous, so that you can view any past, present, or future activity on the physical plane.

- The presence of spirit guides, other departed souls and fellow astral voyagers are reported.

- Distances are traveled at the speed of light. All the astral body has to do (when properly trained) is think of a location and arrive there in an instant.

- Some astral voyagers remain in the same location with the physical body, while others travel thousands of miles away.

- Sensations of "tugging" at the back of the head are felt when the OBE is too long in duration. This precedes the return to the physical body.

- A common fear is that the unattended physical body will die—the most common trigger for the astral body to reunite with its physical counterpart. A loud noise can also bring about the end of this metaphysical sojourn. This final step occurs in an instant.

Astral Voyaging vs. Clairvoyance

A common misconception, as well as an argument used by skeptics, is that reports of astral voyaging are nothing more than examples of clairvoyance. Clairvoyance is defined as the ability to perceive events occurring now without the use of any of the five senses, but with a sixth sense, ESP.

This is demonstrated by the experiences of early twentieth-century psychic Vincent Turvey. Turvey differentiated between clairvoyance and astral voyaging (both of which he experienced numerous times) by stating that clairvoyance consisted of "seeing" through a tunnel cut through the various physical objects in his path (mountains, forests, buildings, etc.). He was quite aware of being in his astral body, and could see his physical body when he projected out of it. Turvey also had a vivid sense of projecting through space on his way to a specific destination.[1]

Clairvoyance occurs when the projector's mind simply receives current information from a distance that is beyond the individual's five senses. A "medium" or "channel" contacting a "control" is an example of this phenomenon.

---

1   L. Chevreuil, *Proofs of the Spirit World* (New York: E. P. Dutton & Co., 1920).

When Astral Voyages Occur

Some of the classic writers in this field, who themselves experienced many OBEs, stated that soul travel took place when they were physically ill. These writers include Oliver Fox, Eileen Garrett, Vincent Turvey, and Sylvan Muldoon.

It must be remembered that these individuals were sickly throughout their lives. Robert Crockall[2] states that over eighty percent of astral voyages occur when the body is healthy. Most of his experiences coincided with the hypnagogic (pre-hypnotic) state just prior to falling asleep. My clinical research coincides with Crockall's viewpoint.

Whether it is physical fatigue, illness, or extreme stress, a looser connection is created between the physical and astral body, enabling the separation of these bodies. One positive side effect of this astral excursion is that the astral body collects additional energy and recharges the physical body upon its return.

Astral Voyaging and Karma

The Hindus refer to astral bodies as "light bodies." There is only a certain amount of learning the soul can do on the astral plane. It must travel to other planes (causal, mental, etheric, and the soul plane) to acquire advanced levels of instruction (see chapter 5). Each dimension or plane has spirit guides instructing your soul. Naturally, your Higher Self is present with you during this process.

Dual consciousness is the term applied to being aware of the astral body, or other dimensional body, and the physical body at the same time. This may appear confusing at first, but this division of consciousness is in no way harmful. No astral voyage technique will endanger you. The only issue is how much benefit you can obtain with the least amount of discomfort (rigidity or paralysis), and how fast this will occur.

There is absolutely nothing to fear about out-of-body experiences. You will always be both protected and assisted by your Higher Self (especially if you follow the scripts in this book or use my tapes). Eventually

---

2   Robert Crookall, *The Study and Practice of Astral Projection* (London: Aquarian Press, 1961).

your astral body will return to your physical body, with perhaps just a light jolt.

The purpose of these nightly excursions into other dimensions is to encourage the spiritual growth of the soul so that we may eliminate our karma and the need to reincarnate. There are four types of karma. Fate karma is the first type, consisting of the actions from previous lifetimes resulting in our present circumstances.

The second type of karma is primal karma. The original creative force (God) somehow removed our soul from the thirteenth plane and placed it in the lower five planes, so that we are required to purify ourselves by our own initiative and efforts in order to rejoin this perfect energy source. The reason for this is speculative. Was it some form of original sin? Could this have been the result of perfect energy beings somehow violating natural laws and being trapped in the physical body as punishment? Your guess is as good as mine.

Reserve karma is the third type. This category places us at the mercy of the Lords of Karma, and states that we are assigned a certain amount of karma at their discretion. We supposedly have no input about this decision. I have always rejected this concept, due to the lack of participation of our free will.

Last, there is daily karma. This comprises the karma we incur or eliminate from our day-to-day actions and intentions.

An Astral Voyage in History

Charles Lindbergh's 1927 transatlantic flight made aviation history, but it was for him memorable for an additional experience. During the twenty-second hour of his flight across the Atlantic, battling extreme fatigue, Lindbergh left his physical body. In his book *Autobiography of Values* he stated:

> *I existed independently of time and matter. I felt myself departing from my body as I imagine a spirit would depart—emanating into the cockpit, extending through the fuselage as though no frame or fabric walls were there, angling upward, outward, until I reformed in an awareness far distant*

from the human form I left. . . . I remained connected to my
body through a long-extended strand, a strand so tenuous that
it could have been severed by a breath.[3]

The Ancient Greeks

Plato wrote about near-death experiences and conscious dying in Book
X of *The Republic*. Plato also described astral voyaging in his *Phaedo*,
when he related the details of the last hours of Socrates. Socrates states,

And what is the purification but the separation of Soul from the
body, as I was saying before; the habit of Soul gathering and col-
lecting herself into herself, out of all the courses of the body; the
dwelling in her own place alone, as in another place alone, as in
another life, so also in this, as far as she can; the release of Soul
from the chains of the body?[4]

Pythagoras, the Greek adept and mathematician of the fifth century
B.C., was able to utilize soul travel at any time. Alexander the Great used
soul travel, while victorious at the battles of Gaugamela, Hydaspes, and
Issus. However, neither of these great generals succeeded in the end.
Napoleon was forced into exile and Alexander died at a young age.

Roman Senator Curma

During the fifth century A.D., Augustine, Bishop of Hippo in Numidia,
North Africa, described the astral voyaging of the Roman Curma. When
Curma was seriously ill he had a near-death experience in which spirits
on the astral plane informed him that a goldsmith had just died near his
(Curma's) home.

Senator Curma reported that the astral plane contained souls of both
"dead" people and those still functioning on the physical plan, a common sight in the astral world. Upon awakening from this state, Curma
ordered a messenger to his home region. This messenger returned with
confirmation that the local goldsmith had recently died.

———

3   Charles Lindbergh, *Autobiography of Values* (New York: Harcourt Brace Jovanovich, 1978).

4   Plato, *Phaedo*, translated by R. Hackforth (London: Cambridge University Press, 1955).

Zoroaster

Zoroaster, or Zarathustra, was the founder of the ancient Persian religion bearing his name. He mastered soul travel and visited the third plane. Later, Zoroaster was given the mission to reform the old religion of pantheism and transform it to monotheism. He had many communications with his Masters and Guides that facilitated the downfall of Persian idolatry.

Mohammed

Mohammed made similar journeys as Zoroaster, on a "white horse." This prophet described the seven heavens he witnessed in the Koran.

Other Examples

Maria Corelli, author of *Ardath*, was a well-known occult novel writer during the nineteenth century. Many of her books were based on her astral voyaging.

Paramahansa Yogananda, in his *Autobiography of a Yoga*,[5] describes how, through soul travel, he was able to meet his former guru Sri Yukesteswar, who was then deceased.

The Benefits of Astral Voyaging

We all have the natural ability to travel beyond our physical body into other dimensions. Developing this skill can bring us wisdom, freedom, and spiritual growth, and help us overcome the fear of death. Freedom from all physical, mental, emotional, psychic, and spiritual entanglements is usually the principal reason someone is attracted to soul travel.

Another advantage encountered in soul travel is the attainment of wisdom and love. By transcending the physical body we are exposed to and absorb this spiritual knowledge and behavior and bring them back to the physical plane. This becomes part of our spiritual growth, regardless of our initial motives for astral voyaging.

One of our primary illusions on the material Earth plane is that outside factors control our lives. It is always our own consciousness that

---

5 Paramahansa Yogananda, *Autobiography of a Yoga* (Los Angeles: Self-Realization Pub., 1974).

creates our reality. The new physics clearly establishes this. A thorough discussion of this concept is presented in my book *Soul Healing* (St. Paul: Llewellyn Publications, 1996).

Since our consciousness creates our universe, a change in consciousness is necessary in order to travel to the other dimensions. That is why I present preliminary or preparatory exercises before the basic techniques of astral voyaging.

The difference in our states of consciousness can be illustrated by looking at an object. You may analyze it, compare it to other objects, and even define it. These are mental or cognitive approaches. You can only know an object or idea spiritually by becoming it.

This is much more than merely focusing your concentration. When you narrow your awareness upon a single idea (soul travel) exclusively, you also focus your attention on the feeling of this astral journey, so that all other thoughts and distractions are blocked from your consciousness. This will now bring about the out-of-body experience you so desire, and a safe return to the physical body.

You can actually correct current problems by soul travel. For instance, thought is a component of the mental plane, while imagination is characteristic of the astral plane. By traveling to the appropriate plane, you can use its respective mechanism to alter circumstances in your present to a more pleasant outcome. Once you leave the physical body, there is no time as we know it. Past, present, and future all mesh together providing an ideal opportunity to correct mistakes.

Please don't consider this some form of "cheating" the universe. The karmic laws are perfectly just, and this knowledge would be unattainable ("forbidden knowledge") if it was out of line with the universe's plan.

Summarizing Astral Voyaging

Leaving the physical body may occur when we are healthy or ill. It takes place every night when we sleep (particularly during our dream or REM cycle), during physical or emotional trauma, and at times when we are intensely focused or preoccupied with something.

Voyagers report seeing a tunnel and white light, the presence of spirit guides and other souls in another dimension, having sharper perception, seeing a pulsating silver cord attaching the astral body to the physical one, visiting both living and dead people, and bringing back information they simply could not have obtained through their five senses.

Westerners assume that our waking world is real and the dream world unreal. This strict separation is not shared by many primitive cultures; there the dream world, daily life, and the past and present are merged into a single reality. The anthropologist Edward Tylor stated:

> *Certain of the Greenlanders . . . consider that the soul quits the body in the night and goes out hunting, dancing and visiting. . . . Among the Indians of North America, we hear of the dreamer's soul leaving his body and wandering in quest of things attractive to it . . . . The New Zealanders considered the dreaming soul to quit the body and return, even traveling to the region of the dead to hold converse with its friends. . . . Onward from the savage state, the idea of the spirit's departure in sleep may be traced into the speculative philosophy of higher nations as in the Vedanta system, and the Kabbala.*[6]

Who are we so-called rationalists and scientists to blindly dismiss the age-old space-time continuum and parallel universe approach to the world? I do not consider this approach folly.

---

6   E. Tylor, *Primitive Culture* (London: J. Murray, 1871).

Initial Out-of-Body Experiences

The most common report of initial astral voyages is that of falling asleep while practicing a relaxation exercise and experiencing a spontaneous out-of-body experience (OBE). A sinking and floating sensation represent the first stages of this OBE.

A roaring or gushing sound filling your ears; a paralyzed body; the flickering of light as bright flashes under your now closed eyelids; seeing your physical body from the perspective of one hovering above it; feeling completely released from the confines of the physical body; experiencing a momentary blackout and then immediately awaking back within your physical body—all of these sensations are often reported by people having their first OBE.

Modern psychiatry will try to rationalize this phenomenon by classifying it as one of three perception anomalies: *autoscopy*—the seeing of one's own apparition; *distraction of body image*, during which we confuse the body's physical boundaries; and *depersonalization*—a sense that our physical body is no longer real.

The fact that astral voyagers can exert direct control over their OBE nullifies the last two disorders. OBE subjects also exhibit a veridical, or truth-telling characteristic. By correctly noting exactly what is going on hundreds of miles from their physical body, voyagers prove a true psychic phenomenon is occurring, eliminating the first classification.

Astral trips are as common as other forms of psychic experiences, such as precognitive dreams and telepathic "hunches" or intuition. Studies clearly show that people who have OBEs are fairly well adjusted and just like you or me in most ways.

Psychological expectation is the single most important factor in generating an OBE. If you truly believe a certain technique will work, it most likely will. Anyone can learn the techniques presented in this book. There are absolutely no dangers in leaving your physical body. OBEs are as natural to our functioning as breathing. The great majority of OBE subjects polled reported their time out of the body as enjoyable (some said ecstatic) and most wanted to have many more OBEs.

There is no possibility of being prevented from returning to the physical body. This will occur involuntarily in the beginning and instantly. Keep in mind that we spend three hours each night out of our body during the dream or REM cycle. All dreams are OBEs. I suspect we spend the entire sleep period in another dimension.

The occasions that are most favorable to astral voyaging are just prior to falling asleep, at times of utter stillness, and during warm, humid weather. People can bring on an OBE solely through the concentrated application of their willpower. This is not the most important factor, however. When our subconscious desires an OBE as a chief goal, these astral trips will begin to occur spontaneously. I refer to this as an "astral kickback" effect.

Unquestionably, success in the art of soul travel is due to this combination of subconscious motivation and a pre-existing ability we all have for experiencing an OBE.

During its projection, our astral body becomes disengaged from our physical body and floats slightly above it. Next it rises, moving somewhat in front of the physical body and becoming upright. This process is reversed when the astral body returns to the physical body and reunites with it.

When you have your initial OBE, I strongly suggest you do not move. If you do move, your OBE will be disrupted and your astral voyage will be cut short. When you want to end it, focus your concentration on moving a part of your physical body (blinking your eye, twitching a finger, etc.) and you will immediately return to your physical body.

Approximately twenty to thirty percent of OBE subjects report a momentary blackout at the precise instant the astral body disengages from the physical body. Do not be alarmed—this is perfectly safe and normal. A sense of dual consciousness—being aware of being both in and out of the body—is also quite common.[1]

Leaving the physical body will most commonly take place through the head. Many people describe this sensation as if their soul was being sucked out through a hole in the top of their head. On rare occasions a spinning out of the body is described.

Initially you may find yourself viewing your bedroom even though you know your eyes are closed and you are trying to fall asleep. By simply willing your consciousness to leave the physical body, your first OBE will very likely be induced by your own conscious efforts.

Another interesting phenomenon about your experience in the astral world is that your sense of hearing will be heightened. Muldoon and Carrington[2] report the story of Fraulein Sophie Swoboda in Germany. Sophie lay down to rest on a day when she had a severe headache. Her mother was in her room keeping her company.

After awakening from a deep sleep, Sophie saw her mother leave her room and enter their living room to keep Sophie's father company. Sophie's headache was gone and she followed her mother into the living room, where she heard her father reading out loud from a book.

When Sophie returned to her room, she observed her physical body sleeping. Instantly she returned to her physical body. Some time later she told her mother word for word what her father had read from the book. Sophie also accurately related the conversation that subsequently took place between her parents. One interesting factor here is that there were two rooms between Sophie's bedroom and the living room, and all of

---

1 Robert Crookall, *Casebook of Astral Projection* (New Hyde Park, NY: University Books, 1972).

2 Muldoon and Carrington, cited in Robert Crookall, *The Mechanisms of Astral Projection* (Moradabad, India: Darshana Internation, 1969), pp. 87–88.

the doors were closed! This especially developed sense of perception (hyperthesia) is not uncommon in astral voyaging.

The Silver Cord

I have already briefly described the silver cord that attaches the astral body to its physical counterpart. A pulsating silver cord most commonly is connected from the forehead (or sometimes the solar plexus or stomach area) of the physical body to the back of the astral head.

We do not see this cord when out of the body unless we turn around and look back. My patients have described this attachment as a tape, thread, ribbon, or an umbilical cord. This last description is most accurate; it is theorized that all the learning and spiritual advances our astral body make are fed back into our physical body through this silver cord.

The majority of descriptions state that this cord is about two or three inches thick when within ten feet of the physical body. It pulsates (I feel it is our consciousness that creates this pulsating, and that it thins out as the astral body distances itself from the physical.) This connection is always maintained until the death of the physical body. Even near-death experiencers describe this attached silver cord.

I believe the mental, spiritual, and physical nourishment that is transmitted along this silver cord to the physical body makes it function much like the umbilical cord of a developing fetus. This silver cord is probably also responsible for our sharpened senses when astral voyaging.

One reason it is nearly impossible to examine your physical body closely while astral voyaging relates to the pulsating silver cord connecting the two bodies. This cord creates a light pulling or tugging sensation throughout the projection. The closer you get to your physical body, the greater this pull becomes.

There is a critical point, usually just a few feet from the physical body, where the cord's pull suddenly brings the astral body back into its physical counterpart. I have had this experience several dozen times myself.

Moving Physical Objects

An astral voyager may walk around a room or outside, or glide and also move in an up-and-down, wave-like motion. An astral body travels at the speed of light and often from vantage points high above the ground. When you become an experienced voyager, the mere thought of a location or person will instantly send your consciousness to that location or individual.

The above description is generally accepted by authorities and astral voyagers. What is controversial (bear in mind that this entire discipline is controversial) is whether an astral body can move a physical object.

Two very different conditions may exist with astral voyagers. In one case the astral body traverses physical objects by passing right through them. These souls, however, are unable to physically move an object on the earth plane. Those of you that saw the feature film *Ghost* will easily relate to this principle.

The second type of experience occurs when the astral body is able to move physical objects, make physical contact with people, and create sounds. A voyager capable of the first type of response usually cannot effect the second type and vice versa.

Theories abound to explain this most interesting phenomenon. One hypothesis is that our astral double is composed of varying amounts of a semi-physical body, and a body of pure energy or soul. The greater the semi-physical component, the less able the astral body is to pass through physical objects and the greater its ability to move material things, create sounds, and make actual physical contact with people on the physical plane.

Authorities disagree about the ability of the astral double to touch its physical counterpart. Celia Green describes a woman who touched her own body and stated it was "warm to the touch." Another voyager shook her own shoulder, resulting in her physical body waking "with a strong start, sitting upright in bed."[3]

Green's work at Oxford since 1961 has greatly expanded the field of astral voyaging. Her research has demonstrated that between twenty and

---

3   Celia Green, *Out-of-Body Experiences* (Oxford England: Institute of Psychophysical Research, 1986).

thirty percent of people surveyed reported at least one OBE. About six percent describe having six or more trips out of the body. Most OBEs began in childhood, and those who had only one OBE tended to do so between the ages of fifteen and thirty-five. The incidence of astral voyaging appeared to diminish with age.

Some first-time projectors describe a feeling of immobility and rigidity, leading to frustration in not being able to control their physical body. This feeling decreases once separation of the two bodies is complete. A blackout is experienced at the precise moment of separation. The silver cord is visible. In the initial voyage, the weightless astral double has very acute powers of perception (hyperthesia). Bright, vivid colors and unusual sounds are detected. Dual consciousness is exhibited, with the astral body being the real self and the physical body now viewed as a shell.

Most beginning astral travelers can pass through physical objects, but are unable to touch or move them. They usually discover that travel is at lightning speed. Most initial voyages end due to fear of danger to the physical body. This unwarranted concern results in an instantaneous return to the physical state. This initial experience is considered very enjoyable, and most voyagers want to have many more of these astral trips.

Some astral voyagers describe what transpersonal psychologists refer to as a peak experience. This is also a component of Eastern disciplines such as yoga and meditation. Dr. Raynor Johnson reported one such case from Australia:

> . . . about eleven P.M. I suddenly found myself out of the body floating over a Highland moor, in a body as light or lighter than air. . . . The life in the wind and the clouds and the trees was within me also, flowing into me and through me, and I offered no resistance to it. I was filled with glorious life. . . . I knew where my earthly body was, and that I could return to it instantly if danger threatened. The experience may have lasted a few minutes or a few seconds. . . . I was outside time. I came back greatly invigorated and refreshed. . . . If this was what the so-called dead experience, how much more vitally alive they are than we are here.[4]

---

4 R. Johnson, *Watcher on the Hills* (London: Hodder & Stoughton, 1959).

It is not difficult to see how significantly an OBE can affect an individual's life. Just ponder for a moment how you could use this experience to understand the meaning of life, your karmic purpose, and how you could better comprehend the true nature of reality and our universe.

Time, desire, and patience are the requirements of soul travel. You will note some differences while in these other realms. The laws governing these planes are quite different than those we are accustomed to on the physical plane. You may experience only a partial conscious awareness or a dual consciousness, and a feeling of being energized and cleansed accompanies these soul travels.

Soul travel is an excellent starting place for spiritual growth. This type of excursion will undoubtedly open you up to more spiritual experiences, often resulting in a realization that there is a process of spiritual learning and purification going on here in the physical world as well as in the other dimensions.

The Purpose of Sleep

Sleep functions to renew the vitality of our astral and mental bodies. The separation of the astral body from the physical body actually produces sleep. The vital force of the astral body is facilitated by its exposure to cosmic energy at night.

A second function of sleep is communication with our Higher Self and Masters and Guides for the purpose of spiritual growth, or raising the frequency vibrational rate of our soul. I refer to this as cleansing. The Eastern Yogis (and others) have known this principle for thousands of years. The formal function of sleep is necessary for preservation of life on the physical plane. This second purpose is only required for spiritual advancement.

The Five Stages of Astral Projection

Although each individual will have a somewhat unique experience, there are certain commonalities to astral voyaging. They can be described as five separate stages.

Stage One

The sleep state is characterized by the astral body moving out of alignment with its physical counterpart. This allows for a comprehensive recharging of both the astral and mental bodies, as the physical body attains its nightly rest. We leave our body every night during the sleep cycle (especially in the dream or REM phase).

This stage can also be exhibited when we are fully conscious. While attending the University of Maryland School of Dentistry in Baltimore in the early 1970s, at Christmas I would drive down to Ft. Lauderdale, Florida—a twenty-one-hour drive. As a determined physical plane soul, I drove this distance continuously, stopping only for gas. I would rent a room in a house for the holidays each year.

During one of my trips I recall arriving at my destination and dragging myself to the bed, but being unable to sleep due to my hyper-alert mind. In reality I was still on the highway and nearly dozing off. I was jolted back into consciousness. My astral voyage ended and my now-recharged physical body was able to successfully complete the trip. This was a stage one astral projection out of my exhausted physical body while my mind was awake.

As an aside to this experience, when I arrived in Florida my routine was to purchase a newspaper and look through the classified advertisements for a room to rent. This trip was unique in that the room I eventually did rent was exactly the room I saw on the highway several hours before! This is one example of precognition that may occur during an astral voyage.

Stage Two

This stage is characterized by the astral body being projected several feet away from its physical body. Often this is noted as a result of an accident or trauma. The projector leaves his or her body to avoid pain, and watches others attending to its physical counterpart from a distance. Joggers running long distances report this type of OBE.

Stage Three

The astral double in this stage is sent several hundred or thousand feet away, but always within familiar surroundings. You can travel to a target of your desire at this time. The occult law, "Energy follows thought," applies here. A strong-enough desire to be with a loved one or a special place can result in the astral body traveling great distances.

Stage Four

The distance traveled by the astral body is rather significant in this stage. Since the astral double can travel at the speed of light, it arrives instantly at most destinations. The distance traveled is directly proportional to the desire and will of the astral body.

Stage Five

Spiritual growth at its highest level is a characteristic of the fifth stage. A Master or Guide, or our Higher Self, is with our soul at this phase. Some may refer to these perfect entities as angels, but the role is the same. Voyaging now takes on new meaning, as enlightenment is the main goal.

The Mechanics of the Astral Plane

There is a basic framework of permanent structures on the astral plane, but this vast dimension has very different laws that control it. This astral dimension is composed of emotional substance that responds to every thought, desire, and emotion we have on the physical plane.

Our negative thoughts and emotions create evil and bizarre creatures and conditions on the lower astral planes. All of the things we hate, fear, and want no part of manifest themselves on the lower astral plane. It is easy to see why Hell became so entrenched in human thought. This is what the Swedish mystic Swedenborg sometimes saw. The Mystery Schools depicted this as the "river of death." Hell was also the Greek and Roman "Hades," the ancient Egyptian "Amenta," the Jewish "Sheol," the ancient Hindu and the Theosophist "Kama Loca," the Tibetan "Bardo," the Scholastic theologian "Limbo," and the "Plane of Illusion," "Graylands," etc., of various communicators.[5]

The upper astral planes represent our thoughts and desires of love, beauty, truth, and so on. These are the planes of the Christian Heaven,

---

5   H. F. Prevost Battersby, *Man Outside Himself* (London: Rider and Co., 1940).

the Buddhist Devachan, the Norse Valhalla, the Native American Sum-
merland, and so on.

Whatever we think or feel is recorded in astral form at some location
in the astral plane. When I first started inducing my own astral voyages,
I often experienced circumstances characteristic of both planes.

For instance, in 1983 I purchased my first miniature schnauzer and
named her Karma. During that year I had occasion to watch the third
Star Wars movie and had an astral voyage later that night. During my
astral trip I was accompanied by my dog Karma and we spent a beautiful afternoon in a park on the Astral Plane.

Suddenly, the figure of the evil Darth Vader came out of the woods
nearby and started chasing us. His figure was immense, and I quickly
instituted a counterattack to send him on his way. My astral sense of
humor was in attendance, as I created a can of spinach, opened it with
miniature lightning bolts, and consumed this can of power immediately.

Just like Popeye, my fists grew in size, and I punched Darth Vader
right through his helmet. He stood there stunned for a moment, and
then ran away. Karma jumped into my arms and licked my face, showing her undying love for me.

Was I on the upper or lower astral plane? I really can't say for sure.
Considering the total quality of this voyage, I would tend to vote for the
upper dimension. Perhaps even the upper astral plane has its occasional
"bad guy" show up once in awhile.

A possible explanation for the "Bogey Man" so often reported by children comes from the ectoplasm they produce when frightened. Very often
children are scared just because it is dark. In a darkened room this ectoplasm (see chapter 3) can materialize into creatures. White light dissipates
ectoplasm, so never deny a child a light in their room while they sleep.

Our imagination actually does create conditions in the astral world.
What we term imagination is nothing more than the use of our astral
senses. A mere thought is enough to cause an entity or circumstance to
appear in the astral world.

On the physical world we may fantasize about going to a certain city,
or being with a particular person. This results in a mere thought to us on
the earth plane, but a reality is created on the astral plane.

How the Astral Body Separates from Its Physical Counterpart

No two astral voyagers experience separation of the astral and physical body in the same way. My study of metaphysical literature,[6] interviews with thousands of patients, and my own personal experience support this.

However, certain mechanisms have been reported consistently enough during the past hundred years or more to present a paradigm. The following are some components of this mechanism.

The astral body begins its ascent from the solar plexus to the throat and eventually leaves the body at the top of the head during the course of actual physical death.

With practice, an astral voyager may project the double out from any part of their physical body, although the exit from the head is most commonly reported. This astral body can also leave all parts of the physical counterpart at once, "oozing out like steam and drawing together outside."[7] Hollywood producers must have been reading the old literature when they wrote scripts for the vampire movies of the 1940s and beyond.

The movement of the astral body is most commonly a zig-zag or spiral movement. Following this, a straight line path is exhibited.

This astral body contains a higher proportion of "semi-physical" substance in the early stage of its separation, and is more influenced by the physical body at this time. Later on this proportion is reduced and the double can now move through solid objects with greater ease. The greater the spiritual development of the projector, the higher the percentage of astral matter.

The astral body tends to continue in motion, and sees other objects in motion which are at rest on the physical plane. My recommendation is to remain still when you initially leave the body to properly orient yourself to this astral dimension. Refrain from touching objects until you are stabilized.

The previous discussion explains how astral projection is accomplished by such disorienting techniques as the "whirling dervishes." On

---

6   Robert Crookall, *The Techniques of Astral Projection* (London: Aquarian Press, 1964).

7   Ernesto Bozzano, *Discarnate Influences in Human Life* (London, John N. Watkins, 1938).

the physical plane our body stops when it reaches a barrier. The astral body keeps moving in this direction, and is susceptible to projection by inertia.

One of the most efficient methods of stabilizing the astral body is to look at a bright object.

A trail of light is seen as the astral double moves on the astral plane. Some projectors have described this as a "phosphorescent streak" or a "white luminous cloud." One theory suggests this gave rise to the concept that angels have wings and fly by these means.

Partial astral projection is common in severe illness, but projection can be inhibited by crossing the hands and feet.

A blackout is experienced when the astral body separates and eventually rejoins its physical component. The projector often experiences a sensation like moving through a tunnel, rising upon separation, and then a falling sensation when reuniting with the physical body, followed by a "click" in the head.

Dual consciousness (awareness of both the physical and astral bodies and their respective dimensions) is common.

Reports of lower astral plane (Hades) voyages accompany projectors who are lower in spiritual growth and whose astral body composition is higher in semi-physical substance. Discarnates encountered on this plane are known as "hinderers," who attempt to irritate and manipulate the voyager.

The upper astral plane (Paradise) is experienced by those who are higher in their spiritual evolution, and whose astral body composition shows a greater proportion of astral matter.

The pulsating silver cord usually observed is an extension of both the astral and physical bodies.

Commonly, a newly-released astral body lies horizontal, just above the physical body. It may then travel one of two paths: it either uprights itself immediately over the physical body, or it rises about four feet above the physical body while remaining in the horizontal position.

The return to the physical body can happen in one of three ways: fear will usually cause a straight fall accompanied by a jump, a spiral fall, or a slow, vibratory fall. Fear speeds up a fall. By merely letting yourself go and allowing yourself to fall, you can end a falling dream.

A lack of memory of the OBE follows a rapid projection or reentry of the astral double.

Dreams of rising are caused by being conscious of leaving the physical body. Flying or floating dreams are due to being conscious of traveling horizontally in the astral body. Being conscious of returning to the physical body results in dreams of falling.

Your astral body is not an exact replica of your physical structure. The astral double almost always appears younger and can exhibit a different hair color, tattoos, and other distinctions common to the physical body, as well as the absence of beards and mustaches, or the absence of glasses.

An Astral View of the Physical Plane

There is a rather significant discrepancy in reports of astral voyagers as to the nature of the physical plane from which they left. Occasionally voyagers describe different colors of rugs, curtains, etc., and an incorrect description of other elements in the physical room they are observing.

This is confusing to the projector because the experience seems so real, yet the facts don't quite check out with the reality of the physical plane. How can we explain this discrepancy without destroying the validity of the OBE?

The answer lies in the field of quantum physics. My book *Soul Healing*[8] thoroughly discusses this new physics concept, both explaining and demonstrating the principles of our mind creating our reality and the existence of parallel universes.

Suffice it to say that we create a parallel of the physical world when we are in our astral double. This simulated world is imperfect and subject to our thoughts and whims on the very emotionally charged astral plane.

For example, if we thought that the wallpaper in our bedroom had blue dots, but in reality they were green, our astral creation of the simulated physical world would have these blue, not green, dots. We see blue dots because that is what we expect to perceive. The limitations and creative ability of our consciousness (subconscious mind) affect the world we create.

---

8   Bruce Goldberg, *Soul Healing* (St. Paul: Llewellyn, 1996).

One question to be considered is: why do we create a physical plane at all? Why not just travel and experience the astral world as it is? Due to the basic insecurity of our nature, we must be continuously reassured that we are not delusional. Apparently the easiest way to accomplish this is to create an environment that reflects the physical plane that we have come to call home.

Human nature is imperfect. We all make mistakes. Even the pencils of doctors and other scientists have erasers. We have the free will and creative capacity to construct any type of world we choose. This capacity, properly harnessed, will result in the eventual purification of our soul and the elimination of our karmic cycle.

Our Other Bodies

Always remember a cardinal rule of the universe when considering our other bodies. This rule is: all bodies are created and shaped by our subconscious (consciousness). This principle also applies to the universe that we perceive. Quantum physics clearly supports this concept.

Before you can appreciate the other bodies we possess, it is necessary to discuss the chakras and the human aura.

The Chakras

Chakra is a Sanskrit term that means "wheel of light." Most of the literature on this topic describes the seven major chakra energy centers in our body (see figure 1, page 30). Two additional chakras—the *Atman* and *Brahman*—are included in the Hindu's description of this system.

Each chakra spins, creating an electromagnetic radiation energy field that surrounds our physical body that is known as the aura.

A chakra is always "open," since it is the union of spirit and matter manifested as consciousness. The soul as consciousness pervades and holds its bodies of manifestation together as a cohesive, functional unit through certain focal points. In the Indian tradition, these points or centers of force are called chakras. In a person of high spiritual development they are seen to revolve at great speed, and eventually to become spheres of radiant energy. In those of lesser spiritual development, the centers are not so active, giving the impression of saucer-like depressions on the surface of the etheric body. The chakras are often called lotuses, each petal representing certain constituent energies.

The theosophist C. W. Leadbeater places the chakras on the front of the body. Tibetan and Indian literature places them along the cerebro-spinal axis. The Master Djwal Khul says that they lie some three inches behind the spinal column. These divergent views regarding the locations of the chakras can be a product of the nature of the energies a person uses to function clairvoyantly. If he is an astral psychic, he will tend to work with certain astral involutionary energies, which will predispose him to seeing the chakras as located on the front of the torso. If he is a mental psychic, then he works in matter of more rarified quality which is evolutionary in nature, and his inner vision will show him that the centers lie along the spine.

A chakra is constantly spinning and recycling energy to our aura. Although a chakra may never be closed, it may be blocked. This can lead to energy imbalances and disease.

Chakras may be described as short, swirling, miniature black holes of color from our tailbone to the top of our head, aligned along the spine. They are identical in shape and size.

The main function of the seven chakras is to mediate all energy coming into, within, and leaving our physical body. This distribution mechanism is necessary for our physical, mental, emotional, and spiritual functioning.[1]

---

1 Jonn Mumford, *A Chakra & Kundalini Workbook* (St. Paul: Llewellyn Publications, 1994).

The First Chakra

The root, or first chakra, is the most primitive energy center and regulates our basic survival mechanisms. We associate the color red with this chakra. The immune system, our will to live, and our ability to reproduce are its domain. The first chakra also absorbs energy from the earth.

At the base of the spine between the sacrum and coccyx, or tailbone, is where the root or first chakra is found. This chakra is sometimes called the basal chakra. It is our basic life force center, and properly stimulated it can ease fears and make us aware of past-life talents. This center is also the seat of the Kundalini (the serpent energy considered to be the most powerful stream of energy in our body).

When this chakra is disrupted the following symptoms may be observed: sexual obsession; aggression, impulsive and reckless behavior; possessiveness, insecurity, and immediate gratification urges; hyperactivity, power concerns, and manipulative behavior; and immune system problems.

The Second Chakra

The second or spleen chakra is found just above the genitals and below the navel. This center monitors our basic emotions, creativity, the lower digestive tract, the excretory system, the kidneys, adrenal glands, bladder and pancreas. It concerns itself with detoxification of the body. The second chakra's color is orange.

Imbalances in this chakra produce the following symptoms: a lack of vitality; accelerated aging, arrogance, conceit, and vanity; antisocial behavior; and a loss of identity.

The Third Chakra

The third energy center is also referred to as the solar plexus chakra. It is located just below the breast bone, at the base of the sternum, and it appears yellow. This chakra is the point of personal power and the expression of creativity through the balanced use of that power. Astral traveling is also associated with this chakra.

The third chakra is also concerned with the powers of the mind, emotions, the stomach, and upper digestive tract. The assimilation of nutrients, psychic experiences, rational (left brain) thought processes and atonement to the influence of nature's elements within our lives are part of this chakra's domain.

Imbalances in this chakra produce the following symptoms: timidity and fear in general; anger and rage; isolation; judgmental and dogmatic behavior; feeling deprived of recognition; and aloofness.

The Fourth Chakra

The heart chakra is the other name for the fourth chakra. It is located in the center of the chest at approximately the level of the heart muscle, between the ribs and on the sternum. The color green is assigned to this chakra.

This energy center influences the thymus gland of our immune system, the circulatory system, tissue regeneration and right brain functions. It is our center of higher love, healing, understanding, and compassion. This chakra is the gatekeeper to the higher chakras, and must be unblocked for us to grow spiritually.

The heart chakra is a crossroad of transformation and balance. It stands midway between physical and spiritual life. Both forms of energy are processed here. If spiritual energy coming from the upper three chakras is blocked, this will deny the lower three chakras the vital energies required for preparing our physical body for its spiritual growth.

Imbalances in this chakra can result in these difficulties: an attitude of coldness, devoid of compassion and morality; asthma; financial and emotional insecurities; jealousy and possessiveness; mistrustfulness of life; self-doubt; and blaming others.

The Fifth Chakra

The fifth chakra, or throat chakra, is located in the throat region near the lower cervical vertebrae. This is the center of communication and clairaudience. It is associated with the thyroid, lungs, and organs of the throat and upper chest, and its color is blue.

This chakra also concerns itself with creativity, right brain functions and psychic abilities such as clairaudience and telepathy.

Imbalances with this energy center may result in the following symptoms: neurotic obsessions and obesity; excessive vocalizing or the inability to express oneself (stuttering); constant giving in to authority figures; clinging to tradition and fixed ideas; resisting change and dogmatic behavior; authoritarian behavior and being slow to respond to input from others.

The Sixth Chakra

The "third eye" or brow chakra is the sixth chakra. It is also referred to as the agna chakra, and deals with intuition and higher sense perception (such as clairvoyance). This chakra is found in the center of the forehead, just above the eyebrows. The color indigo is associated with this chakra.

This energy center is the seat of our psychic and mental functions. It also exerts an effect on the pituitary gland and the entire endocrine system, the immune system, the eyes, ears, and sinuses. This chakra functions as a balancing center for the left and right brain. It also deals with creative visualization, imagination and spiritual vision.

Imbalances to this chakra can bring about mental or psychic distress, including hallucinations and delusions. An imbalance here may also be responsible for sleep disorders; eye problems, and hormonal imbalances; pursuing idolized relationships; lateness, impatience, and inefficiency; fear of the future and superstitiousness; forgetfulness, oversensitivity to the opinions of others, and excessive worrying.

The Seventh Chakra

The crown, or seventh chakra, is located at the top of the head, and functions as an inlet for and link with spiritual energies. Violet is its characteristic color. This center is also referred to as the "Thousand Petalled Lotus" and functions to maintain a continuity of consciousness. It is the first chakra to receive spiritual energy from cosmic sources, and the last energy center to process energy flowing up from the lower chakras.

A block in this chakra means there is no flow of spiritual energy in either direction. Life now becomes meaningless and stagnant. All possibilities for spiritual growth will cease and the physical body will die if this chakra is blocked. A proper balancing of this chakra can release information of our Higher Self with our physical body (conscious out-of-body experience or COBE to be discussed in chapter 9).

Imbalances to this chakra result in one or more of the following symptoms: depression; intense erotic fantasies; feeling misunderstood, shameful, and expressing a low self-image; an inability to maintain relationships; self-denial; and an excessive need for sympathy.

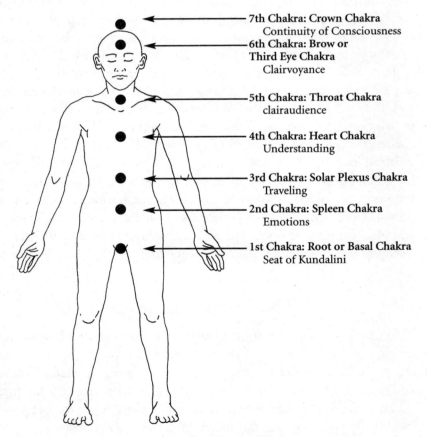

7th Chakra: Crown Chakra
Continuity of Consciousness
6th Chakra: Brow or
Third Eye Chakra
Clairvoyance

5th Chakra: Throat Chakra
clairaudience

4th Chakra: Heart Chakra
Understanding

3rd Chakra: Solar Plexus Chakra
Traveling

2nd Chakra: Spleen Chakra
Emotions

1st Chakra: Root or Basal Chakra
Seat of Kundalini

Figure 1. The Seven Major Chakras

We, as spiritual beings, are immersed in the energy field of the universe. This consists of all five of the lower planes. You may only be conscious of events occurring on the physical plane, such as fragrance of perfume, an itch on your body, or the sound of a bird chirping. This does not limit us to the physical plane. A complete depiction of the other planes will be given in chapter 5.

The reason we don't perceive these other dimensions is that our consciousness simply cannot handle the extra data. The true nature of our being is spiritual and energy based. Normally, our energies are in complete balance and harmony. We have a Higher Self, the perfect part of our soul, which regulates these energies. Chakra energies are a significant component of this system.

Our soul is simply energy that is created in duality and is trying to return to its original source (God). The subconscious mind is another term for the soul.

As spiritual beings composed of energy, we are dynamic in motion, and it is natural for us to reach out and interact with other energies. This interaction contributes to our realignment in our own energy systems.

The Aura

The aura is a collection of electromagnetic energies of varying densities in the form of colored lights. Light has occupied a unique position in the history of our universe. The first thing God created, according to the Old Testament, was light. God said, "Let there be light!" and there was light.

Light is the origin of everything and is consistent with the Big Bang theory. Energy was first created approximately fifteen billion years ago. Visible light became a part of the universe about 500,000 years after the Big Bang. This primordial light became the microwave radiation which makes up the cosmic background today. Matter was formed out of energy after the universe was cooled down sufficiently.[2]

The aura is composed of colored light that is normally beyond the visible light spectrum. These colors are pink/red, blue/green, blue, mauve and yellow. Our health, balance and spirit energy is reflected by these colors.

---

2 Kuthumi, *Studies of the Human Aura* (Colorado Springs: Summit University, 1975).

The electromagnetic layer is closer to the physical body and reflects the colors of the inner center. This electromagnetic energy field is affected when the body is fatigued, distressed or unbalanced. The normal strong and uniform glow of this field can appear thin and weak in color under duress or illness. When we are excited and charged with energy, this layer glows brightly all around the physical body.

The aura may be seen psychically as an oval-shaped ring of light that either pulsates or appears as a swirling pattern of several colored lights. There are seven interwoven rings of light in the aura and each component represents a different aspect of our being:

- Ring 1 represents the health of the physical body.
- Ring 2 represents the emotions.
- Ring 3 represents the intellect.
- Ring 4 represents the subconscious, especially imagination and intuition.
- Ring 5 represents the Higher Self.
- Rings 6 and 7 are not visible on most people and represent advanced cosmic aspects of our soul's energy.

The Meaning of Aura Colors

There are several schools of thought concerning the significance of the colors of an aura. Some colors affect the physical body because of their lower frequencies, while others influence the mind due to their higher frequencies. The following chart summarizes these effects[3]:

Physical
Green, Light Blue: Restful
Red: Stimulating
Orange: Revitalizing

---

3   Ted Andrews, *The Healer's Manual* (St. Paul: Llewellyn Publications, 1993), p. 110.

Emotional

Turquoise, Sky Blue: Restful
Orange: Stimulating
Peach: Revitalizing

Mental

Indigo: Restful
Yellow: Stimulating
Emerald Green: Revitalizing

Spiritual

Blue: Restful
Violet, Purple: Stimulating
Gold: Revitalizing

Each color represents a "certain light frequency" and "can be depressing or stimulating" to our functioning.[4] There is no one guaranteed effect from a certain color. We each respond based on many factors in our own aura and the environment in which we live.

Kirlian Photography

Kirlian photography was developed by Semyon and Valentina Kirlian in Russia in 1939. This method demonstrated that an aura surrounds all living things and can be documented on film. The aura seen on an organism varied in size according to the amount of vital force present.

This energy field grew smaller as the health of the plant or animal diminished. The brightest auras were registered on the hands of healers.

The work of the Kirlians gives us scientific evidence that auras exist. It also appears to explain the depiction in portraits of saints and other holy people throughout history with halos of light surrounding them.

---

4   Jack Schwarz, *Human Energy Systems* (New York: Dutton, 1980).

The Auric Bodies

The aura is affected by changes in our physical, mental, emotional, and spiritual activities. This energy field is the sum total of these effects and may be seen as different colors or felt as various intensities.

Thoughts have a natural tendency to attract energies with similar vibrations. For example, if you feel depressed, your thoughts attract similar patterns of energy and you may quickly sink deeper into this negative mood. The opposite occurs when you force yourself to think of something positive. This now attracts more positive energy and the depressed mood lifts.

Normally there are no leaks or holes in our aura. This electromagnetic energy field may send energy out to the environment, but this energy is eventually returned to the body. There is never a loss of energy from our aura. Our motivations, personality, and physical health are represented in our aura.

Three separate and distinct auric bodies compose our aura. These are the physical auric body, the etheric auric body, and the vital auric body.

The Physical Auric Body

The light-blue or bright white band is seen from the edge of our skin extending out ⅛ to 1½ inches. Often this physical auric body appears as a colorless gap sandwiched between the physical body and the colored auric bodies.

A bulge in this auric body is observed near an area affected by injury or disease. This is the densest auric body of the three. Ill health can be seen in this auric body long before it will exhibit medical symptoms. A bulging physical auric body can disrupt the etheric auric body and create a hole in the latter. The result is a decrease in the radiance of the vital auric body.

The Etheric Auric Body

The etheric auric body is composed of a non-physical substance and is a perfect replica of the physical auric body. The ancients referred to this etheric auric body as *First Matter* or *Hyle*. The matrix upon which the physical body exists is this etheric auric body. Its substance is called ectoplasm. The physical body would decay without its etheric counterpart.

Other names for this body are the *vehicle of vitality* (Hindu), the *Kesdjun Body* (Gurdjieff) and the *body of formative forces* (Rudolf Steiner).

The etheric auric body carries off the soul's energy to the nonphysical world at the moment of death (discussed in greater detail in chapter 9).

This etheric auric body extends from one to four inches in all directions from the physical auric body. It can be seen as a hazy light-blue or gray smoke emanating from the physical body. Occasionally, violet, blue, green, orange, and yellow are observed.

The underlying basis of an individual's actions, their growth mode, and their emotional state can be assessed by an analysis of the etheric auric body. The etheric body has its own organs. It energizes the physical tissues and therefore cannot be separated from the physical body for long. Dislodgement of the etheric matrix soon brings death to the overlying physical body. It cannot be projected.

The Vital Auric Body

The vital auric body extends from two to six inches from the outer edge of the etheric auric body. This body is very bright and composed of radiant fingerlets of lines of energy extending out in all directions.

This auric body is in contact with the astral body and absorbs emotional disruptions, pulling them into the inner layers of the aura and sending them to the appropriate chakra for processing. Your charisma or personality is projected to others by way of this vital auric body. At the same time, this body's radiant energy line goes out to the minds of others and picks up their personality vibrations.

There is a definite and regular shape to a well-conditioned aura. An aura that is lacking in certain places and bulges in others signifies that its owner is out of balance. The healthier the individual, the more regular his or her aura will be. The aura soaks up vibrations from everything around it. A large aura can dissolve people's thoughts. This can deplete the owner of this energy field. Weaker souls are more susceptible to other people's energies and may take on their projections.[5]

In my book *Soul Healing*, I described the case of Mark Smith, who had a near-death experience when he was just a few days old. He has had several regular OBEs since then. His NDE facilitated his ability to see auras. The following exercise is taken from his book *In a New Light*.[6]

To See Your Own Aura

1. Stand in front of a mirror at least eighteen inches away, further if possible.

2. Place yourself with a white or neutral color surface visible in the mirror behind you, again eighteen inches or more is ideal.

3. Relax, breathe deeply and sway gently from side to side.

4. Focus on the texture of the surface of the wall behind you.

5. As you stare past the outline of your head and shoulders you will see the envelope of light around your body move with you as you rock gently.

6. Remember to breathe as you do this, since you are now both viewer and subject.

7. Lighting should be subdued, neither too bright, nor too dark. Experiment. Auras can not be seen in total darkness, and bright light will wash out all but the most vibrant of auras.

8. Color of clothing is unimportant. You might find that your auric color, when you become accustomed to seeing it, will clash with certain items in your wardrobe, but you will see your true colors regardless of what you wear.

5   Joseph Ostrom, *You and Your Aura* (Northamptonshire, England: The Aquarian Press, 1987), pp. 22–27.

6   Mark Smith, *In a New Light* (Bethesda, MD: Aurora Publishing, 1995), pp. 115–117. Used with permission of the author.

9. Experiment with projecting a color. Think of a color and try to visualize it. You can change your baseline colors temporarily through this kind of exercise, and the change can be seen.

10. As you exhale, notice that the aura should get larger. Reciting the numbers 1 through 30 in a normal speaking voice will help liberate your energy. Take a breath after every two numbers.

11. Speed up the count from the number 20 on without taking a breath and watch your aura shrink in size and vibrancy. As you resume normal quiet breathing, the aura will return to its former size, but might appear a little brighter.

Thought-Forms

A thought-form is composed of a non-physical substance and may be created as a result of disruptions in any of the three auric bodies. These thought-forms may appear as sharp-edged, muddy-colored and ugly energies that range in size from a pea to the size of a grapefruit. Their color and form correspond to the nature of the wish, desire, or thought of the individual.

The presence of the thought-forms (foreign energies) irritate the radiant lines of the vital auric body. This compromised vital auric body can create an opening for the thought-form to attack the etheric auric body, which in turn directly affects the etheric body.

The etheric auric body is the very framework upon which physical life depends. Any insult to these auric bodies and penetration of a thought-form causes its entrance into a chakra and subsequent disturbance to the function of this chakra. Often two or three chakras are affected by a single insult.

These thought-forms represent a certain vibrational configuration created by our mind. It will disappear, unless reinforced, after a short time.

The Mental Body

The mental body interacts with the three other bodies (physical, astral and etheric). It is composed of the least dense matter and can project itself across the planet and even into other galaxies. The mind is our reality, while the other bodies are simply creations of the mental body. There are three components of the mental body. These divisions are:

- The conscious level. This controls the physical body and its various functions.

- The subconscious level. This is our soul and connects with the Higher Self.

- The superconscious level. This is the perfect part of our soul, often called the Higher Self.

The Astral Body

Since most out-of-body voyages will occur on the astral plane, let us discuss the astral body in greater detail. The astral body has been described by most cultures since ancient times. It was called *ka* by the Egyptians, *doppelganger* by the Germans, *vardger* in Norwegian, *taslach* in Scottish, *fetch, waft, task* and *fye* by the English, *ruach* in Hebrew, *eidolon* in Greek, *larva* by the Romans, *bardo* by the Tibetans, *pranamayakosha* by the Hindus, *rupa* by the Buddhists, *thankhi* in China, and *desire* body by the theosophists.[7]

The astral body, when viewed by our physical body's eyes, appears to sparkle and resembles our physical body in size and shape. It appears somewhat transparent, yet filled with many tiny white stars.

We project our astral body every night as we sleep. In addition, we possess a mental body. Both the astral and mental bodies are comprised of non-physical matter. When we feel, we act in our feeling or astral bodies. When we think we act mentally in our mental bodies. The astral body is made up of finer substance than the etheric body, but not as fine as that of the mental body.

7 Robert Crookall, *The Study and Practice of Astral Projection* (London: Aquarian Press, 1961),

We project out of our etheric-physical body and dwell in our astral and mental bodies during sleep. The astral body is the main vehicle for our movements in the astral realm. When we awaken, the astral and mental bodies slip back into their usual position in close alignment with the physical and etheric bodies. All of these bodies are recharged due to exposure to cosmic forces as a result of these nocturnal sorties.

When spirits are in the normal conditions of astral life, they appear as glimmering lights. When they wish to manifest themselves to mortals, they assume (in order to be recognized) the physical appearance similar, but often much younger, to that they had in their physical body. They may also appear quite different from their earthly form. When viewed from a distance, their normal appearance is that of small blue lights. These astral inhabitants look like a round blue object up close. The astral body may appear much younger than the biological and chronological age of the physical body, especially when observed in a mirror.

Astral bodies may look ovoid in form within an egg-shaped envelope. They are larger and taller than the physical body. They may also appear luminous and give off a glow that can illuminate a completely darkened room.

The astral body will be dressed in clothes associated with something that the projector is thinking about, or an event that occurred in the past. Garments may be an exact replica of current clothes worn by the voyager, or an improved version of it.

Since our astral body is associated with sensation, passion, and other intense emotions, it is continually altering its appearance to reflect our current emotional state. When psychics observe the astral body they may see various colors that reflect our emotional state (see chart on page 40).[8]

---

8   Annie Besant and C. W. Leadbeater, *Thought-Forms* (Adyar, Madras, India: Theosophical Publishing House, 1978), pp. 22–24.

Color	Emotion or State of Mind
Black	Hatred and Malice
Deep Red	Anger
Scarlet	Oppressed or Injured
Sanguinary Red	Sensuality
Crimson	Love
Dull Brown-Red (Rust)	Avarice
Brown-Gray	Selfishness
Greenish-Brown with Deep Red or Scarlet Tint	Jealousy
Leaden Grey	Deep Depression
Livid Grey	Fear
Orange	Pride or Ambition
Yellow	Intellectuality
Gray-Green	Deceit and Cunning
Emerald-Green	Versatility and Ingenuity
Pale, Luminous Blue-Green	Sympathy and Compassion
Dark Blue	Religious Feeling
Light Blue	Devotion to a Noble Spiritual Ideal
Lilac-Blue with sparkling Golden Stars	Higher Spirituality

Desires affect the development of the astral body. We can refine our astral body by turning our desires inward toward spiritual growth. Rising beyond our animal instincts and physical desires results in this form of spiritual development. Our actions will determine our future physical surroundings. The surroundings will be favorable or unfavorable depending on whether you make others happy or unhappy. When our physical body dies, this astral body is the temporary home of our soul until the reincarnation process is completed.

The Causal Body

According to the Theosophists, there are three components to the Higher Self. They are the Atma, Buddhi, and Manas. The Manas are also referred to as the causal body. The lower self is the astral soul and enters the astral field of Kamaloka upon the death of the physical body. Indestructible elements, known as "permanent atoms," make up the physical, astral, mental and etheric bodies. Along with the aura, these permanent atoms register the experiences of each lifetime.[9]

A Buddhic web of life extends from the Higher Self into the etheric body and from here it manifests itself, eventually, into the physical body. These life threads (the silver cord) withdraw at death and wrap themselves around a core in the heart and take the shape of a purple and gold frame. Here they migrate to the third cerebral cavity and, along with the permanent atoms, leave the body through the top of the head.

The fate of the astral-etheric part of the lower self is Kamaloka, the astral field surrounding the earth. The soul can now indulge in any desires without fear of retribution. The spent desires remain as *skandhas* or astral elements, and will return in the succeeding incarnation. The permanent atoms withdraw into the mental body.

It is these skandhas (astral-etheric or etheric-physical) that are the carriers of karma. The Higher Self falls asleep at the end of the Kamaloka tenure and reawakens in Devachan. This is the world of thoughts. It is free of causes and consists only of effects. Indulging in one's thoughts is the only action in this dimension.

The mental body is discarded after the soul leaves Devachen and it arrives in Manas, the Higher Self-component, housed in the causal body.

A golden thread of Buddhic matter signifies the return to a new incarnation. The permanent atoms of the Higher Self accompany this substance and bring along all remaining skandhas left behind on the other lower planes.

The condition of the permanent atoms and accompanying skandhas determine the conditions of the new life.

---

9   Charles W. Leadbeater, *Dreams: What They Are and How They Are Caused* (London: Theosophical Society, 1903).

Ectoplasm

Our body gives off in minute quantities an ephemeric substance called ectoplasm. This is mainly albumin and some amino acids, obtained from the orifices of the body. Only rare individuals have the capacity to produce it in vast quantities, especially during the trance state. This person would be known as a materialization medium.

Ectoplasm is easiest to observe in red light—white light is completely antagonistic to this substance. In a materialization seance huge amounts may be produced by the entranced medium and then it can act as a reservoir from which astral entities can draw. They will then be able to materialize for all to see and will remain so until the ectoplasm supply dissipates.

Occasionally, when there is a supply of ectoplasm available, an astral body of someone in projection will materialize. This occurs in the case of bilocation. In these cases, the other individuals present donate their ectoplasm to the astral body of the voyager, and a solid form of that body appears.

When one projects to a place or a person where ectoplasm is available, materialization of the astral form or just part of it, say a face or hand, is possible. Sometimes the one to whom the projection is made may provide the ectoplasm. The research of Dr. Eisenbud with Ted Serios provides a well-documented example of this.[10]

Serios could hold a Polaroid camera to his brow and think strongly. In some instances, with the camera lens removed, he could "deposit" an image of his thought onto the camera plate. Many books written by Hans Holzer show rather convincing photographs of these ectoplasm ghosts.

The Solid Astral Double

The following is a rather dramatic example of our astral body appearing as a physical body to others on the earth plane. The projector is usually aware that they have materialized elsewhere. But ordinary people are not so fortunate.

---

10 Allen Spraggett, *The Unexplained* (New York: New American Library, 1967).

The solid astral double is often involved in business or other professional circumstances. Spraggett[11] reported a case involving Dr. Mark Macdonnell, a member of the British House of Commons. Macdonnell was laid up at his home and very ill when an important bill came before the House for a vote.

Macdonnell's solid astral double was seen by dozens of witnesses to be debating this bill in the house for two days. His vote is on record, although there are other witnesses proving that he never left his house during those two days.

Susy Smith[12] relates a story of what is known as the arrival phenomenon. A New York businessman named Gorique went to Norway for the first time. He was quite shocked when several people, including the hotel clerk, greeted him as someone they knew well. Gorique had never met these Norwegians before. One person approached him and said, "Delighted to see you again, Mr. Gorique."

The metaphysical explanation for this rests on the fact that Gorique had been planning and thinking about this trip to Norway for several weeks before his departure. He either projected his astral body to Norway, or created a temporary thought-form that represented him across the Atlantic, but he was not consciously aware of either process. The projection of ectoplasm is another explanation.

11 Spragget, op. cit.
12 S. Smith, *The Enigma of Out-of-Body Travel* (New York: Garrett-Helix, 1965).

Astral Entities

Just what type of beings are you likely to encounter during your astral voyages? We will explore the answer to this question in depth in this chapter.

Dating back to at least 50,000 B.C., shamans used rituals placing themselves in communication with nonphysical entities. The Mystery Schools of ancient Egypt, Greece, Persia, Rome, and India also dealt with contacting spirits. This approach appeared to reach a zenith in the nineteenth century with the Spiritualism Movement. Today we see a resurgence of interest in angels, the Higher Self, and channeling in general.

Every major religion acknowledges the reality of discarnate entities or spirits. These may be called saints, angels, the holy spirit, and so on. However, Hollywood films, television, and novels have incorrectly fostered the idea that some evil process is necessary to contact one of these spirits.

The media's conception of spirit contact has led to the false assumption that the individual who establishes this contact must be in great danger. In reality, this communication is natural, relatively simple, and is a wonderful experience. Spirit communication removes the fear of death or bereavement, and results in a form of spiritual empowerment. We can prove our immortality, and in addition receive enlightenment from beings far more spiritually evolved than us.

The statements above specifically refer to receiving communication from an astral entity on the physical plane. When we voyage to the astral plane or other dimensions, we will encounter several different type of entities.

Fellow astral voyagers who are alive and well represent the first class of astral entities. These souls may appear somewhat younger than their physical plane counterpart, and are usually in good "spirits." One group of not so happy campers you may encounter are souls going through a near-death experience. These beings are stressed, moody, and most likely will not be very sociable. They are harmless.

A third group is composed of discarnates who are between lifetimes. These souls have not yet entered the white light (their Higher Self) and are wandering around the astral plane, often unaware of the fact that they have died. These ghosts or poltergeists may be friendly or antagonistic, but they usually are harmless and just want to be left alone. Included in this group are departed loved ones from your physical planet life. They are usually more receptive to you, as they recognize you instantly.

Your own Higher Self or superconscious mind most commonly will be represented as a brilliant white light. The light may appear in a human-like form to make it easier for you to communicate with this perfect source of your soul's energy. This is the fourth type of encounter you may experience on the Astral Plane.

The best way to relate to what your Higher Self is like is to experience it yourself. I developed a self-hypnotic technique called the superconscious mind tap that is the main therapeutic technique I use in my Los Angeles office (you may wish to tape-record the script that follows).

A superconscious mind tap is simply training the subconscious mind (soul) to communicate with the superconscious mind (Higher Self). The mind tap is particularly valuable in our discussion because it trains you to raise the quality of your own soul's (subconscious mind's) frequency vibrational rate. The mind tap promotes contact and communication with lost loved ones and spirit guides, and overviews past and future lives with spirit guides or anyone in your life today.

Superconscious Mind Tap Script

The following superconscious mind tap exercise is perfectly safe and easy to master:

Now listen very carefully. I want you to imagine a bright white light coming down from above and entering the top of your head. Filling your entire body. See it, feel it and it becomes reality. Now imagine an aura of pure white light emanating from your heart region. Again surrounding your entire body. Protecting you. See it, feel it and it becomes reality. Now only your spirit guides, Higher Self, and highly evolved loving entities who mean you well will be able to influence you during this or any other hypnotic session. You are totally protected by this aura of pure white light.

In a few moments I am going to count from 1 to 20. As I do so you will feel yourself rising up to the superconscious mind level where you will be able to receive information from your Higher Self and spirit guides. You will also be able to overview all of your past, present, and future lives. Number 1 rising up. 2, 3, 4, rising higher. 5, 6, 7, letting information flow. 8, 9, 10, you are halfway there. 11, 12, 13, feeling yourself rising even higher. 14, 15, 16, almost there. 17, 18, 19, number 20 you are there. Take a moment and orient yourself to the superconscious mind level.

PLAY NEW AGE MUSIC FOR 1 MINUTE

You may now ask yourself questions about any issues, or you may contact any of your spirit guides or departed loved ones from this level. You may explore your relationship with any person. Remember, your superconscious mind level is all-knowing and has access to your Akashic records.

Now slowly and carefully state your desire for information or an experience, and let this superconscious mind level work for you.

PLAY NEW AGE MUSIC FOR 8 MINUTES

You have done very well. Now I want you to further open up the channels of communication by removing any obstacles and allowing yourself to receive information and experiences that will directly apply to and help better your present lifetime. Allow yourself to receive more advanced and more specific information from your Higher Self and Masters and Guides to raise your frequency and improve your karmic subcycle. Do this now.

PLAY NEW AGE MUSIC FOR 8 MINUTES

All right now. Sleep now and rest. You did very very well. Listen very carefully. I'm going to count forward now from 1 to 5. When I reach the count of 5 you will be back in the present, you will be able to remember everything you experienced and re-experienced, you'll feel very relaxed, refreshed, and you'll be able to do whatever you have planned for the rest of the day or evening. You'll feel very positive about what you've just experienced and very motivated about your confidence and ability to play this tape again to experience the superconscious mind level. All right now. 1, very very deep, 2, you're getting a little bit lighter, 3, you're getting much much lighter, 4, very very light, 5, awaken, wide awake and refreshed.

As with all self-hypnosis and meditations, I highly recommend making a tape of these exercises. If you would like professionally recorded tapes of these techniques, simply contact my office for a comprehensive list of these tapes.

Subpersonalities

A subpersonality is the result of a splitting of our consciousness (soul) into several fragments of energy. This can be brought on by physical or emotional trauma, or through negative projection techniques (malicious magic).

This split of our consciousness produces a partial personality from the original core personality we possess. A subpersonality is trapped in the incident that created it and strives to fulfill the factors that led to this split in the first place. These energy components continue the dysfunctional emotional states propagated by the traumatic event, and may exist on both the astral and physical planes simultaneously.

We do not see a complete takeover of the personality or "possession" of the individual on the physical plane in these instances. The manifestations are more commonly that of unusual eating habits, or alterations in mood and social responses to others. In extreme cases these may manifest as two or more separate personalities, now termed Dissociative Identity Disorder (DID), previously referred to as Multiple Personality Disorder (MPD). In reality, the personalities are attached entities.

These subpersonalities may even be a carryover from a previous lifetime. A subpersonality may be formed when the individual is very young and it can remain attached, yet inactive, for many years. It is only when an additional traumatic event occurs that some of these fragments of the patient's being become activated. These entities will appear as discarnates on the Astral Plane and may not be so easy to differentiate unless you communicate with them.

You may not be very likely to assist these entities during your OBEs. It is critical to reintegrate a past life subpersonality or present life fragment before initiating visualizations and other techniques to guide it into the white light. The fragmented personality is invited to rejoin its past life persona in the process of integration. Then the moment of death in that incarnation can be reviewed and the soul fragment can now be properly directed into the light. The patient will now feel a fullness and warmth, where previously there had been a void.

Integration Exercise

The following exercise is an example of this integration approach that you may use if you feel you have such an attached entity:

1. Sit quietly, apply protection, and breathe deeply. Scan your auric bodies and look for voids, dark spots, holes, empty places and hollow regions. Focus on these areas. See any defects in your aura as a dark, loose thread.

2. Concentrate on the thread that is most prominent. This may be the darkest, thickest, or brightest. Follow this thread until it

results in a scene of something traumatic from this life or a past lifetime.

3. As you recall these events, observe the details of the thread. Feel the emotions associated with these memories. Now reframe this event in a positive manner so you can grow spiritually as a result. Change whatever facts or circumstances necessary to alter this episode so that it ends happily.

4. Now focus on the thread again. Direct it so that it blends in with the other threads of the aura. Repair or replace it so all voids, holes, dark spots, or empty and hollow areas are brought back to a normal and healthy state.

5. Meditate on this process for five minutes. Feel the stabilization of emotions and the raising of your soul's energy as you complete this exercise. Come out of the trance by opening your eyes.

As a result of integration and cleansing techniques, a deep and lasting change results in spirit attachment (subpersonality) cases. The discarnate sent to the Light can never return to the previous host. You may actually see these subpersonalities entering the white light on your astral voyage, and we immediately observe an elimination of the dysfunctional symptoms and behaviors. My patients have described this effect as a burden lifted or a blockage removed. They are now able to return to normal function, feeling stronger than they ever felt before.

Techniques Used in Treating Subpersonality Cases

Sometimes it is necessary to regress the host to a past life to relive the exact moment of attachment of the discarnate. I always enlist the aid of the host's Masters and Guides and Higher Self during these procedures. Occasionally I will request that entity discard all negative emotions such as anger, hate, jealousy, rage, and the desire to control others.

Another approach to treat subpersonality cases deals with a form of chakra healing. The host is regressed to the moment the past life personality made this attachment. It is often the death scene in this previous life. The patient is asked to remove a dagger, bullet, or other object that caused a violent death.

Laser Healing Technique

A superconscious mind tap is initiated and the Higher Self is asked which chakras were damaged in that past life. I instruct the patient in the following laser healing technique:

1. Begin transmitting a fine blue light and another green light of energy from the third eye area. Then hold these two beams of light until you feel a tingling, cold, or warm sensation on your forehead.

2. When this is felt, add the appropriate color to these beams that reflects the problem. Mauve is added for communication, yellow for fear, green for creativity, and blue for depression.

3. Now move these laser beams of light down from the forehead to the affected chakras. Hold them in one position for ten seconds and then fan them out over this area.

4. Now move these beams about twelve inches over your head and combine them with your aura. These light beams are then fanned down the body to the feet.

5. Meditate for three minutes. Next place your hands together and then brush them against your thighs. This technique functions in activating and revitalizing healing energy and results in strengthening the aura, as well as realigning the appropriate chakras.

A variation of this visualization technique is to use these laser beams of healing energy to reattach severed limbs, replace a head that was cut off, and so on, to affect an integration of the past-life personality. This "welding" of laser body parts is quite effective. This can also be applied to cancer and other systemic diseases suffered in the past life.

If the past life personality cannot quite complete this surgery, I advise them to pick up their severed head or limb and take it with them to the Light. Subpersonalities have been both misunderstood and misdiagnosed throughout history. These cases are surprisingly easy to treat, and result in a very special form of empowerment to the patient.

Masters and Guides

The sixth type of astral entity is the most positive and spiritually uplifting entity (outside of your Higher Self) that you will meet on the Astral Plane. These beings are referred to as Masters and Guides, or just spirit guides.

These beings are perfect. They once had a karmic cycle, but have learned all of their spiritual lessons and have raised the frequency vibrational rate of their soul to a perfect level.

In reality these souls have merged with their Higher Self and may ascend to the higher planes to join God. Instead, they choose to remain on the lower planes to assist other souls (who are imperfect) in their quest for ascension. I will discuss the other planes in greater detail in chapter 5.

Some refer to these spirit guides as angels. Must of our main religions mention angelic beings in the various scriptures and sacred texts. Other classes of spirit guides that you may meet are:

◆ Protectors. Spirit guides that assume the form of strong animals such as elephants, dragons, and panthers are called Protectors. They can also appear to us as a Viking or American Indian, and have great presence.

◆ The Doctor. A spirit helper who assists in our mental, physical, or emotional healing is called a doctor. This guide had lives on earth as a healer or physician.

◆ Teacher. Spirit guides who help us understand the world in which we function are called teachers. They are especially involved with our spiritual growth and evolution.

◆ Message Guides. The psychic abilities you have such as intuition, clairaudience (hearing spirit guides), clairvoyance (seeing spirit guides), and so on, are developed with the assistance of message guides. These entities help you receive messages and other forms of information from the "other side."

◆ Gatekeepers. These spirits assist you in your spiritual protection from negative entities and evil forces. They function as guards, allowing only positive beings to communicate with you.

◆ Chemist Guides. It is important for your physical body to be able to handle the more intense vibrations from the spirit planes. Chemist Guides assist your physical body in altering its body chemistry to more easily adjust to this spiritual communication.

You have an inner band of a select number of guides who work with you on a regular basis. An outer band of these spirit guides assist you when you are ready for a particular spiritual lesson in growth. It is an infrequent communication compared to that of the inner band. One member of the inner band acts as a representative and contacts you most frequently.[1]

Occasionally, a spirit guide will communicate with you while you are in your physical body. Here are some principles you should know about your communication with a guide.

◆ You are in no danger at any time from establishing communication with a spirit guide. Do not be concerned with being "possessed," or harmed in any way.

◆ The compatibility of your purposes and goals is the main reason why a particular guide or group of guides chooses to work with you.

◆ The higher level guides serve as sources for clarity, direction, and guidance. Their main concern is your higher purpose.

◆ The control and direction of all communication with your spirit guides always rests with you. If you are not ready or willing to be contacted, you can simply dismiss this guide. This usually is not a problem, as your spirit guides can telepathically read your mind and are well aware of when you are most and least receptive to them.

◆ A spirit guide will assist you in any way you request, as long as it does not result in harm to others or interfere with your own spiritual growth. No spirit guide is going to learn your karmic lessons for you. You must do that yourself.

1 Ted Andrews, *How to Meet and Work with Spirit Guides* (St. Paul: Llewellyn, 1992), pp. 17–21.

- ◆ There are no short cuts to spiritual growth. Your spirit guides will assist you with their communications, but you always have the free will to reject their advice. Contact with these beings will efficiently speed up your spiritual growth, but do not expect instant revelations each time contact is made.

- ◆ Do not follow a spirit guide's advice blindly. You are encouraged to test them.

- ◆ Spirit guides communicate with you only with your permission.

- ◆ As a result of contacting spiritual guides, you can expect the following to occur: you will be enlightened spiritually; your compassion toward others will grow; your goals that may not have been attained in the past will now be achieved; you may experience physical, mental, emotional, or spiritual healing; and an increase in your psychic abilities will be noted. You are always left feeling confident and empowered. All messages and advice are designed to give you freedom to choose your actions. You are always left feeling changed for the better in some way. There is no difficulty in understanding the information provided. It agrees and expands upon your own basic knowledge. You will find new information presented that always betters your life in some way as you apply it. Others will be attracted to you because of your new and higher energy.

A sense of sincerity, simplicity, humility, and spirituality will always be demonstrated as a result of these contacts. This entity will never make demands or brag about their abilities or knowledge.

Your true spirit guide will be able to accurately perceive not only future trends in your life, but how you will respond to them.

I have mentioned the concept of testing a spirit guide to make sure they are, in fact, a true angelic entity. One way to do this and to see your own future is to conduct a simple exercise. On the astral plane time as we know it does not exist. You may very well observe the future of your physical body. This is not so easy to do in your initial voyages.

Future Viewing Exercise

This next exercise will assist you in seeing your own future so that you may benefit from this knowledge now:

1. Sit comfortably, apply white light protection and breathe deeply. Visualize a symbol for the future. This may be a radio, book or anything you like. Mentally toss this symbol out into the future and perceive it broadcasting information back to you about your future. Turn your recorder on and verbalize any information you acquire.

2. Ask your spirit guide to assist you in this exercise. Now imagine that it is exactly one week from today. See and feel what you are doing. Let any images, thoughts and feelings come into your awareness. What is different about your life at this future date? Record your impressions. Dissolve these images.

3. Now perceive it is one month from today. Ask your spirit guide to further help you with this step. What is it exactly that you are planning, doing and thinking? What has changed since the one week information was given to you?

4. Follow these same steps and look at three months, six months, one year, and finally five years into your future. Investigate any issues you consider important in your life. Give yourself advice from the perspective of these probable futures.

5. Ask your spirit guide to comment on your advice and the accuracy of your probable futures.

6. Here are some questions to ask your guide:

   What can I emphasize in my life during the next week (month, three months, etc.) that will facilitate my spiritual growth?

   What specific decisions and choices can I make right now to achieve my highest aspirations?

   What behaviors, thoughts ,and actions can I implement to accelerate my spiritual path?

   Think of a current situation in your life and ask, "What am I learning from _____?"

How can I improve my skills as an astral voyager? What can I do physically, mentally, emotionally, and spiritually to raise the frequency vibrational rate of my soul?

Lower Astral Plane Entities

In chapter 5, I will discuss the make-up of the astral plane in greater detail. For our current discussion, let me state that this dimension is divided into an upper and lower level. This depiction so far has dealt primarily with the upper astral plane. Ninety-five percent of your astral voyages will be to this part of the astral dimension.

In rare instances, you may find yourself in the lower astral plane. This accounts for the five percent of NDEs being reported as negative. A similar percentage of regular OBEs are depicted as scary or stressful. You are never in any real danger, especially with the white light protection techniques I present in this book.

The astral entities I am about to present represent the seventh category of astral entities. I have briefly discussed the concept of thought-forms already. Any thought you have on the physical plane creates a manifestation of this image on the astral plane.

This thought-form is only temporary and eventually disappears. Sometimes the thought-form enters the physical plane, as in the example of bilocation. You will run into all kinds of these temporary creations while voyaging. These may be objects, people, or creatures.

Ectoplasm Attackers

Ectoplasm attackers resemble thought-forms in physical appearance. The difference is one of longevity. These entities, once created, take on a life of their own. They will eventually disappear, as will thought-forms, but their existence is for a greater length of time than a simple thought-form.

The thought-form follows the direction and instructions of its creator. Ectoplasm attackers have their own agenda and may function independently of our thoughts. In addition, it is our negative thoughts and emotions, such as jealousy, hatred, and anger that generate this creature. A thought-form may also be created by positive thoughts and feelings.

Initially the ectoplasm attacker will follow the guidance of its creator. Then it goes off on its own track and does whatever it wants to do. Since it is formed from negativity, the actions generated are never healthy.

Thought-form Removal Exercise

If you are worried about running into your own thought-forms, here is a simple exercise to remove them. To do this exercise, have a piece of paper and a pen available.

1. Sit comfortably, apply protection and breathe deeply. Write down on your paper an issue that is currently troubling you. Now ask your Higher Self how this problem interferes with you reaching your maximum potential. Write down these answers.

2 Reflect in your own mind on images of events from the past that caused this issue. This may be a former life. Detach yourself from this scene and gather as many details as you can.

    Where were you? How old were you? Who was there with you? What feelings did you have then? What feelings do you have now? Quickly jot down the answers to these questions and move on to another time which might be related in some way to your present-day problem. If an image is foggy, or you're just not sure how it goes, don't worry about it, work with what you've got.

3. Now imagine that you are in a playhouse watching the scene your mind gave you in step 2. As you watch this painful scene unfold, see yourself yelling "STOP" from the audience. The characters freeze where they are.

4. Visualize yourself running onto the stage and taking the part of yourself. You are now going to complete this scene so that you are empowered and the cause of this emotional or other pain is eliminated.

5. As you begin, yell out "ACTION." The other characters come to life again and you are able to control their actions and dialogue. At the end of this scene say to each character, "I love you and release you from this action, regardless of your motivation."

6. Now say out loud, "I love myself and I release these old thought-forms from my aura and discharge them into the universe where they will instantly disintegrate."

Demonic Entities

Demons represent pure evil. These spirits never existed in human form. Their objective is to possess a human body and take over the Earth. You are not likely to meet these during your voyaging. Even if you do encounter a representative of this category, it will most likely be a minor demon.

When seen on the physical plane, a demonic entity exhibits certain traits. It moves from right to left, counterclockwise, or in a circular fashion. Prayer and light immobilize it. Lower level demons write in a haphazard fashion. The higher level types are capable of writing in a neat, attractive, and orderly script, backward (from right to left) and with sophisticated knowledge of Latin, Hebrew, and Greek.

Fear, hate, and death fuel this entity. Demons often try to come across as your spirit guide. There are several warning signs to look for to determine what type of entity you are dealing with. It is easy to spot a demon.

Something is wrong if you are blindly accepting the information coming through a spirit guide contact merely because it sounds sophisticated. Always use your own background and common sense with this type of data.

Always check for consistency in the data given. Keep a log or diary of the spirit guide information. If your spirit guide gives contradictory material, or if it goes against what other recognized teachers have presented, be wary of its accuracy.

Test the data given by this spirit. The material provided should be new and not merely soundbites from current metaphysical philosophy. It should be verifiable and accurate. If you feel uncomfortable in any way as a result of exposure to this entity, something is wrong. A true spirit guide will leave you with a sense of positivity and empowerment.

Fear

Fear is the only real inhibiting factor in soul travel. I have already discussed fear of leaving the body and fear of what may (but won't) happen to your physical body while astral voyaging.

No matter how frightening an experience is on these other planes, no harm can possibly come to you. If you encounter a scary situation, there are several things you can do to make yourself more comfortable. You can try remaining completely passive—any threatening person or creature will also become quite passive. You can initiate an aggressive behavior such as punching the creature, regardless of its size. It will not counter with depression, but it will depart. You can say: "In the name of God (Allah, or whoever you pray to), go away!" Remind yourself that nothing can harm you. Vizualize yourself completely surrounded by white light that follows you everywhere.

Although you are in no danger when you voyage out of your body, your physical body and psyche may be attacked at any time, whether or not you engage in soul travel.

Summarizing the Astral Plane

The astral plane was named by medieval alchemists who were describing the purgatory dimension of Christianity and the underworld, or Hades of the Greeks. This astral plane is a real world, with inhabitants, houses, objects, and other structures.

It is difficult for most of us physical plane dwellers to conceive of something we cannot see, unless astral voyaging is mastered. The same can be said of the air that surrounds us. We cannot see air, yet hurricanes and tornadoes are known to wreak havoc to our buildings, sink ships, and so on.

Because our imagination and emotions create actual beings and objects on the astral plane, it is often referred to as the realm of illusion. Objects are seen on the astral plane from all sides at once. The inside of a "solid" being is as visible as the outside.

In the past psychics and sensitives were able to view and describe the astral plane. We all have latent psychic abilities, and practicing the exercises presented in this book will assist you in being a first-hand observer of this most interesting dimension.

The Astral Plane is much larger than its physical counterpart, and its borders extend literally thousands of miles above its surface. This dimension is what physicists seem to refer to as the fifth dimension, for all past, present, and future events occur simultaneously on the Astral Plane. Every material object and particle on the physical plane has an astral counterpart, composed of astral matter.

Entities on the astral plane are conscious only of objects on their dimension. They cannot see physical matter from our plane. However, an astral inhabitant may use a medium or attach itself to the aura of a resident of the physical plane, and thereby gain access to our world.

Another oddity of the astral plane is the Astral Light. This is a vehicle that assists in the movement of beings on that dimension. This Light also has access to the Akashic records (stored on the causal plane), analogous to a computer terminal tapping into a mainframe.

Animals have souls too, so their astral counterparts are present on the Astral Plane. Every monster we have seen in a film, ghost-like character, cartoon figure, and representatives of any and all of our thoughts, desires, and emotions will be present on the Astral Plane.

This includes such nature-spirits as elves, pixies, trolls, satyrs, fauns, imps, goblins, fairies, and so on. All types of thought-forms become a reality on the Astral Plane, even though their presence on the physical plane is temporary.

Occultists used the term "elemental" to refer to these thought-forms. These manifestations of our love, kindness, jealousy, insecurity, and evil thoughts and emotions give rise to an entity on the Astral Plane.

The Upanishads states: "Where heaven and earth meet there is a space wide as a razor's edge or a fly's wing through which one may pass to another world."

In the next chapter we will discuss the other planes that exist, and that you may voyage to beyond that of the Astral Plane.

The Other Dimensions

T he premise of this book is that there are other planes of existence (dimensions) beyond the earth plane to which our soul may travel (and does at least nightly) in the form of pure energy (electromagnetic energy). In this chapter we will discuss the plane concept in detail.

The sources for this chapter are drawn from metaphysical literature, the reports from my more than 11,000 patients, and my own personal data from soul traveling I have done. As is the case in almost any type of literature, there are different systems and minor disagreements as to the details of what I present.

For example, the Theosophists (drawing from the Buddhist Masters) declare, with absolute certainty, that there are seven planes. My classification shows thirteen planes. Do not be concerned about these discrepancies. Use this data that I present as background, and make up your own mind as to your belief system. There are no absolute truths, including what I just stated.

First, let's overview the lower five planes in which our karmic cycle is manifested. Each plane is characterized by a unique frequency vibrational rate, or level of awareness. The physical plane is the densest, and this density decreases as the soul moves up to the other dimensions. On these other planes are locations where the soul receives spiritual lessons from Masters and Guides. Some authorities refer to these centers as temples of wisdom.

The Lower Five Planes

The Earth or Physical Plane

This plane is where we are now. It is the realm of illusion of reality (maya), science, body, matter, space, time, and energy. The physical plane is the most stressful dimension, but offers us the greatest opportunity to remove or add karma to our soul's spiritual level of evolvement. Some have suggested visiting various temples of wisdom in certain Tibetan monasteries and in the mountains of Peru. The metaphysical sound associated with this plane is thunder.

The Astral Plane

Psychic phenomena (ghosts, telepathy, clairvoyance, telekinesis, etc.) originates here. The Astral Plane is divided into the lower and upper Astral Planes. The lower Astral Plane is where a soul who has lived a rather evil or completely dysfunctional life would go upon clinical death. There are demonic entities on this dimension, and many who have traveled here would equate it with Hell. You are in no danger of entering this dimension as long as you are protected by the white light. Christians would describe this as purgatory or the bardo state of the Tibetans.

The upper Astral Plane is determined by the concept of imagination and form. You create your own reality by using your imagination to immortalize form. Emotions run high on this plane. In the case of most people, the soul goes here following physical death on the earth plane. Most ghosts (poltergeists) are astral bodies. All buildings on this dimension appear immense in size and almost beyond description. The Temple of Askleposis is a learning center on this plane. This building has been likened to a grand European cathedral. The sound characteristic of this plane is the roar of the sea.

Also in this city is a great museum. All inventions originate on the Astral Plane, since every earth plane inventor has merely traveled to this museum in order to get their ideas. Edison, Da Vinci, Alexander Graham Bell, Nikoli Telsa, Marconi, the Wright brothers, and many others have used this technique to develop things that better mankind.

You can use this museum to work out and improve the destiny of your own life. It is said that George Washington traveled here from Valley Forge during the American Revolution, and he was shown the future of America. This inspiration changed the course of world history.

There is an old metaphysical expression, "So above, so below!" By simply using your imagination at a certain place and time and thinking about a place or event, you are actually sending your astral body there.

You may not create a true bilocation, but you can nevertheless obtain needed information and experience in this way. In recent times we refer to this as remote viewing. Both the United States and Russian governments have spent many millions of dollars on researching the use of astral voyaging for espionage (this technique is discussed in chapters 11 and 14).

Another expression that is relevant here is, "wherever thought goes, the body must follow." I am specifically referring to the astral body, but the mental, causal, and etheric bodies also adhere to this rule.

The Causal Plane

The causal plane is the location of our Akashic records. These records are a detailed account of all our actions and the results of these behaviors in each of our past, present, parallel, and future lives. The progression of our soul's spiritual growth is reflected in these records. In addition, each lesson we have learned or failed to attain is kept on file.

These files have been described as tiny objects resembling electromagnetic computer cards from a storage apparatus. You have the option of reading them directly, or viewing a hologram displaying scenes that depict the entire range of your current life or a past or future incarnation.

It is possible to access these Akashic records from any of the other planes through the use of alpha techniques, or by visiting a learning temple. A medium or psychic is actually reading these records when they give you an accurate psychic reading. The Lords of Karma also have complete access to these "charts." The tinkling of bells can be heard when you voyage to this dimension.

The Mental Plane

On the mental plane, thoughts, philosophy, ethics, moral readings, and intellectual functions dominate. Masters on the physical plane (Jesus, Buddha, etc.) did their work here during their waking state when they occupied a physical body. Most of the time these and current-day Masters are out of the physical body and residing on the mental plane. The God(s) of orthodox religion is/are located here.

Form and creativity manifest themselves as abstracts, numbers, and geometric figures. The souls that live here build their homes in the style of abstract design. The soil is blue and is used to build their roads, which have a deep blue appearance. All souls here wear a white flowing cloak and give the appearance of angels. The sound of running water is heard on this plane. The "Aum" or "Om" sound originates here.

The Etheric Plane

Truth and beauty are the most significant lessons our soul learns on the etheric plane. This plane is the source of our subconscious and primitive thoughts. This dimension appears flat to the soul traveler, due to its vast size. Brilliant white lights dominate the sky of this plane, and the sound of buzzing bees is heard continuously.

Psychic surgery on the etheric body is performed here, which heals the physical body by way of accelerating the self-renewal functions of the physical body. This is accomplished through our aura, or electro-magnetic energy field, representing an extension of our soul. Through color and sound, the etheric body is linked to our Higher Self and this connection brings about healing to our physical body.

The Soul Plane

The soul plane is the ultimate destination of the soul upon its death on any of the lower five planes. It is here where our Higher Self and Masters and Guides educate us and assist us in the selection of our next lifetime. Here on the soul plane with the help of our spiritual advisors, we may access our Akashic records from the causal plane. The sound of a single note from a flute is characteristic of this plane.

It must be remembered that even with the help and advice of our perfect Higher Self and equally perfect Masters and Guides, we always have free will to accept or reject their assistance. If you have a difficult life and keep making the same mistakes over and over again, don't blame anyone else, or the universe. Your life and karma are completely your responsibility. Shakespeare stated it best: "To thine own self be true."

As we shall see when I discuss conscious dying in chapter 9, the soul plane is where our soul embarks from during the process of rebirth and enters into following the end of its previous incarnation.

Summary

We can summarize the characteristics of the astral through etheric planes as follows:

Physical Nature

All dimensions beyond the earth plane are composed of higher vibrational energy. This level increases as we go from the astral to etheric plane, resulting in each world appearing to be less physical than our realm. Time does exist to a degree on these planes, but it is not as significant as within our three-dimensional universe. There are no real outer boundaries.

All worlds seem to occupy the same areas of space throughout all of space, each able to function independently of the other worlds because they are each vibrating at a different rate of energy. An inner plane spoken of as being higher or lower than another simply refers to a difference in vibration, not separation by linear distance.

Most of the people, buildings, and landscapes of these other planes appear earthlike. Some of the dimensions and structural configurations do seem a bit distorted by our earthly standards.

Physical Laws

There are no physical laws on these dimensions as we know on earth. Gravity is non-existent—we can fly anywhere by merely thinking of a location. We appear to be weightless, but can walk on the ground if we choose. Buildings and other structures remain on the ground because our thoughts plant them there; this is not due to gravitational laws.

People

Most of the inhabitants on these planes appear earth-like in every way. There are people of different races, ethnic background, and of various ages. Only a small percentage of these souls resemble alien-like creatures or cartoon characters. The lower Astral Plane is the home of elements from occultist literature.

Language

English is spoken, if that is your native language on the physical plane. Whatever language you are comfortable with will be spoken on these other planes. Most communication is by telepathy.

The Seven Higher Planes

The soul can go no further than the soul or 6th plane until it has achieved perfection. When this state is finally achieved, the soul ascends into the higher planes on its way to God (All That Is, heaven, nirvana, and so on). This is now possible because the soul's frequency vibrational rate is high enough to enter the 7th plane. When a further increase in its frequency vibrational rate occurs, it moves to the 8th plane and so on until it finally reaches the 13th or God plane. Another option for our perfect soul is to remain as a Master or Guide and assist other less evolved souls to reach their state of ascension or perfection.

I particularly like this plane concept in its debunking of the concept of Hell. There is a heaven, but no Hell as the various religions describe. The lower Astral Planes represent a type of temporary Hell, but you can escape from this dimension and move on. Traditional concepts of Hell require the devotee to accept the "one-way ticket" paradigm.

Always bear in mind that it is your thoughts (motives) and actions that determine your frequency vibrational rate. This level of consciousness or spiritual growth is completely within your control. I refer to this as a form of psychic empowerment. As you can see, a belief in God is very much a part of metaphysics and soul travel.

The following chart illustrates this plane concept:

GOD or NAMELESS PLANE (PLANE 13)		
Seven Higher	Plane 12	
Planes	Plane 11	
	Plane 10	
	Plane 9	
	Plane 8	
	Plane 7	

SOUL PLANE (PLANE 6)		
Karmic Cycle	Etheric Plane (Plane 5)	Subconscious
(Lower 5 Planes)	Mental Plane (Plane 4)	Mind
	Causal Plane (Plane 3)	Akashic Records
	Astral Plane (Plane 2)	Emotions
	Earth Plane (Plane 1)	You are Here

Figure 2. The Plane Concept

One question that students of metaphysics have concerning the various planes is their exact location in relationship to each other. These planes do not lie one above the other, but function as different realms of existence. They may occupy the same space at the same time, just as temperance, sound, and light coexist. Our consciousness is the result of the interaction of these planes with our Higher Self and filtered down to our subconscious mind.

The Lords of Karma

One of the more controversial aspects of the working of the karmic cycle involves the Lords of Karma. *Lipika* is another name for these cosmic administrators. Their function is to supervise the process of reincarnation.

The Lords of Karma function like the IRS, registering all actions and experiences of each soul in the akashic records of each individual. Next, they parcel out karmic tests as a form of education to each one of us.[1]

---

1   Hans Ten Dam, *Exploring Reincarnation* (Middlesex, England: Penguin Books, 1990), p. 59.

This karmic audit in the form of tests seems quite unfair, and suggests a violation of the free will principle. However, the Lipika have been reported from many sources throughout history, so we must consider their existence a possibility.

The importance of sound must be mentioned at this time. Two characteristics universally experienced in soul travel are changes in light and sound. This creative energy sound, Vedanta, has been called *Nada Brahma* by the Buddhists, *Vadon* by the Sufis, and *Shabda Dun* by the Hindus and Bani.

A sound wave is created that functions to carry the soul, like an escalator, to other dimensions. Repeating this sound facilitates this mechanism. It is not necessary to do this, but many find it helpful in the early stages of astral voyaging.

Our chakras are responsible for the development and perception of these sounds. The metaphysical literature suggests that this sound is produced by the humming of atoms as they flow out from God's center into the worlds below via the great sound wave, which touches all things (world-soul). This sound expands through our seven chakras.

The main purpose of this sound is to awaken the inner consciousness and connection with God. The bells and gongs of religious services, Gregorian chants, mantras used by the Orientals, the horns blown by the yogis, and the double flute of the Sufi dervishes are other examples of this principle.

The great sound wave is the mode of transportation our soul utilizes to transcend the physical body. Our consciousness actually rides this current of sound right out of the physical body. Often this sound will be heard as a faint high whistle, a tinkling of bells, the buzzing of bees, the sound of a whirlpool, a deep humming, a single note of a flute, a heavy wind, the roar of the sea, or the sound of thunder. Most commonly these sounds are detected in the right ear only.[2]

I have already described the lower five planes and the sounds associated with them. People often ask me: "How do I know which plane I am on when I soul travel?" There are three methods to distinguish your dimensional location. Your Masters and Guides or Higher Self can

---

2   Paul Twitchell, *Eckankar: The Key to Secret Worlds* (San Diego: Illuminated Way Press, 1969).

inform you of which plane you are currently on. The landmarks and uniqueness previously described can assist in your identification as to which dimension is available to your consciousness. Each plane has a characteristic sound associated with it. For example, if you heard the roar of the sea, this would indicate the Astral Plane. The tinkling of bells tells you that the Causal Plane is your current location and so on. A voyager from another plane who does not have an Earth life would hear the sound of thunder as they enter the Physical Plane.

Each plane is also characterized by a different pattern of light. This cosmic light brings us love, wisdom, and bliss when we are exposed to it during our astral voyages. We may also experience it on the physical plane.

Saul of Tarsus experienced such a brilliant light on the road to Damascus, leaving him blind for days, and transforming him into Paul, the disciple of Christ, as a result of this experience.[3] Anyone who is ready to receive this light will be its beneficiary. George Fox, the founder of the Quakers, received this light while in prison. The Roman Emperor Marcus Aurelius and St. Teresa of Avila are other noteworthy recipients.

Once out of the physical body, thought, light, and sound must be integrated. With proficiency we can move anywhere by thought and pass to wherever we desire on beams of sound. These procedures will all be in accord with our thought commands.

Each plane has its own bureaucracy of Masters and Guides that supervise the activities on that particular dimension. These Masters utilize the great sound wave to keep the planes balanced and free from destruction by negative forces. They are in charge of creativity, space, time, and other physical workings of the lower universes. They possess unlimited freedom and have immense powers, along with great wisdom to carry out the management of their universe.

They are perfect beings and have no karma to work out. These entities are subject only to the laws of the worlds within which they reside.

We as soul travelers will encounter some of these Masters during our out-of-body excursions. Learning and spiritual growth is always possible during these encounters.

The more open we astral voyagers are in consciousness, the greater will be the spiritual, illuminating enfoldment of us. This spiritual illu-

---

3   Acts 9:3, op. cit.

mination is not achieved by knowledge alone, but by practice and living the spiritual life.

It is rather difficult to obtain information about the higher planes. Souls with karma simply cannot enter these dimensions. Our Masters and Guides can relay information about these regions if we are prepared to receive them. At the end of this chapter you will find an ascension technique to assist you in traveling to the soul plane where you can access information first hand concerning the higher planes.

When you are on the soul plane your Masters and Guides are able to educate you concerning these dimensions. The more spiritual you become, the greater the likelihood you will be permitted conscious memories of these planes.

The higher planes are hard to describe. These worlds lack any form of negativity. There is a freedom from what we call cause and effect, or causality. The reason for this is that we can only have an effect in relation to a finite mode of being. There is no such state on the higher plane, merely a nowness, isness, and hereness.

Cause and effect is an illusion created by the lower planes, because on these planes a succession exists; one life leads to another, a change of season occurs as a cycle, and so on. None of this happens on the higher planes.

In the higher planes, logic does not exist, and there are no perpetrators or victims. Each energy unit makes its own postulates and functions by them. There is no possibility of harming another soul. In addition, we do not possess any form of body. We are pure and perfect energy voyaging home to God, from whence we came.

Soul Plane Ascension Technique

Now listen very carefully. I want you to imagine a bright white light coming down from above and entering the top of your head. Filling your entire body. See it, feel it and it becomes reality. Now imagine an aura of pure white light emanating from your heart region. Again surrounding your entire body. Protecting you. See it, feel it and it becomes reality. Now only your Higher Self, Masters and Guides and highly evolved loving entities who mean you well will be able to influence you during this or any other hypnotic session. You are totally protected by this aura of pure white light.

In a few moments I am going to count from 1 to 20. As I do so you will feel yourself rising up to the superconscious mind level where you will be able to receive information from your Higher Self and your Masters and Guides. Number 1, rising up. 2, 3, 4, rising higher. 5, 6, 7, letting information flow. 8, 9, 10, you are halfway there. 11, 12, 13, feel yourself rising even higher. 14, 15, 16, almost there. 17, 18, 19, number 20, you are there. Take a moment and orient yourself to the superconscious mind level.

PLAY ASCENSION MUSIC FOR 1 MINUTE

Now from the superconscious mind level, you are going to rise up and beyond the karmic cycle and the five lower planes to the soul plane. The white light is always with you and you may be assisted by your Masters and Guides as you ascend to the soul plane. Number 1, rising up. 2, 3, 4, rising higher. 5, 6, 7, letting information flow. 8, 9, 10, you are half way there. 11, 12, 13, feel yourself rising even higher. 14, 15, 16, almost there. 17, 18, 19, number 20. You are there. Take a moment and orient yourself to the soul plane.

PLAY ASCENSION MUSIC FOR 1 MINUTE

From the soul plane you are able to perceive information from various sources and overview all of your past lives, your current lifetime, and future lives, including all of your frequencies. Take a few moments now to evaluate this data and choose your next lifetime. Get a feel for the entire process.

PLAY ASCENSION MUSIC FOR 6 MINUTES

You have done very well. Now I want you to further open up the channels of communication by removing any obstacles, and allow yourself to receive information and experiences that will directly apply to and help better your present lifetime. Allow yourself to receive more advanced and more specific information from the higher planes this time. Your Higher Self and Masters and Guides may assist you in receiving this all-important information which will help you raise your frequency and improve your karmic subcycle. Do this now.

PLAY ASCENSION MUSIC FOR 8 MINUTES

All right now. Sleep now and rest. You did very well. Listen very carefully. I'm going to count forwards now from 1 to 5. When I reach the count of 5 you will be back in the present and on the earth plane. You will be able to remember everything you experienced. You will feel very relaxed, refreshed, and you will be able to do whatever you have planned for the rest of the day or evening. You will feel very positive about what you've just experienced and very motivated about your confidence and ability to play this tape again to experience the soul plane. All right now. 1, very, very deep, 2, you're getting a little bit lighter; 3 you're getting much, much lighter; 4, very, very light; 5, awaken, wide awake and refreshed.

This technique is admittedly a difficult one for the novice to master at first. It is an advanced form of my superconscious mind tap. I recommend the superconscious mind tap prior to trying this technique.

Preparing for Your Astral Voyage

I have practiced astral voyaging since 1971, and have trained thousands of my patients to experience the techniques presented in this book. The most common complaints I receive from patients, as well as people whom I have never worked with who purchase my tapes, is that they simply could not leave their body when they played so-and-so's tape, or attended another practitioner's workshop.

The main reason for these failures has, in many cases, little to do with the tapes they played, or the clinicians they saw. Belief in the credibility of the technique and/or the person training you is as significant as, if not more than, the technique you utilize. Another important factor is preparation for this OBE.

This book contains dozens of approaches to induce astral voyaging. They will all work, but not necessarily with you. By this I mean you may be far more successful with certain techniques as compared to others. Your friends, family, or even complete strangers may have the most dramatic OBE with methods that only succeeded in frustrating you.

"All roads lead to Rome" and any technique can lead you to an OBE. To make your attempts easier and to facilitate your initial astral voyages, I am going to present certain things you can do to insure your rapid success and maximize your OBE.

Preparation is everything in life. The better-prepared attorney (not necessarily the smarter one) wins his or her cases most often. The better-prepared football team (not necessarily the one with the most talented players) wins the big game on Sunday with greater frequency.

Some of these initial recommendations may seem tedious and unnecessarily cumbersome. Think of them as training wheels on a bicycle. When you no longer need them, simply remove them. I would rather see you over-prepared than under-prepared when you attempt to leave your physical body.

Diet and OBEs

Prescott Hall was an amateur psychic investigator from Brookline, Massachusetts during the early part of the twentieth century. He was a member of the American Society for Psychical Research, and fairly active in his investigations of mediums and claims of paranormal abilities. Hall had occasion to investigate a Boston medium named Minni Keeler from 1909 to 1915 concerning dietary methods for inducing OBEs that were not already published. Keeler detailed much information on the nature of astral projection, far more advanced than anything available in the literature at that time.[1]

Diet Recommendations

Several of my patients have found Minni Keeler's diet recommendations helpful in their initial attempts at astral voyaging. She suggested cutting down on food intake or fasting prior to OBE attempts.

Do not eat anything in the hour just prior to the actual OBE exercise. Fruits and vegetables would be advisable earlier, but avoid meat and nuts of any kind, especially peanuts. Carrots, raw eggs, and liquids of all types aid in OBEs. Keeler recommended abstaining completely from all alcohol, tobacco, and other drugs.

1 Crookall, *The Techniques of Astral Projection,* op. cit.

Visualization Exercises

Keeler also proposed certain visualization exercises to facilitate astral voyaging. Here is a selection from her suggestions:

See yourself swirling through the center of a whirlpool becoming a single point. Now expand this image as you emerge from this whirlpool out of the body.

Imagine your body being transported along a great wave of water, or perceive yourself flying to the Himalyas.

Mentally perceive yourself hanging on to a coil of rope, and slowly emerging from the body of it.

See yourself as a point of light in a large tube that is being slowly filled with water. Imagine now that you spot a tiny hole in the side of the tube and you push yourself through this hole to escape.

Look at yourself as though you were looking at your image in a mirror. Transfer your consciousness to that image.

Concentrate on a spot above your head and try to rise up to it, or imagine your physical body falling through space. Mentally see yourself as a soap bubble floating in space.[2]

Environmental Considerations

Here are some hints concerning the environment of the room where you intend to practice astral voyaging.

Warm weather favors astral voyagers. Keep your room a few degrees above normal room temperature. Do not attempt astral projection during a thunderstorm. The weather should be dry and clear with high barometric pressure. Remember the sound of thunder is associated with the physical plane and will retard your OBE.

Wear very loose clothing or none at all.

Make your initial attempts in complete darkness, or in very dim light. Make sure there is silence, and practice alone.

Time your trials late at night, right before you normally retire. Get yourself in a comfortable position. Lie on your right side for best results, but absolutely never lie on your left side—it will inhibit your success.

---

2 Ibid.

Techniques for Preventing Paralysis

Another of the complaints I hear from people concerning their OBEs deals with the paralysis they experience immediately prior to leaving the body. This catalepsy has been reported many times in the literature during the past 100 years.

It is really quite simple to remove this annoying effect. This temporary paralysis is in no way harmful, but it does help to create fear in the projector. Fear is your chief enemy, for it will either prevent you from leaving your physical body, or result in a very quick trip.

Two simple techniques will prevent this paralysis. One is the superconscious mind tap presented in chapter 4, and the other is white light or spiritual protection technique. You will note I include a white light technique in my script of the superconscious mind tap. Some projectors either ignore it completely, or delete the white light component when they practice these techniques. These are the very same individuals who complain about paralysis just prior to their astral voyage.

Protection Exercise

Try these simple protection techniques to insure no paralysis interferes with your astral trips:

1. Imagine that your physical body is a honeycomb. You are so porous that any energy coming toward you will flow right through you without affecting you in any way. Keep your attention completely focused on this image.

2. Now visualize a trap at the back of this honeycomb mesh screen. This receptacle traps any form of negative energy and immediately neutralizes it.

3. Perceive all of the negative energy that you are exposed to passing through your aura without affecting you in any way. This negative energy now is trapped in this receptacle and is immediately neutralized.

Visualization of Higher Self Assistance

Another visualization that you can apply is the one that follows, which also brings your Higher Self in to assist you:

1. Sit in a comfortable position with your spine straight. Keep still and clear your mind of all thoughts. Breathe in deeply and imagine a ray of white light entering the top of your head. Breathe out slowly.

2. See this white light now surrounding your entire body and a second ray of white light originating from your heart region. This second ray of light merges with the first light and completely surrounds your body and the room in which you are located.

3. Accept the presence of this protective light. Try not to think about it, just focus on your breathing and the presence of this light.

4. Say to yourself or out loud, "I am completely protected and balanced by this white light. Only my Masters and Guides, Higher Self, and loving beings who mean me well can influence me now."

5. As you breathe in, say, "The light and the positivity of the universe becomes a part of my consciousness and protects me."

6. As you exhale, say, "I am merging with my Higher Self and my soul's energy is protected."

This procedure should be practiced for fifteen minutes. The best way to do this is by making a tape of this exercise and playing it with New Age music in the background.

Protection Exercise

Here is another protection exercise that is one of my personal favorites:

1. Sit comfortably or lie down, dressed in loosely fitting clothes, and with your shoes off. Breathe deeply for two minutes.

2. Breathe in deeply and as you exhale, visualize a circle of energy in the form of a white light above your head. Sense this energy moving in a clockwise direction as it moves down your body.

3. This circle of white light now takes the shape of a funnel and appears as a corkscrew as it slowly descends down your body. See certain fragments of negative energy being ejected from your aura as it makes its descent.

4. Imagine this energy field finally moving into your feet. Now see a gold band of energy moving up from your feet to your head. As this gold band rises, it leaves a thin gold shield around your aura. This is a protective covering that only allows positive energy to enter your auric field.

5. Spend five minutes with this last visualization. Now take a few deep breaths and relax.

Chakra Aligning Exercise

The next exercise will align the four upper chakras (energy centers) of the body, and help you to maximize and balance your soul's energy. I refer to this as the *higher chakras link*.

1. Sit comfortably or lie down. Breathe deeply and apply protection. Focus your attention on the Third Eye region of your forehead. This is located between your eyes and is the 6th chakra.

2. As you inhale, imagine a glowing white light being drawn into this Third Eye area and creating a sensation of warmth. Hold this focus for a count of eight. Now exhale and repeat this procedure two more times.

3. As you inhale again, see this glowing white light being drawn up to the crown chakra located at the top of the head. See a rainbow bridge being formed here above the crown chakra. Hold this focus of the rainbow bridge for a count of eight at the crown chakra, exhale and repeat this procedure two more times.

4. Visualize the rainbow bridge moving into the Third Eye chakra and finally into the throat (5th) chakra. As you inhale, feel this warm sensation permeating your throat. Hold this focus of the rainbow bridge in the throat chakra for a count of eight, exhale, and repeat this procedure two more times.

5. Imagine this rainbow bridge moving from the throat chakra into the heart (4th) chakra. This is the area in the middle of the chest at the level of the heart.

6. As you inhale, feel this warm sensation permeating the heart chakra. Hold this focus for a count of eight, exhale, and repeat this procedure two more times.

7. Finally, inhale deeply and hold your breath for a count of ten. As you hold your breath, visually link up the rainbow bridges in your heart, throat, Third Eye, and crown chakras with a band of glowing white light. Feel this link as a warm, tingly sensation. Exhale slowly and repeat this procedure two more times.

You have activated your highest spiritual centers to facilitate your astral voyage.

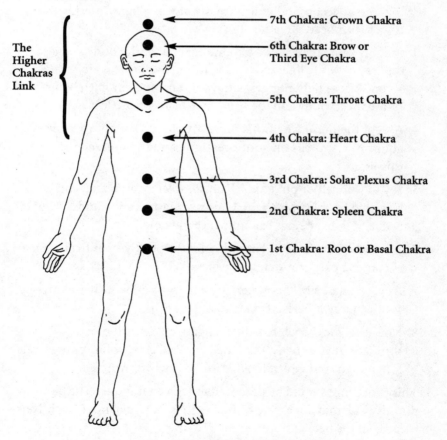

Figure 3. The Higher Chakras Link

The next two groups of exercises will train you to balance your soul's energy and connect further with your spirit (Higher Self) energy.

Exercise to Balance Your Own Energy

The following exercise will assist you in balancing your own energy.

1. Wear loosely fitting clothes and no jewelry. Sit in a comfortable position with your spine straight. Keep still and clear your mind of all thoughts.

2. Place the palms of both of your hands on your thighs in a comfortable manner, without applying pressure to either thigh. Breathe in deeply and imagine a ray of white light entering the top of your head. Breathe out slowly.

3. See this white light now surrounding your entire body and a second ray of white light emanating from your heart region. This second ray of light merges with your aura and completely surrounds your body and the room in which you are located.

4. Accept the presence of this protective light. Try not to think about it, just focus on your breathing and the presence of this light.

5. Say to yourself or out loud, "I am completely protected and balanced by this white light. Only my Masters and Guides, Higher Self, and living beings can influence me now."

6. As you breathe in say, "The light and the positivity of the universe becomes a part of my consciousness."

7. As you exhale say, "I am merging with my Higher Self and my soul's energy is perfectly balanced."

8. Now imagine the white light changing colors as it moves throughout your body. See it become red, green, blue, orange, yellow, indigo, and violet. Let this image stay with you.

This procedure should be practiced for fifteen minutes. The best way to do this is by making a tape of this exercise and playing it with New Age music in the background.

Exercises to Connect with Your Spirit Energy

1. Sit quietly, relax, and breathe deeply. Apply protection (see the superconscious mind tap exercise) and ask your Higher Self to assist you in connecting with your spirit energy.

2. Place the backs of both hands against your forehead. Point both of your thumbs down and continue breathing deeply. Now lift your hands up and move them out in front of you at the level of your shoulders.

3. Turn your hands around so that the palms face you and make sure one hand is on either side of your head. Slowly exhale and say, "OM." While you are doing this, bring your hands to rest in front of your throat, again with their backs facing you and the thumbs pointing downward.

4. Place both hands with their backs toward you on your forehead. Point both of your thumbs down and continue breathing deeply. Now lift your hands up and move them out in front of you at the level of your shoulders.

   Turn your hands around so that the palms face you and make sure one hand is on either side of your head. Slowly exhale and say, "OM." While you are doing this bring your hands to rest in front of your heart, again with their backs facing you and the thumbs pointing downward.

5. Repeat the sequence in Step 4 two more times.

6. Sit in this relaxed position for two minutes. Enjoy this state as you breathe deeply. You have successfully connected with your spirit energy. End this exercise by opening your eyes.

The next exercise is designed to balance your psychic energy with your physical body. If you wish to do this, do not end the preceding exercise but continue with this one as follows:

1. Breathe slowly with your hands palm down on your lap. Focus your energy as a white light, and visualize it rising through your body from your toes to the top of your head.

2. This is your soul's energy. As you continue breathing rhythmically this white light will be joined by other colors. During this time

you are very relaxed and experiencing a feeling of harmony, peace, and balance.

3. Stay in this state from five to ten minutes. End this trance immediately by opening up your eyes. If you feel a floating sensation or perceive yourself leaving your physical body, stay with the experience. You are perfectly safe if you have an out-of-the-body experience at this time.

Focusing Exercises

One of the traits you will have to acquire to successfully leave your body is focused concentration. Try this method to assist you in this goal:

1. Sit comfortably or lie down and breathe deeply. Take a deep breath and hold it for a count of six. Let it out slowly. Take a second deep breath and hold it for a count of nine. Let it out slowly.

2. Select a positive goal or quality that you would like to attract in your life. Emotional fulfillment, peace, compassion, and love are examples.

3. Concentrate on this quality and think about the different ways it could be a part of your life. How would this change your attitude toward life? Imagine how this would affect your family and friends. Keep images of these thoughts and impressions in your mind for six minutes. Set a timer to assure this amount of time.

4. Monitor your thoughts and filter out the unrelated ones. Keep your attention on the images and thoughts concerning this positive quality that you now have incorporated in your life. Note your feelings and make this a part of your reality.

You can try several variations of this exercise by focusing on an object. A favorite piece of jewelry, a flower, or crystal works well. As you concentrate on this item, note its texture, color, and size. Do this for six minutes.

Here is another exercise designed to assist you in focusing:

1. Place a lit candle at eye level and sit in a chair within four feet of it. Make sure there are no drafts in the room. Set a timer for ten minutes and end this exercise the moment the timer sounds.

2. Relax and breathe deeply. Ask your Higher Self to assist you in projecting colors onto this candle flame. Concentrate on the color blue and mentally project that color on to the flickering candle flame. When you see the blue color look away from the candle and begin again.

3. Stare at the candle flame once more, only this time focus on the color green and repeat this procedure.

Your conscious mind might tempt you with outside thoughts. Ignore these mental distractions and continue gazing at the candle flame. You cannot succeed with this exercise if you focus on outside thoughts. You must discipline yourself to deal only with the candle. This applies to any other potential distraction that may be around the room or your home.

In future sessions, you might want to make the candle flame higher or lower with your mind as you develop your psychic powers and your ability to focus on one thing at a time.

Relaxation Exercises

Physical relaxation is quite conducive to the spontaneous occurrence of OBEs. The following regimen will allow you to progressively relax your physical body.

1. Lie on your back or right side, making sure to keep your hands at your sides.

2. Take a deep breath and hold it for as long as you can. Try to force this breath into your stomach. Let this breath out slowly.

3. Repeat this step seven times.

4. With your eyes closed, focus all of your concentration on the top of your head. Now tense the scalp muscles and relax them.

5. Repeat this step with the neck muscles, upper arms, and then move down through the entire body.

6. Focus your attention on your heart, and both listen to and feel its rhythmic beat.

7. Move your awareness of your heartbeat to your scalp and feel the pulsation of your heartbeat in your scalp. Do not merely imagine this pulsation, but actually feel it.

8. Move this feeling of heartbeat down to your forehead, then your cheeks, neck, stomach, lower abdomen, thighs, calves, and feet.

9. Reverse these steps and transfer this feeling of your heart's pulsating rhythm from your feet to your scalp.

10. Last, focus all of your attention on the heart and slow down this beat.

By slowing down your heartbeat you are simulating the state your physical body is in during normal sleep, while you consciously remain awake. This is exactly what happens during an OBE. Modern research on biofeedback demonstrates that with practice it is not difficult to slow down or speed up the heartbeat at will. There is no danger in causing a heart problem, or any other medical difficulty, with this approach. Yogis have been successfully doing this for thousands of years.

Yogic Breathing Exercises

East Indians have used breathing techniques to soul travel for thousands of years. Try these out to prepare for your astral excursions.

1. Either sit or stand in an erect position. Breathe slowly through your nostrils, not from the chest. Let your abdomen extend.

2. Swell the lower chest by pushing out the lower ribs as you breathe through your diaphragm.

3. As you continue breathing, extend the upper chest, again pushing out the lower ribs.

4. Hold this breath and then slowly exhale through the nostrils and/or mouth forcing all the air out of the lungs.

This next exercise prepares you for the actual pranayama devised specifically for soul travel.

1. Lie down in a comfortable position.

2. Establish a steady and rhythmic breathing pattern. Imagine your breath rising up the body through the bones of the legs and finally being forced out of them.

3. Repeat this step but now focus on the bones of your arms, then your skull, stomach, and genitals.

4. Visualize your breath rising up your backbone as you inhale, and descending down it as you exhale.

5. See your breath being inhaled and exhaled through every pore in your skin.

6. Now, as in the previous step, send your breath to your forehead, back of the head, base of the brain, heart, solar plexus, navel region, and genitals.

7. Finally, exhale all of your breath from your lungs and relax.

Deep breathing relaxes the body, calms brain activity, induces hypnosis, and relieves the body of tension. This combination helps bring on an OBE. Yogic scripture stresses incorporating these breathing exercises with other yogic practices, under the guidance of a teacher.

The Bellow's Breath

This form of yogic breathing will facilitate your ability to leave the body. To do this:

1. Sit upright in a comfortable chair and breathe in deeply through your nostrils, so they become flared. Repeat this several times at the frequency of one breath per second.

2. In the beginning, limit yourself to four deep breaths to prevent dizziness. With conditioning you should reach the level of ten breaths.

By practicing this simple technique, you are insuring its natural application by the physical body during your astral voyage. Bellow's breathing allows you to reach a desired target on the astral plane, and maintain your presence on this other dimension for longer periods of time.

Another advantage of this ancient breathing technique is that it assists the astral double in its ability to ward off attack by unfriendly astral entities, should you venture into the lower astral plane. Furthermore, you now exhibit greater control over your astral voyage, and this adds to your maintaining a greater degree of continuity of consciousness. We will discuss the advantages of conscious out-of-body experiences (COBEs) in chapter 9.

Shifting Focus Techniques

In order to shift your focus of awareness out of the body, you will need to develop your ability to visualize. These next two exercises will assist you in this endeavor:

1. Sit in a comfortable chair facing a bare wall.

2. Place a simple object directly in front of your line of vision.

3. Stare at this object until you are certain of its color, design, shape, and contours.

4. Close your eyes and visualize both the object and the room. Recreate all aspects of the room and the location of this object in your mind's eye.

5. See this object as if you could look through your closed eyes with X-ray vision. Do not open up your eyes until this image of the object and the room fades.

6. Repeat this process two more times.

After you have mastered this exercise try the next one:

1. Repeat the steps in the previous technique, only this time use a clock. Memorize the time.

2. Close your eyes and mentally perceive the clock. After several minutes think of what time it is now. Open up your eyes and check your proposed time with the actual time on the clock.

Your visualization ability is excellent if your estimated time is close to that of the clock.

These exercises train you to project some part of your consciousness away from your body, but not so far away that you cannot control it. During your visualizations you may not be able for a moment to determine whether your eyes are closed or open. This is a preliminary shift in consciousness that precedes an OBE. Try suggesting that your consciousness leave your body when this happens.

Hypnotic Trances

Trances are usually associated with either hypnosis or meditation. You might consider it a connection between the physical body and the non-physical subconscious and Higher Self. Many consider trances to be an altered state of consciousness.

Daydreams are simply waking levels of natural trance states. During this state you are relaxed, focused, more creative and less aware of the passing of each moment of time. These altered states of consciousness are when most of your insights, creative inspirations, and problem solving talents surface. You are also more balanced and centered at this time. I have already mentioned the hypnagogic state and its association with soul travel.

Applying the trance state to astral voyaging, we may say that this frame of mind sets aside one level of consciousness (willpower, ego, or conscious mind) to allow another level of consciousness (spirit guide or Higher Self via the subconscious) to come through, or to leave the physical body.

One of the common misconceptions many people have with trance states is that they think spirits are possessing them. To be possessed, certain traits would have to be exhibited.

For one thing, your entire being would literally be taken over by a new personality. In addition, you would experience a sudden change in consciousness and have no memory of what transpired during the possession. The projection techniques I have already presented will protect you from any form of psychic attack. A detailed discussion of these psychic attacks is presented in my book *Protected by the Light* (St. Paul: Llewellyn Publications, 1998).

Types of Trances

A trance may take two very different forms. The mediumistic trance is characterized by the withdrawal of the conscious mind (ego) from the physical body, allowing a spirit guide to communicate directly with you. Another type of this category results in a partial withdrawal of the ego during this process. These are passive states during which the individual's memory is either limited or nonexistent.

The second trance category is referred to as a shamanic trance. In this type, the individual's ego withdraws from the physical body, but the latter is left protected. A more active process ensues in that the soul leaves the physical body to communicate with spirit guides in other dimensions, and returns to the physical body with complete memories of these experiences. This is the type that we will deal with in astral voyaging.

Developing Your Hypnotic Trances

You can develop any trance state with relative ease by using visualizations and guided imagery approaches. These methods help focus the mind with images, while at the same time calming it. You can now become more aware of the inner realms (subconscious and Higher Self) of your mind and allow yourself to travel to the other planes.

To maximize your trance levels, you need to develop creative imagination, visualization, and concentration skills. The result will be an increase in your perception of the spiritual dimensions, and spiritual growth.

Creative imagination enables your subconscious to create scenes and images associated with the information received from the spirit guides. These three-dimensional representatives are equivalent to a daydream or night dream, during which you lose your awareness of the ordinary world around you. You are now more receptive to communication from the higher spiritual realms and are better prepared for soul travel.

The ability to create a mental image or picture and hold it within your mind is what we mean by visualization. This life-like representation allows you to identify with the object or experience. Some of the techniques I have already presented involved visualization, as did the previous section.

Concentration refers to your ability to maintain the image you created in your mind without wandering on to another thought or impression. It implies the technique of putting aside all mundane and distracting thoughts, feelings and impressions that would compete with the initial image you created.

Your soul gains entrance into these spiritual dimensions by using these three abilities characteristic of a trance: creative imagination, visualization, and concentration. This results in direct spiritual perceptions by the subconscious, rather than symbols or metaphors that require translation and interpretation.

The exercises in this book will train you to enter into trance states. Whether it be meditation or self-hypnosis approaches, the trance state will have certain basic characteristics. Among them are a general feeling of relaxation, and a sense of time moving quickly. You will actually have no idea how much real time has elapsed. Your concentration will be more focused. Your eyes may move back and forth (rapid eye movement or REMS), but you will notice a lack of movement in your body.

When you have an OBE you are in a truly altered state of consciousness (ASC). In this deeper trance state you may observe feelings of rejuvenation. A new sense of hope, joy, and purpose is exhibited by the experiencer. You will be aware of changes in meaning or significance. Feelings of profound insight, illumination, and truth are frequently observed in ASC. You may also experience body image changes. A sense of depersonalization, de-realization, and a loss of boundaries between self and others or the universe are observed. These encounters can be called "expansion of consciousness," or feelings of "oneness" in a mystical or religious setting. Not only may various parts of the body appear or feel shrunken, enlarged, distorted, heavy, weightless, disconnected, strange or funny, but spontaneous experiences of dizziness, blurred vision, weakness, numbness, tingling, and analgesia are likewise encountered.

Alterations in thinking may also occur. Subjective interruptions in memory, judgment, attention, and concentration characterize this feature. Some people who experience an ASC appear unable to communicate the essence of their experience to someone who has not had one. Amnesia is also noted.

A disturbed time sense can be evident. Common to this are subjective feelings of time coming to a standstill, feelings of timelessness, and the slowing or acceleration of time.

Some people may worry about loss of control. Someone experiencing an ASC may fear that he or she is losing grip on reality and self-control.

Changes in emotional expression may be evident. Displays of more intense and primitive emotional expressions that are sudden and unexpected appear. Emotional detachment may also be exhibited at this time.

There are certain basic principles of suggestion you should know to maximize your ability to use the scripts in this book or my tapes. Suggestions should always be worded in such a way that they are both clear and unambiguous. The word "must" should never be employed.

You will want to work on only one issue at a time when using auto-hypnosis. The most important and crucial suggestions should always be left until the end.

It is always much easier to secure the acceptance of a positive suggestion than a purely negative one. No matter how deep the trance, no suggestion should ever be given that you might find distasteful or objectionable. In phrasing suggestions aim for a definite rhythmical pattern, and remember, repetition is essential. Keep these suggestions simple.

It is easier to secure the acceptance of a suggestion if it is coupled with an appropriate emotion. A permissive suggestion is more likely to be carried out than a dominating command.

You must have motivation to experience hypnosis. Time must be allowed for a suggestion to be accepted by the subconscious and then carried out. If a post-hypnotic suggestion is used (most therapeutic suggestions are post-hypnotic), always incorporate a cue for the termination of the suggestion if it should be ended. If the post-hypnotic suggestion should not be terminated, be very careful not to give a cue for termination inadvertently.

In my book, *New Age Hypnosis* (1998), I presented specific recommendations for making your own self-hypnosis tapes and how to prepare your practice room for these exercises. A simple recommendation, known as the "Ganzfeld stimulation," will help you produce a slight disorientation and daydream-like imagery to facilitate your OBE.

Tape halved ping-pong balls over your eyes and stare into a red light. I would suggest you play New Age music through headphones as white noise until you attain a satisfactory level of trance routinely. This Ganzfeld effect, developed by William Brand and Charles Honorton, has been shown in their laboratories, and many others, to lead to statistically significant results.[3]

---

3   C. Honorton, "Psi and Internal Attention States," in *Handbook of Parapsychology*, ed. B. Wolman (New York: Van Nostrand, 1977).

Self-Hypnosis Relaxation Technique

The following is a simple self-hypnosis exercise that will relax you and prepare you for more advanced techniques:

Lie down comfortably, close your eyes and begin to relax. Allow yourself to become more and more relaxed. Breathe very deeply and send a warm feeling into your toes and feet. Let this feeling break up any strain or tension, and as you exhale let the tension drain away. Breathe deeply and send this warm feeling into your ankles. It will break up any strain or tension and as you exhale let the tension drain away. Breathe deeply and send this feeling into your knees, let it break up any strain or tension there, and as you exhale let the tension drain away. Send this warm sensation into your thighs so any strain or tension is draining away. Breathe deeply and send this warm feeling into your genitals and drain away any tension.

Send this warm feeling into your abdomen now; all your internal organs are soothed and relaxed and any strain or tension is draining away. Let this energy flow into your chest and breasts; let it soothe you and as you exhale any tension is draining away. Send this energy into your back now. This feeling is breaking up any strain or tension and as you exhale the tension is draining away. The deep, relaxing energy is flowing through your back, into each vertebra as each one assumes its proper alignment. The healing energy is flowing into all your muscles and tendons and you are relaxed, very fully relaxed. Send this energy into your shoulders and neck; this energy is breaking up any strain or tension, and as you exhale the tension is draining away. Your shoulders and neck are fully relaxed. And the deep relaxing energy is flowing into your arms; your upper arms, your elbows, your forearms, your wrists, your hands, your fingers are fully relaxed.

Let this relaxing energy wash up over your throat, and your lips, your jaw, your cheeks are fully relaxed. Send this energy into your face, the muscles around your eyes, your forehead, your scalp are relaxed. Any strain or tension is draining away. You are relaxed, most completely relaxed.

And now float to your space, leave your physical body and move between dimensions and travel to your space, a meadow, a mountain, a forest, the seashore, wherever your mind is safe and free. Go to that space now. And you are in your space, the space you have created, a space sacred and apart. Here in this space you are free from all tension and in touch with the calm, expansive power within you. Here in this space you have access to spiritual information and energy. Here is the space where you can communicate with your spirit guides. Your flow is in harmony with the flow of the universe. Because you are a part of the whole creation you have access to the power of the whole of creation. Here you are pure and free.

Stay here for a few minutes and when you are ready let yourself drift up and back to your usual waking reality. You will return relaxed, refreshed and filled with energy. And you will return now, gently and easily. Open your eyes and stretch your body.

Always bear in mind that the most important factors in inducing soul travel are subconscious desire to have an OBE and practice. Once you attain these goals, astral voyaging will occur spontaneously and naturally. I refer to this as an "astral kickback effect." Previous OBEs lead to spontaneous soul travel.

Trance Conditioning Technique with an OBE

Let yourself relax completely . . . and breathe quietly . . . in . . . and out. And as you do so . . . you will gradually sink into a deeper, deeper sleep. And as you sink into this deeper, deeper sleep . . . . I want you to concentrate on the sensations you can feel in your left hand and arm. You will feel that your left hand is gradually becoming lighter and lighter. It feels just as though your wrists were tied to a balloon . . . as if it were gradually being pulled up . . . higher and higher . . . away from the chair. It wants to rise up . . . into the air . . . toward the ceiling. Let it rise . . . higher and higher.

Just like a cork . . . floating on water. And, as it floats up . . . into the air . . . your whole body feels more and more relaxed . . . heavier and heavier . . . and you are slowing sinking into a deeper, deeper sleep.

Your left hand feels even lighter and lighter. Rising up into the air . . . as if it were being pulled up toward the ceiling. Lighter and lighter . . . light as a feather. Breathe deeply . . . and let yourself relax completely. And as your hand gets lighter and lighter . . . and rises higher and higher into the air . . . your body is feeling heavier and heavier . . . and you are falling into a deep, deep sleep.

Now your whole arm, from the shoulder to the wrist, is becoming lighter and lighter. It is leaving the chair . . . and floating upward . . . into the air. Up it comes...into the air,...higher and higher. Let it rise . . . higher and higher, . . . higher and higher. It is slowly floating up . . . into the air . . . and as it does so...you are falling into a deeper, deeper trance.

Recall a spiritually uplifting moment in your life. It may have been a feeling of reverence during a religious service or in a planetarium looking up at the stars.

Visualize a floating sensation spreading throughout your entire body. Continue breathing deeply and feel your soul leaving your body through the top of your head, as it rises up beyond the earth plane to the astral plane.

Note the warm feeling now spreading and permeating throughout your entire body. Stay with this feeling for three minutes.

Experience a feeling of total love and peace. Let yourself immerse your complete awareness in a sense of balance and centering of your soul's energy. Stay with this feeling for four minutes and slowly return to your physical body. Open up your eyes and stretch.

The Mirror Technique Exercise

1. Sit in a chair placed in front of a full length mirror and place yourself in a hypnotic trance. Many of my patients play my OBE tape prior to practicing this exercise.

2. Open your eyes and look at yourself in the mirror as if your consciousness was in the mirror looking out at its reflection (you in the chair).

3. Stand up and stare directly at your mirror image eyes. Stay in this position until you feel unsteady and begin to sway.

4. Return to your seat and continue staring at your reflection's eyes. Say your name out loud over and over in a monotone voice.

5. Complete this consciousness transfer by imagining your mirror image is speaking your name, while your physical body is moving its lips, but no sound comes out. Hold this image for five minutes.

One concern many projectors have expressed to me is that of going to the lower astral planes on their voyages. I have already described how negative (although harmless) that environment can be. Only five percent of projectors have this encounter in near-death experiences.

The easiest way to avoid this problem is to enhance your own spiritual development. Your soul's frequency vibrational rate will determine which aspect of the astral plane you enter. You do not want to experience the murky atmosphere and unpleasant entities that characterize the lower astral plane.

How does one raise their level of spiritual growth to avoid the lower astral planes? The best way is to work with a competent soul healer to train you in your own growth. If you cannot afford private sessions, I highly recommend my tapes to facilitate your psychic empowerment. Instructions on selecting a soul healer and additional methods to increase your soul's development are presented in my Llewellyn books *Soul Healing* (1996), *Peaceful Transition* (1997), and *New Age Hypnosis* (1998). The advantage of self-hypnosis is that it allows for an automatic partial projection of the astral body, which functions to recharge and vitalize it. This results in an energization of the physical body also. A continuity of consciousness it now maintained.

One indication that you are about to project is a sudden release of disconnected visual images which yogis call *vrittis*. These bring on the actual projection, and represent thought-forms. They are often mistaken for mere visualization.

Basic Astral Voyaging Techniques

In this chapter, I will present a variety of basic techniques designed to facilitate your initial controlled astral voyage. These methods are time-tested and all work. Try each of them and decide which works best for you, then concentrate on that technique.

Although you may enter the causal, mental, etheric, or soul plane, most of you will voyage to the astral plane. There are two possibilities in this dimension, as illustrated in the following chart:

LOWER ASTRAL PLANE	UPPER ASTRAL PLANE
Feelings of confusion and bewilderment	Feelings alert, secure, peaceful, and happy
Misty or foggy environment	Earth-like and beautiful environment with human inhabitants
The presence of bizarre and evil inhabitants	Telepathic, clairvoyant, and precognitive experiences

Figure 4. Astral Plane Dimensions

You can increase your likelihood of traveling to the upper astral plane by following the exercises presented in this chapter.

Often projectors describe themselves in a blue-grey zone that separates the physical from astral plane. Our soul enters this neutral zone in its astral form, commonly described as a sheath appearing as "a thousand sparkling stars."

The soul is drawn to this buffer zone at lightning speed. This region sometimes resembles the underground silo of an enormous rocket, perhaps two hundred feet in diameter and more than two thousand feet deep. The ceiling of this circular pocket is open and may display a brilliant canopy of white light, or you may see a night sky sprinkled with specks of twinkling stars. There may even be a pastoral scene by a river.

Using Stones, Herbs, and Oils to Project Your Astral Body

Stones

A very simple technique to induce an astral voyage is to place an unset stone under your pillow at night and simply go to sleep. I recommend you only use one stone at a time.

Amethyst: This violet stone has been used to treat anger, hallucinations, fear, hate, and grief. Its high vibrational rate makes it ideal for producing OBEs.

Aquamarine: It is supposed that this stone gives clarity to mental visions. A gem of this clear blue or blue-green color assists our astral judgment and clears our mind.

Azurite: This stone is reported to aid our psychic development.

Crystal, Quartz: The rock crystal also assists in facilitating our ESP powers.

Lapis Lazuli: The ancient Egyptians referred to this as the "Stone of Heaven." It is said to promote sound sleep and aid in spiritual vision.

Malachite: This dark green stone creates a feeling of positivity and general well-being.

Moonstone: Your ability to unmask enemies and facilitate dreams will be experienced by using this stone.

Peridot: This light green stone promotes a good nights rest.

Tourmaline, Blue: This stone may be red, green, yellow-green, pink, honey-yellow, violet, or black instead of blue. This stone gives us confidence, inspiration, and tranquillity.

Herbs and Oils

Ancient cultures used the scent of certain oils to improve their psychic senses and induce astral voyaging. You may smell crushed herbs or fresh flowers instead. Do not ingest either the herbs or the oils. Use only one at a time to keep both your physical and astral head clear.

Bay: This herb promotes psychic awareness.

Calendula: Marigold is another name for this flower. It reportedly induces psychic dreams.

Chamomile: This herb relieves tensions and produces restful sleep.

Cinnamon: You will improve your psychic awareness by smelling this fragrance.

Clary sage: The musty scent of this herb promotes calmness and dreams.

Deer's tongue: Smelling this vanilla-like herb will facilitate OBEs.

Frankincense: Become more aware of other planes: unleashing the superconscious and reducing stress are effects of this oil.

Honeysuckle: Your psychic awareness will be increased by smelling this sweet flower.

Hyacinth: This flower is used to eliminate nightmares and promote a restful sleep.

Iris: The odor of this flower root or oil is associated with strengthening the connection between the conscious mind and the psychic centers.

Jasmine: You will have more psychic dreams and feel less nervous while using this oil.

Lilac: Use of this scent will aid in the recall of past lives.

Lotus or Water Lily: Inhaling the scent of this flower creates peace and tranquillity.

Mace: The odor from this nutmeg enhances psychic awareness.

Mimosa: Dreams of the future will be facilitated by the sweet fragrance of this yellow flower.

Mugwort: This plant induces astral voyaging.

Myrrh: The bitter scent of this herb will improve your awareness of other dimensions.

Sandalwood: Your frequency vibrational rate will be improved from its scent.

Yarrow: The rich scent of this garden flower promotes psychic communication.

Visualization Techniques

Visualization has usually, in some form, been involved in inducing OBEs. It is a significant component of hypnosis and most other forms of alpha (meditation, biofeedback, yoga, etc.). Going as far back as the ancient Egyptians, we find records indicating that they believed that mental images could materially affect the physical plane. They felt that a desired event could be brought about by the mere act of visualization.

The most ancient of metaphysical practitioners were (and are) shamans. These healers took their sick on mental journeys to other worlds in search of their soul, and eventually returned it to the patient's body. This soul hunting was called "ecstasy."

During the first century A.D., St. Ignatius of Syria wrote a spiritual manual in which he specified visualizing various holy scenes as a way of creating a state of ecstasy. Visualization approaches are a component to most religions, and are found in all cultures throughout the world.

I wrote a scientific article detailing the current medical and psychological use of visual imagery to treat cancer in 1985.[1] Mnemonic memory systems for learning tasks and disciplines have been around since ancient Greece. The advantage of these visualization techniques for astral voyaging is that they will train you to perceive your whereabouts from a perspective completely independent of the physical body.

---

1   Bruce Goldberg, "The Treatment of Cancer through Hypnosis." *Psychology: A Journal of Human Behavior* 3 (4) 1985: 36–39.

There are five major steps in using visualization to induce OBEs:

1. Develop the ability to construct and control mental images. Try to hold in your mind's eye the image of one of the following symbols for ten minutes without losing it: a blue circle, a white crescent, a red equilateral triangle, a yellow square, or a black oval.

   Try a different symbol at each consecutive trial to eliminate boredom and dependency on any one image. These are known as *tattwa symbols*, and we will use them later in this chapter as doorways to the Astral Plane.

2. Learn yogic breathing. I have already presented a sample yoga exercise in chapter 6. This form of breathing energizes the physical and astral bodies and allows the astral body to initiate the separation process.

3. Master the art of transferring your consciousness into an inanimate object. For example, place a glass across the room from where you practice astral voyaging. Focus your concentration on it, and try to merge with this glass. This exercise succeeds when you are one with the glass and experience yourself as the glass.

4. Learn to project your consciousness away from your physical body to any other location. Try projecting your soul across a room and think from that perspective. Do not visualize or lift out or separate from your astral double. End this session by simply willing your consciousness back to your physical body. Now you can see where the old term "traveling clairvoyance" came from.

5. Practice projecting your consciousness far away from your physical body. This step begins much like step 4, but now you visualize your astral double floating up and away from your physical body. Once this is achieved, will it to travel at least several miles away by concentrating on a person or location. Terminate this step by simply visualizing the astral double reuniting with its physical counterpart.

Cooling Down Technique

Keith "Blue" Harary, the Duke University student who was the subject of a research project by Dr. Robert Morris (see chapter 14), developed a "cooling down" method to prepare himself for his astral voyaging in laboratory experiments. His position is that this quieting down of his body would spontaneously bring on an OBE.

Relax each part of the body by the use of the self-hypnosis exercise I presented earlier. You may use any technique that results in a progressive relaxation of the muscles of your body. This one is taken from my book, *New Age Hypnosis* (1998):

Now I want you to concentrate on the muscle groups that I point out to you. Loosen them, relax them while visualizing them. You will notice that you may be tense in certain areas and the idea is to relax yourself completely. Concentrate on your forehead. Loosen the muscles in your forehead. Now your eyes. Loosen the muscles around your eyes. Your eyelids relax. Now your face, your face relaxes. And your mouth . . . relax the muscles around your mouth, and even the inside of your mouth. Your chin; let it sag and feel heavy. And as you relax your muscles, your breathing continues r-e-g-u-l-a-r-l-y and d-e-e-p-l-y, deeply within yourself. Now your neck, your neck relaxes. Every muscle, every fiber in your neck relaxes. Your shoulders relax . . . your arms . . . your elbows . . . your forearms . . . your wrists . . . your hands . . . and your fingers relax. Your arms feel loose and limp; heavy and loose and limp. Your whole body begins to feel loose and limp. Your neck muscles relax; the front of your neck; the back muscles. Keep breathing deeply and relax. Now your chest. The front part of your chest relaxes and the back part of your chest relaxes. Your abdomen . . . the pit of your stomach, that relaxes. The small of your back, loosen the muscles. Your hips . . . your thighs . . . your knees relax . . . even the muscles in your legs. Your ankles . . . your feet . . . and your toes. Your whole body feels loose and limp. And now as you feel the muscles relaxing, you will notice that you begin to feel heavy and relaxed and tired all over. Your body begins to feel v-e-r-y, v-e-r-y tired and you are going to feel d-r-o-w-s-i-e-r and d-r-o-w-s-i-e-r, from the top of your head right down to your toes. Every breath you take is going to soak in deeper and deeper and deeper, and you feel your body getting drowsier and drowsier.

Allow all outside thoughts during this relaxation phase to drift passively through your mind.

Suggest to yourself that at any time you may experience an OBE, and this projection would be terminated if your physical body felt in any way uncomfortable.

Finally, concentrate on a desired location, or person to visit, and allow yourself to travel there in your astral double.

Here are some additional visualization techniques to facilitate your astral plane exploration:

1. Make yourself comfortable in an easy chair, couch or bed. Relax and close your eyes and reduce as much tension as possible in your body. Take a few deep breaths. Focus your attention on the place between the eyebrows, known as the Third Eye. Many individuals find it helpful to repeat "OM" several times.

2. In your mind's eye create a blank black screen in the Third Eye area. Keep it free from any pictures if at all possible. If you need a substitute for any mental pictures flashing up unwanted, place there the image of something you find pleasurable or comforting.

3. You may begin to detect a faint clicking sound in one ear or the sound of a cork popping. This indicates you are about to leave your physical body.

4. Choose a destination where you wish to visit and focus on this location. Use your five senses at this time; see the colors, smell the flowers, etc. If you are having trouble with visualization, merely think about this destination.

    Soon you will find yourself standing in the center of this scene. Wherever you place your thoughts, the rest of you is bound to follow. This is the astral plane. Be wary of your thoughts at this time, as each cognition will direct the astral body to relocate in a "twinkling of an eye." To return to the physical body, all you need to do is think about it and that will be accomplished instantaneously.

5. Sit comfortably, apply protection, and place yourself in a trance. Concentrate on sending your soul's energy to either the astral, causal, mental, etheric, or soul plane.

6. Breathe deeply, and as you exhale say "OM." Inhale and hold your breath for a count of seven. While you are breathing, focus on the plane you want to travel to and let your spirit guide assist you with this trip. Remain in this trance for at least fifteen minutes.

Through visualization, an individual can achieve a focused awareness while remaining detached from thoughts, emotions, and the dispersion of energy characteristic of ordinary consciousness. Induced visualization, when used while in a state of passive concentration, is a very powerful tool to mobilize the resources of both the body and mind. Visualization has been aptly described as a bridge between the different levels of the self.

The Body of Light

This visual imagery technique is begun by using any standard self-hypnosis or other relaxation technique. Keep your eyes closed at all times.

Phase One

1. Visualize yourself no longer lying down (or sitting in a chair) but instead standing in your room approximately six feet away from your physical body. See yourself in detail, noting your clothes, jewelry, accessories, and so on in great detail. Visualize in great depth, with particular emphasis on color.

2. Now visualize yourself back in your chair or bed and see yourself get up and walk around the room. Mentally note each object in your room in detail. Make sure you are walking in a clockwise direction around your room.

    Notice how the perspective of the room changes as you walk around it. If this is too difficult, open up your eyes, stand up, and physically walk around the room. Then resume this exercise.

3. Repeat step 2, but now move in a counterclockwise direction around your room. Now move your imaginary body to another room in your home and repeat steps 2 and 3. Finally, see yourself wandering through your entire house using these parameters. Do not move on to other rooms until you have mastered visualizing your practice room.

4. Next explore a more distant and less familiar environment. Begin with indoor locations, and later move on to outdoor sites. Always focus on the details of your environment as you move around it. Do not add other people to any of these visualizations.

When you have successfully completed phase one, go on to phase two to develop the technique of visualizing an image of yourself standing at a distance from your physical body while walking around several locations and examining them in detail.

Phase Two

1. Now keep your eyes open and recreate the image of yourself. When you have focused on this image, see yourself looking out from its eyes.

2. Imagine your room from the vantage point of this image of yourself. Scan the room and observe every detail, including your own physical body, either seated or lying down.

3. Have this figure now walk around the room in a clockwise manner and repeat steps 2, 3, and 4 from phase one.

You will experience one of two things happening when you master this phase. Either you will vividly see the room from this new body, or your consciousness will suddenly jump into this created image of yourself.

This technique now becomes more interesting, as you can begin exploring completely unfamiliar locations and travel to other planets. Return to your physical body by reversing this procedure: visualize how the room appears from the vantage point of your physical body while in your "phantom" body.

Your phantom body is not truly an astral double. It can pass through solid objects and travel to any part of our universe. You may also explore the other planes and end up on the soul plane. You have created this astral body out of your mind's energy, rather than separating it from your physical body.

The Body of Light technique projects your focus of consciousness into an astral shell for the purpose of animating it. This is quite different than a classic OBE with a separation of the astral from physical body. This astral phantom can be directed to bring back information you could not possibly know from another location to prove the fact that this is not merely your imagination. Many consider this a mechanism for clairvoyance.

I have considered this mechanism a possible explanation for some (but not all) of the results obtained from remote viewing experiments. You may feel that you are still in your physical body. It is only when you start moving through solid objects, or are unable to touch a physical object, that you convince yourself that "you're not in Kansas anymore."

The phantom body you create can look any way you desire it to appear. This is one reason why the Theosophists refer to this astral body as the "desire" body. If you create an astral phantom twenty years younger and fifteen pounds lighter than you appear today, that is what your astral body will look like during the entire course of your astral trip. In other words, you may shape-shift at will and "be all you can be." It's a most intriguing form of psychic empowerment.

Doorways to the Astral Plane

There are vast pre-formed regions of the Astral Plane that are the result of various influences and energies. To this framework we add our own thoughts and feelings. Metaphysical literature reports doorways that that allow a relatively easy and quick entrance into this other dimension.[2]

The Norse doorway is a bridge of light (the Bifrost Bridge) that has Heimdal (a golden youth) as its guardian. A spring flowing from a cave represents the Celtic doorway. A knight in black armor on a black horse is its guardian.

The Italian, Spanish, French, and Phoenicians all use the same doorway image: a rock island shrouded in a mist, with a discarnate wailing

---

2 Jonn Mumford, *A Chakra & Kundalini Workbook,* op. cit.

voice and a boat as its guardians. A cool cave in a hot, dark desert environment is the doorway of the Native American. Its guardian is a howling coyote. Finally, the Hindus used a tantra yoga kundalini doorway back through the egg and sperm to their original source.

The tattwa symbols developed by Hindu philosophers are associated with the ancient alchemical elements of Ether, Earth, Fire, Water, and Air. When placed on the forehead over the third eye, they assist us in our astral voyages. These are actual doorways to the Astral Plane.[3]

The tattwa symbols are shown below:

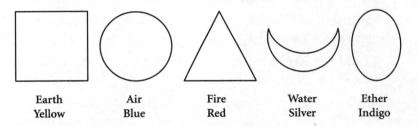

Earth	Air	Fire	Water	Ether
Yellow	Blue	Red	Silver	Indigo

The best way to practice this exercise is to make a set of tattwa cards. Cut white cardboard into two-inch squares. Leave the back of each card white and recreate on the front of the card one of the five symbols in its corresponding color. It is best to use oils or acrylic paint, but pasting colored paper cutouts on the cards works also. The purity and clarity of the colors should be as close to the primary color spectrum as possible. Coat these cards with clear gloss varnish to preserve the symbols and enhance their colors.

Tattwa Exercise

The procedures for this exercise are as follows:

1. Sit in a comfortable chair and relax. I suggest my standard self-hypnosis exercise with white light protection. Select your tattwa card and gaze intently at the colored symbol for thirty seconds. Now turn this card over and stare at the back. The symbol will appear on the back of the card. This optical illusion is quite normal and results in a complementary color appearing. For

---

3   Jonn Mumford, *Magical Tattwa Cards* (St. Paul: Llewellyn Publications, 1996).

example, lavender or mauve will be substituted for the yellow earth symbol.

2. Close your eyes and mentally see this symbol in your mind's eye. It is best to visualize yourself drawing in the glowing symbol.

3. Mentally enlarge this symbol so you can pass through it into the astral plane.

4. Visualize yourself stepping through this now enlarged symbol. Perceive yourself walking a few steps and looking behind you, as you see this luminous door suspended in mid air.

5. Mentally direct yourself to a specific location in the astral plane and begin your journey.

6. To end this session, simply step back through the doorway and return to your physical body.

Another variation of this technique is to stare at a candle. Close your eyes and the after-image of the candle will take the shape of a colonnade of marble pillars or other doorway to lead you to the astral plane.

Guided Imagery

It is easy to equate or confuse guided imagery with visualization. When you initiate a visualization, you are creating a mental picture of a specific thing or event. This is a very active and specific process.

Guided imagery is rather passive and non-directive. This procedure is used to induce a state of relaxation and serenity. You are now taking a mental journey to a comfortable and peaceful place, with no established parameters. This place may be altered at your discretion to make it appear even more relaxing. Often a guide is present to assist you with this journey.

Imagery is a flow of thoughts you can see, hear, feel, smell, or taste. An image is an inner representation of your experience or your fantasies. Imagery is the currency of dreams and daydreams; memories and reminiscence; plans, projections, and possibilities. It is the language of the arts, the emotions, and most important, of the deeper self.

Imagery is a window on your inner world; a way of viewing your own ideas, feelings, and interpretations. It is a rich, symbolic, and highly personal language, and the more time you spend observing and interacting with your own image-making brain, the more quickly and effectively you will use it to travel to other dimensions.

One of the most common misunderstandings about imagery is that it requires you to be able to visualize. While imagery certainly includes what you see in your mind's eye, it also consists of what you hear in your inner ear, sensations and emotions that you feel inside, and even what you smell and taste in your imagination. Some people imagine in vivid visual images with color, sound, smell, and sensation, while others may experience sounds, songs, or thoughts in their heads without any pictures. Some will be more aware of senses or feelings that guide them and let them know when they are close to something meaningful. It doesn't really matter how you imagine—just that you learn to recognize and work with your own imagery. Your purpose is not to get pretty pictures—your purpose is to pay attention to what your body/mind is trying to tell you. Imagery is a vehicle to this understanding, which may come through inner pictures, words, thoughts, sensations, or feelings.

Guided Imagery Exercise with Self-Hypnosis

Here is a sample guided imagery exercise using self-hypnosis:

> Now a feeling of complete relaxation is gradually spreading over your whole body. Let the muscles of your feet and ankles relax completely. Let them go . . . limp and slack. Now, your calf muscles. Let them go limp and slack. . . . Allow them to relax. Now, the muscles of your thighs. Let them relax. . . . Let them go . . . limp and slack.
>
> And as the muscles of your legs and thighs become completely limp and relaxed . . . you can feel a feeling of heaviness in your legs. As though your legs are becoming just as heavy as lead. Just let your legs go . . . heavy as lead. Let them relax completely.
>
> And as they do so . . . your sleep is becoming deeper and deeper.
>
> That feeling of relaxation is now spreading upward . . . over your whole body. Let your stomach muscles relax. . . . Let them go . . . limp and slack.

Now, the muscles of your chest . . . your body . . . and your back. Let them all go . . . limp and slack. . . . Allow them to relax. And as you do so . . . you can feel a feeling of heaviness in your body . . . as though your body is becoming just as heavy as lead. As if it wanted to sink down . . . deeper and deeper . . . into the chair.

Just let your body go . . . heavy as lead. Let it sink back comfortably . . . deeper and deeper . . . into the chair. And as it does so . . . you are gradually falling into a deeper, deeper sleep. Just give yourself up completely . . . to this very pleasant . . . relaxed . . . drowsy feeling.

And now, this feeling of relaxation is spreading into the muscles of your neck . . . your shoulders . . . and your arms. Let your neck muscles relax . . . particularly the muscles at the back of your neck. Let them relax. . . . Let them go . . . limp and slack.

Now, your shoulder muscles. Let them go limp and slack. . . . Allow them to relax. Now, the muscles of your arms. Let them relax. . . . Let them go limp and slack.

And as you do so . . . you can feel a feeling of heaviness in your arms. As though your arms are becoming as heavy as lead. Let your arms go . . . heavy as lead. And as you do so . . . your sleep is becoming deeper . . . deeper . . . deeper. And as this feeling of complete relaxation spreads . . . and deepens over your whole body . . . you have fallen into a very, very deep sleep indeed.

You are so deeply asleep . . . that everything I tell you that is going to happen . . . will happen . . . exactly as I tell you. And every feeling that I tell you that you will experience . . . you will experience . . . exactly as I tell you.

You are about to embark on an imaginary journey, during which your awareness will be introduced to perceptions that are quite different than anything you have encountered before. You absolutely have the ability to voyage to the astral plane or beyond.

Your silver cord will always remain attached to your physical body—protecting you and transmitting communication from your Higher Self to your subconscious.

Continued practice will insure your success. Your voyages will only be to the upper astral plane or beyond. There is no possibility of ending up on the lower astral plane.

Your Higher Self and Masters and Guides are always with you, advising and protecting you. Only positive entities will be a part of this experience.

Now raise your vibrations, feeling them spreading throughout your body from the bottom of the spine to the top of the head. Feel the vibrations accentuate this ascension. Do this now.

PLAY NEW AGE MUSIC FOR 2 MINUTES

Your astral body is now separating itself from the physical. See yourself in your mind's eye leave your body through the top of your head. See it happening in your mind and feel it happening in your body. See your astral body float just above your physical body. Now stand next to your physical body and observe it. Move out of this room and rise up into the air. Fly around your local area. Do this now.

PLAY NEW AGE MUSIC FOR 2 MINUTES

Now continue rising up into the atmosphere as you venture on to a planet of your choosing. For this first voyage select from one of the following: the Moon, Mars, or Venus. Explore this planet at your leisure. On subsequent voyages you can select more distant planets.

PLAY NEW AGE MUSIC FOR 3 MINUTES

You've done very well. Now we're going to send your astral body to the upper astral plane or beyond. If you would like to explore the causal, mental, etheric or even the soul plane, just concentrate on the name of this dimension.

As I count forward from 1 to 10, on the count of 10 you will arrive at your destination. 1, 2, 3, moving toward this plane. 4, 5, halfway there. 6, 7, 8, almost there. 9, 10, you are there.

Now begin exploring this dimension at your leisure. Record everything you see, hear, touch, taste, and feel in your subconscious, to be remembered later. Do this now.

PLAY NEW AGE MUSIC FOR 3 MINUTES

Now begin your trip back to Earth by first entering a brilliant white light that you now see before you. Descend back to your room and merge with your physical body. Note the warm feeling now spreading and permeating throughout your entire body. Stay with this feeling for a few moments.

Experience a feeling of total love and peace. Let yourself immerse your complete awareness in a sense of balance and centering of your soul's energy.

Stay with this feeling for a few more moments.

PLAY NEW AGE MUSIC FOR 2 MINUTES

All right now. Sleep now and rest. You did very, very well. Listen very carefully. I'm going to count forward now from 1 to 5. When I reach the count of 5, you will be able to remember everything you experienced. You'll feel very relaxed, refreshed and you'll be able to do whatever you have planned for the rest of the day or evening. You'll feel very positive about what you've just experienced and very motivated about your confidence and ability to play this tape again to voyage to other dimensions. All right now. 1, very, very deep. 2, you're getting a little bit lighter. 3, you're getting much, much lighter. 4, very, very light. 5, awaken. Wide awake and refreshed.

Contemplation Exercises

This is an approach to clearing your mind and focusing your concentration that lies somewhere between meditation and hypnosis. With meditation you are attempting to achieve a relaxed and passive state of body and mind. This is attained by initially relaxing the physical body and freeing the mind of all thoughts concerning the physical body and material world.

Hypnosis is a more directed type of concentration, during which a rigorous attempt is made to hold specific ideas or visual images in the

mind while the body is relaxed. Although I personally and professionally feel self-hypnosis is the most efficient and easiest method to use for
astral voyaging, some individuals find it difficult to focus their concentration enough to attain the result of leaving the body.

Contemplation is not passive as is meditation, yet not nearly as mentally and physically rigorous as hypnosis. We may define contemplation
as a relaxed focusing of the mind in one specific direction, with a continuous orientation on some feeling, thought, or idea. In contemplation
one does not try to rigidly affix the mind to anything, but instead allows
it to wander and simply brings it back each time it tries to wander.

Contemplation Techniques Preparation

Here are some simple contemplative techniques to prepare you for the
exercises in this section:

1. Imagine yourself in a circular-shaped weightless form.
2. Visualize a black inner screen with your eyes closed. This screen is
   pitch black.
3. Now place one small white speck of light on the black inner
   screen. Vary this technique by using a blue, red, then gold light
   speck.
4. Perceive yourself in a weightless body inside your physical body.
5. Listen for a faint high whistling sound by the top of your head.
6. Before going to sleep, keep a constant but vague awareness of
   your own identity. Then shift your focus from your body into
   blackness.

This method combines a mantra with visualizations.

1. Visualize your inner black screen prior to going to sleep, and
   place one blue speck of light on it. Your eyes are now closed.
2. Say out loud the word "OM," or any mantra you have used in the
   past. Repeat this mantra several times.
3. Imagine yourself watching a sunset with someone you care about,
   or walking in a park.
4. Keep this awareness as you drift off to sleep.

The best results with contemplation approaches occur when practiced in the middle of the night. The easiest way to arrange this is to go to bed at your usual time and set your alarm clock to go off in about four hours. Then get up, go to the bathroom and splash cold water on your face. Return to your bed and begin these contemplation exercises while lying on your back.

Contemplation Technique 1

1. While your eyes are closed, relax your body with any exercise previously presented.

2. Imagine a tingly sensation spreading through your entire body, as if you had just returned from an astral voyage. Focus on creating this feeling in your ankles, feet, wrists, and hands.

Contemplation Technique 2

1. As you lie in bed, focus your mind on relaxing your entire body. When this has been accomplished, pay particular attention to relaxing the muscles across both temples. This area extends from the middle of eyebrow to an inch above the ear (the third eye).

2. Listen for a faint high whistle at the top of your head, or any other sound that is not created by your physical environment.

3. Imagine a tingly sensation moving through this third eye region and flowing downward throughout your physical body.

4. Magnify the sound and perceive it as a current of energy flowing from your eyebrows down your physical body to your feet and back to your forehead. This sound current of energy now creates a vibration that surrounds your physical body.

5. Imagine your astral body vibrating out through the third eye region of your head.

Contemplation Technique 3

1. Relax yourself as you lie in bed and mentally induce a tingly sensation at a spot just under the scalp on the top of your head.

2. Relax your eyes and eyelids completely by spending a few minutes using one of the self-hypnotic exercises already presented.

3. Mentally visualize the black inner screen inside your closed eyes. Now project on the screen an image of your astral body separating from your physical body at the top of your head, just above the site of the tingly sensation you created in step 1.

When you use this technique there are some considerations you need to be aware of: Don't become frustrated if you experience your mind wandering during this contemplation. Remove any expectation of actually feeling your two bodies separating. What is more likely to occur is a shift in your awareness during the early stages of your first sleep cycle of being out-of-body. Eliminate the tendency to expect a full OBE with this approach. Just relax and enjoy this experience.

Contemplation Technique 4

1. Relax your entire body while lying in bed and rotate your eyeballs upward toward the third eye region of your forehead. This will cause a slight strain on the muscles surrounding your eyes.

2. Focus on the inner black screen and perceive only darkness. Do not drift off to sleep yet.

3. Listen for a faint high whistle in the top of your head, or any other unusual sounds. Create one if none occurs by itself.

4. Imagine a tingling sensation spreading from your third eye region down throughout your physical body. Keep focusing on your black inner screen during this time.

5. Visualize this sound as part of a luminous white wave on your inner black screen. See this wave rise and carry your astral body with it, resulting in a complete separation from its physical counterpart.

6. Now remove all thoughts and images of the inner black screen, and merely keep a vague awareness centered around your third eye region.

You will fall asleep after step 6 and be aware of an OBE. If your mind wanders during this or any other contemplation, repeat over and over again to yourself the instructions given here.

Remote Viewing

There is an ongoing debate among scientists and clinicians as to whether remote view is a form of "traveling clairvoyance," or a true OBE. I feel it represents a continuum and one can advance from clairvoyance to a classic OBE, depending on the technique applied and the motivation of the subject. Scientific experiments conducted on remote viewing at Stanford Research Institute (SRI) and other institutions will be addressed in greater detail in chapter 14.

The psychic Ingo Swann is credited with developing remote viewing techniques as an aside from his participation in research at SRI. Russell Targ and Harold Puthoff were the SRI investigators who initially studied this phenomenon.[4]

Swann was able to project his consciousness to a location with only the longitude and latitude coordinates given to him by Targ and Puthoff. Swann then reported what he "saw," with astounding accuracy.

The following exercise is divided into two phases. During the first phase you are training yourself to remote view with complete knowledge of the target location. The second phase tests your ability to remote view without foreknowledge of the target site. This latter phase is a simpler version of what SRI and many other researchers conducted as part of their studies.

Phase One

1. Have a friend take pictures of landmarks in your community. Place yourself in a hypnotic trance and view one of these photos.

2. Close your eyes and visualize your astral double traveling to that site. Make detailed notes of your experience.

3. Compare your notes with the photo. Pay particular attention to the hits and misses.

4. Drive to the target site and note some details that you may have stated that were not on the photo. If your observations are correct, and you have never been to this site before, these "extra" details strongly suggest you were successful at remote viewing.

---

4 Ingo Swann, *To Kiss Earth Good-Bye* (New York: Hawthorne, 1975).

Phase Two

1. Have a friend drive to a randomly selected target site in your city, and call you when he or she arrives at the site, but not tell you the exact location.

2. Place yourself in a trance and visualize your astral body joining your friend at this location.

3. Report everything you "see" into a tape recorder and type up this description.

4. Repeat this experiment five additional times with different sites at each trial.

5. Have your friend read your typed descriptions in random order. See if he or she can match your observations to the target site.

Here are some helpful hints to facilitate your progress in developing your remote viewing skills: Draw what you observe. Report everything you see, even if it doesn't make sense. Don't report what you think, but what you see. Refrain from editing or censoring these images. Note everything you detect. Don't attempt too many trials in a short space of time.

To keep your experiments scientifically valid, there are some parameters to guide you. The person going to the site should interact as much as possible within the target, keeping their curiosity focused only on the target selected. You should spend between fifteen and thirty minutes working on a target. Targets are always selected and put together by someone outside of the experiment. Targets selected should stand alone and be uniquely different from one another.

Self-Hypnotic OBE Technique

Here is a self-hypnotic OBE technique that combines several approaches including white light protection. This method eliminates any possibility of paralysis or any other discomforts as you voyage out of the body.

Now listen very carefully. I want you to imagine a bright white light coming down from above and entering the top of your head, filling your entire body. See it, feel it, and it becomes reality.

Now imagine an aura of pure white light emanating from your heart region. Again surrounding your entire body. Protecting you. See it, feel it and it becomes reality. Now only your Masters and Guides and highly evolved loving entities who mean you well will be able to influence you during this or any other hypnotic session. You are totally protected by this aura of pure white light.

Now as you focus in on how comfortable and relaxed you are, free of distraction, free from physical and emotional obstacles that prevent you from safely leaving and returning to the physical body, you will perceive and remember all that you encounter during this experience. You will recall in detail when you are physically awake only those matters that will be beneficial to your physical and mental being and experience. Now begin to sense the vibrations around you and in your own mind begin to shape and pull them into a ring around your head. Do this for a few moments now.

PLAY NEW AGE MUSIC FOR 2 MINUTES

Now as you begin to attract these vibrations into your inner awareness, they begin to sweep throughout your body, making it rigid and immobile. You are always in complete control of this experience. Do this now as you perceive yourself rigid and immobile with the vibrations moving along and throughout your entire body.

PLAY NEW AGE MUSIC FOR 3 MINUTES

You have done very well. Pulse these vibrations. Perceive yourself feeling the pulse of these vibrations throughout your entire awareness. In your own mind's eye, reach out with one of your arms and grasp some object that you know is out of normal reach. Feel the object and let your astral hand pass through it. Your mind is using your astral arm, not your physical arm, to feel the object. As you do this you are becoming lighter and lighter, and your astral body is beginning to rise up from your physical body. Do this now.

PLAY NEW AGE MUSIC FOR 3 MINUTES

You've done very well. Now, using other parts of your astral body (your head, feet, chest, and back) repeat this exercise and continue to feel lighter and lighter as your astral body begins to rise up from your physical body. Do this now.

PLAY NEW AGE MUSIC FOR 3 MINUTES

Now think of yourself as becoming lighter and lighter throughout your body. Perceive yourself floating up as your entire astral body lifts up and floats away from your physical body. Concentrate on blackness and remove all fears during this process. Imagine a helium-filled balloon rising and pulling your astral body with it, up and away from your physical body. Do this now.

PLAY NEW AGE MUSIC FOR 3 MINUTES

Now orient yourself to this new experience. You are out of your body, relaxed, safe, and totally protected by the white light. Concentrate on a place, not far away, that you would like to visit with your astral body. Now go to this place. Do this now. Perceive this new environment.

PLAY NEW AGE MUSIC FOR 3 MINUTES

You've done very well. Now I want you to travel to a destination much farther away. It can be a location across the country or anywhere around the world. Take a few moments and think of this destination and you will be there in a few moments. Do this now.

PLAY NEW AGE MUSIC FOR 3 MINUTES

All right now. Sleep now and rest. You did very well. Listen very carefully. I'm going to count forward now from 1 to 5. When I reach the count of 5 you will be back in the body. You will be able to remember everything you experienced and re-experienced. You'll feel very relaxed and refreshed, you'll be able to do whatever you have planned for the rest of the day or evening. You'll feel very positive about what you've just experienced and very motivated about your confidence and ability to play this tape again to experience leaving your physical body safely. All right now. 1, very very deep; 2, you're getting a little bit lighter; 3, you're getting much much lighter; 4, very very light; 5, awaken. Wide awake and refreshed.

Near-Death
Experiences

I have used the term altered states of consciousness (ASCs) before when referring to out-of-body experiences. This chapter will concern itself with the type of ASC that has received the most scientific attention and publicity during the past twenty years: the near-death experience (NDE).

There are three classes of ASC, and they can be listed as follows:

- Out-of-Body Experiences (OBEs), such as dreams and astral voyages. This is a natural occurrence that in no way endangers the physical body, and is the main subject of this book.

- Near-Death Experiences (NDEs) requires an actual physical death for a few seconds to a few minutes (usually). This is also a natural process that I feel always precedes physical death and initiates a process known as unconscious dying that will be discussed in the next chapter.

- Conscious Out-of-Body Experiences (COBEs) are produced when the soul maintains a connection with the Higher Self at the precise moment of physical death. This may eliminate the need to reincarnate. I refer to this as conscious dying, a most interesting and empowering form of ASC that we will discuss in chapter 9.

119

NDEs have been reported throughout history. These descriptions of the "other side" have been presented by people who have had near-death experiences, historians, philosophers, clairvoyants, mystics, and others sensitive enough to relate their out-of-body encounters.

The psychiatrist Raymond Moody was the first person to apply the term "near-death experience" to this phenomenon, and he published his findings in his international bestseller *Life After Life*. This 1975 work reflected interviews with over 150 patients over a period of eleven years.

About forty percent of Dr. Moody's patients reported core experiences much like those of ordinary OBEs described earlier in this book, with the exception of the panoramic life review, and a being encouraging the soul to enter the white light.[1]

Kenneth Ring, a psychology professor at the University of Connecticut, was the first researcher to scientifically corroborate Moody's work. In Ring's book *Life at Death*, he reports observations of near-death experiencers that are very similar to those my patients describe, such as traveling through a dark tunnel and finding at the other end a very pleasant and comforting place.[2] Some of Ring's subjects reported seeing angels and hearing beautiful music. He pointed out that the soul can choose to return to the physical body, and may be told that if they go back they are going to suffer, perhaps to endure some real pain.

Ernest Hemingway was a young officer with the U.S. Ambulance Corps during World War I. In July of 1918, near the village of Fossalta in Italy, Hemingway was seriously wounded from a mortar shell explosion.

Hemingway's own NDE inspired him to write his famous 1929 novel, *A Farewell to Arms*.[3] When the character Frederic Henry is wounded in this fictional depiction, he describes trying to breathe but being unable to, and feeling himself rush out of his body: "I went out swiftly, all of myself, and I knew I was dead and that it had all been a mistake to think you just died. Then I floated, and instead of going on I felt myself slide back. I breathed and I was back."

---

1 Raymond Moody, *Life After Life* (New York: Bantam, 1975).

2 Kenneth Ring, *Life at Death* (New York: Quill, 1982): pp. 53–55, 61–62.

3 Ernest Hemingway, *A Farewell to Arms* (New York: Charles Scribner's Sons, 1929), p. 54.

The English poet and painter William Blake (1757–1827) depicted NDEs in his art. His *The Descent of Man into the Vale of Death* shows a soul's journey to a shadowy cave, where an angel holding a light guides these spirits into a cavern. Loved ones are present to counsel these recently transitioned souls.

Blake's *The Soul Hovering Above The Body* depicts a departing spirit quite reluctant to give up her earthly sojourn. His watercolor *Jacob's Dream* shows angels leading souls, some of whom are children, up a spiral staircase toward a white light.

William Blake described the "Halls of Los" in his poetry. It is here that events in our lives are preserved in the form of statues. It is only when we focus our attention on these lifeless figures that they become alive and we can view our actions. Past, present, and future events are depicted in this museum. Does this not describe the Akashic records, or possibly the causal plane itself?

Another famous depiction of the core NDE is that of the painter Hieronymus Bosch (1450–1516). His *Ascent into the Empyrean* shows souls accompanied by angels moving through a dark tunnel toward a white light. Here we have a core NDE depicted 500 years ago!

There are also biblical references to NDEs. The following vision on the road to Damascus was described by the Apostle Paul:

> *At midday, O king, I saw in the way a light from heaven, above the brightness of the sun, shining round about me and them which journeyed with me. And when we were all fallen to the earth, I heard a voice speaking unto me, and saying in the Hebrew tongue, "Saul, Saul, why persecutest thou me? It is hard for thee to kick against the pricks."*
>
> *And I said, "Who art thou, Lord?" And he said, "I am Jesus, whom thou persecutest. But rise, and stand upon thy feet: for I have appeared unto three for this purpose, to make thee a minister and a witness, both of these things in which I will appear unto thee. . . ."*
>
> *Whereupon, O King Agrippa, I was not disobedient unto the heavenly vision. . . . And as I thus spake for myself, Festus said with a loud voice, "Paul, thou art beside thyself; much learning doth make thee mad."*

But I said, "I am not mad, most noble Festus; but speak forth the words of truth and soberness."[4]

And:

But someone may ask, "How are the dead raised? With what kind of body will they come?' How foolish! What you sow does not come to live unless it dies. When you sow, you do not plant the body that will be, but just a seed, perhaps of wheat or of something else. But God gives it a body as he has determined, and to each kind of seed he gives its own body. . . . There are also heavenly bodies and there are earthly bodies; but the splendor of the heavenly bodies is one kind, and the splendor of the earthly bodies is another. The sun has one kind of splendor, the moon another and the stars another; and star differs from star in splendor. So will it be with the resurrection of the dead. The body that is sown is perishable, it is raised imperishable; it is sown in dishonor, it is raised in glory; it is sown in weakness, it is raised in power; it is sown a natural body, it is raised a spiritual body. If there is a natural body, there is also a spiritual body. . . . Listen, I tell you a mystery: We will not all sleep, but we will all be changed—in a flash, in the twinkling of an eye, at the last trumpet. For the trumpet will sound, the dead will be raised imperishable, and we will be changed.[5]

The first relatively recent collection of NDEs is credited to a Swiss professor of geology named Albert Heim. He had an NDE after a fall he suffered while climbing the Santis Mountain in the Swiss Alps in 1871. He depicted his NDE as follows:

What followed was a series of singularly clear flashes of thought between a rapid, profuse succession of images that were sharp and distinct. . . . I saw myself as a seven-year-old boy going to school. . . . I acted out my life, as though I were an actor on stage, upon which I looked down as though from practically the

---

4 Acts 26:13–6, 19, 24–25. Holy Bible, Revised Standard Version (International Bible Society, 1973).

5 I Corinthians 15: 35–38, 40–44, 51–52. Ibid.

highest gallery in the theater. I was both hero and onlooker. . . .
They sounded solemn music. . . . I felt myself go softly backwards
into this magnificent heaven—without anxiety, without grief.[6]

Heim published his finding of more than thirty survivors of near-fatal falls in the Alps in 1892. His work was one of the first to scientifically document the core experience of an NDE. His reports included panoramic life reviews, a freedom of fear of the subjects and he also reported an increased speed of thought.

In a study conducted between 1959 and 1960, researcher Karlis Osis demonstrated that deathbed visions were not hallucinations. Neither drugs nor fevers influenced these visions, and the visions reported significantly differed from the auditory hallucinations characteristic of psychotic patients. These deathbed visions were two to three times more likely to contain dead people, as contrasted with reports of those not near death. Social status, religion, age, and education had little effect on the visions.[7]

Thanatologist and noted author and psychiatrist Elisabeth Kübler-Ross described death as: ". . . a shedding of the physical body, like the butterfly coming out of a cocoon. It is a transition into a higher state of consciousness, where you continue to perceive, to understand, to laugh, to be able to grow, and the only thing you lose is something that you don't need anymore . . . your physical body."[8]

Women are more likely to have an NDE in connection with an illness. NDEs reported by men are more commonly associated with accidents or suicide attempts. Either sex may describe a silver cord that pulsates and connects the astral body to the physical body, usually at the back of the head of the latter (one has to turn around in this altered state of consciousness to note its presence).

The reports of children lend additional credibility to NDE depictions. These young souls are twice as likely to report the brilliant white light and have more vivid recollections than adults. The panoramic life review is absent from these reports. Lastly, children have shown a

---

6   A. Heim, in "Notizen ober dem tod durch Abstorz." *Jahrbuch des Schweizerischen Alpclub* 27 (1892): 327–337. Translated in *Omega* 3 (1972): 45–52.

7   K. Osis and E. Haraldsson, *At the Hour of Death* (New York: Avon, 1977).

8   Elisabeth Kübler-Ross, *On Death and Dying* (New York: MacMillan Pub. Co., 1969).

tendency to temporarily forego their childhood identities and become ageless and wise beyond their years.

NDEs can have a remarkable effect on one's life path. A baby-boomer television writer and producer patient of mine whom I'll call Darlene described her NDE when she was fourteen. She was involved in a rather serious car accident. Her mother had to lift up the vehicle to save Darlene.

As a result of this NDE, Darlene lost all fear of death and became very much involved in spiritual pursuits. She worked on the 1970s *In Search Of* television series, and was a close friend to the late Gene Roddenberry, the creator of *Star Trek*.

Tina is a woman in her mid-forties who had an NDE in 1987 as a result of an accident on the construction site of a home she was having built. This former patient of mine described a spirit encounter with an adolescent astral body both during and subsequent to her NDE.

Tina has since received several communications from her late father, with whom she had a very close relationship. He crossed into spirit in 1991. Tina continues to practice regular astral voyaging to this day. She has lost her fear of death, a significant issue with her prior to her NDE. Finally, my former patient is very much empowered and states that she has a new lease on life.

Ray Moody relates a dramatic example of how these NDE reports cannot be confabulated. One of his interviewees precisely described the various instruments that the emergency room staff used to resuscitate her following her heart attack. This elderly woman even described the correct colors of these instruments. What is most unusual about this case history is the fact that this woman couldn't possibly have fudged or exaggerated this depiction—she had been blind for over fifty years![9]

Science Challenges the Efficacy of NDE

In the scientific community there are no shortage of detractors to the validity of NDE. Certain biological and chemical explanations have been proposed to explain this phenomenon. Let us discuss the most common arguments:

---

9   Moody, op. cit.

- Temporal lobe stimulation—Although the panoramic life review may be produced by what Ring calls: "seizure-like neural firing patterns in the [brain's] temporal lobe."[10] This does not produce the entire range of effects described in the core experience.

- Cultural conditioning from media reports about NDEs—Kenneth Ring's study clearly showed that nearly twice as many of those that had no NDE were aware of this phenomenon and the work of Elizabeth Kübler-Ross and Raymond Moody's work · through the media. This defeats any argument that the experiencers were culturally conditioned to have this result. Furthermore, Osis' study demonstrated that social status, religion, age, and education had no significant effect on the reports of NDEs.

- Anesthetics—The only conceivable way general anesthetics could mimic the core experience would be to elevate the bloods level of carbon dioxide. Carbon dioxide does produce the effect of moving through a tunnel and bright lights, but it cannot simulate beings of light or panoramic life reviews. Atlanta cardiologist Michael Sabom measured the blood oxygen levels of a patient at the precise moment of NDE. He found that the oxygen levels were above normal. Patients are given pure oxygen, never carbon dioxide, as part of any resuscitation procedure. Many NDE experiencers had no drugs given to them at all![11]

- Other drugs—Hallucinogenic drug use results in a distorted and variable description of the trip. As already noted, the core experience in an NDE is clear, real, and fairly consistent.

- Cerebral anoxia—NDE reports are not characterized by a cut-off of blood flow to the brain. Even if that did happen, a state of unconsciousness would result and the patient would have no memories of this time. Again, the entire range of the core experience would not be exhibited by cerebral anoxia. Cerebral

---

10 Ring, op. cit., p. 213.
11 Michael Sabom, *Recollections of Death* (New York: Harper & Row, 1981).

anoxia has been produced experimentally, and no one has yet reported the characteristics of an NDE.

◆ Hallucinations—A flat EEG indicates clinical death due to the absence of brain activity. Some reports of NDE coincided with the precise moment of a flat EEG. If this NDE was a hallucination, the EEG would have registered it as such.

Reports of NDE illustrate that it represents a distinctive state of consciousness. This transpersonal state completely transforms or removes many common features of cognition and perception. The voice is assumed to be the Higher Self or a spirit guide.

We can summarize the research findings concerning NDEs as follows:

◆ Ninety-five percent of NDEs are positive, literally transforming the personality of the recipient. These represent voyages to the upper astral plane or beyond. Many patients do not want to return to the physical body because it is so positive. The five percent of negative depictions, I believe, represent sojourns to the lower astral planes.

◆ The patient sometimes gets information about the future. Some of these precognitions have been documented.

◆ A "Being of Light" often conducts a panoramic life review of the patient during an NDE. Not only is every action observed, but their effects on others are noted. Telepathy is the mode of communication.

◆ NDEs cannot be explained adequately on the basis of drugs, hallucinations, cultural conditioning, etc.

◆ Religion, race, and age are also unrelated to NDEs.

◆ NDEs are reported in thirty-five to forty percent of people who have a brush with death.

◆ The overnight personality changes that occur, including greater zest for life, improved self-confidence, healthier eating habits, and increased compassion cannot be explained by hallucinations or any other conjecture proposed by the skeptics critical of this experience.

An NDE is one of the most powerful events a person can experience. It has redirected lives, created saints, inspired religions, and shaped history. This phenomenon has done wonders in removing the fear of death in those who experienced it.

Some behaviors can facilitate our success in the application of soul travel techniques. This list is from my book *Peaceful Transition* (1997).

- Be loving, unselfish, and kind; love is the most important quality in the universe.

- Be a giver. Eliminate the tendency to take from others. Live a more simple and quality life.

- Decrease the attachment to material possessions. Enjoy them all you want but be willing to lose them without envy, resentment, anger, or other negative emotional responses.

- Be empowered. You may want certain things out of life but never be needy.

- Be God-oriented instead of world-oriented.

- Be humble. Eliminate the desire to be ruthless, aggressive, and conceited. Remove all tendencies to be superficial, vain, and phony.

- Learn not to identify too strongly with your body. Say to yourself, "I am a spiritual soul, immortal, and eternal. I create my own reality." The body eventually dies, but the soul is eternal.

Death challenges us to seek life's meaning. This is nature's way of urging us to discover our true real self—beyond that of the material world. Death is only a transition, a shifting from one dimension to another. Near-death experiencers almost universally report eliminating their previous fear of death. This is a lesson we can all benefit from in our soul's growth.

I presented this chapter to illustrate the strong scientific support for OBEs, and that there is no reason to fear death. Fortunately, we don't have to go through an NDE to experience astral voyaging. The techniques presented in this book are time-tested, perfectly safe, and when used properly, will train you in the art of soul travel.

Conscious Out-of-Body Experiences

Open the being to God,
Abide in stillness,
Life arises, and passes,
Birth, growth, and return,
A rhythmic arc from Source to Source.
In the rhythm is quietude,
A tranquil submission;
In the soul's submission is peace,
Absorption in Eternity.
And so, the great Light!

— Lao-Tzu

The third class of ASC is something I call conscious out-of-body experience (COBE). To understand this concept we must discuss conscious dying. Both the *Tibetan Book of the Dead* and the ancient Mystery Schools professed the principle that if the soul could establish and maintain a linkage with its Higher Self at the precise moment of physical death, it would eliminate the need to reincarnate.

I refer to this connection with our superconscious mind at the moment of death as conscious dying. The spiritual enlightenment that results from this mechanism can immediately perfect our soul and make the process of coming back to another body unnecessary.

The *Tibetan Book of the Dead* represents the collective wisdom of sages who taught that dying was an art that the living could learn to simulate and thereby attain enlightenment.[1] At the same time this method would benefit the loved ones of the departed by shortening the bereavement period.

It is interesting to note the similarities between the early stages of death depicted by the Tibetans during the eighth century, and the core NDE as proposed by modern thanatologists.

Among the descriptions of the early bardo (in-between life) state, the Tibetans talked about the soul being suspended in a void, hearing whistling sounds and a gale-like roaring, and being surrounded by a misty gray light. I have already ascribed the sound of the roar of the sea to the astral plane.

Other aspects of this scripture include:

The dying become aware that they have left the physical body, but disbelieve it at first. They feel no difference, until they try to communicate with their loved ones. Their friends and relatives cannot detect their presence at this time.

The soul now notices their form is shining and able to pass through solid objects. Their thoughts now control their travel. The mere thinking of a location sends them to this place instantly.

This recently departed soul sloughs off emotional attachments to their earthly existence as it moves toward a light. Tests are experienced as the soul confronts spiritual beings who judge them. The soul is presented with a type of mirror reflecting their life and behavior.

A successful completion of this bardo state experience enlightens the soul and allows it to ascend to the higher planes, or return to the cycle of birth and death with a greater understanding of the illusory nature of the physical plane.

---

1 W. Y. Evans-Wentz, *Tibetan Book of the Dead* (New York: Causeway Books, 1973).

The Zoroastrian Scriptures (550–330 B.C.) state that it requires three days for "the spirit of a departed person to find its home in Paradise." The Hebrews shared a similar belief. Their prophet Hosea declared: "Come, and let us return unto Jehovah; for he hath torn, and he will heal us. . . . After two days will he revive us: in the third day he will raise us up, and we shall live before him."[2]

The meditation and self-hypnosis scripts that follow are a modern day version of these approaches. You will find conscious dying techniques and theoretical paradigms in several other sources throughout the history of civilization such as: *Egyptian Book of the Dead;* "Book VI" of the *Aenid* by Virgil; Swedenbourg's *De Coelo et de Inferno*; Christian Masses such as the Requiem; Dante's *Divine Comedy; The Seven Sermons of the Dead* by Basilides; and *Descent Into Hades;* the Orphic Manual of the Greek Mystery School.

Cleansing

When we discuss conscious dying, there are certain terms that must be understood to comprehend this concept. The following are basic definitions that I have developed.

The conscious mind is divided into two main components. One part is termed the conscious mind proper and consists of our analytical, critical and basic left brain activities. This part of our mind literally dies when the physical body crosses into spirit, so it is not relevant to our discussion.

The other component of our consciousness is our subconscious mind (soul or spirit) which is our creative, emotional, and right brain function. This subconscious is pure energy in the form of electromagnetic radiation and is indestructible. It is what reincarnates into a new body when the physical body dies—it is our soul. Although the subconscious may be pure energy, it is far from perfect. The main purpose of reincarnation via the karmic cycle is to perfect the soul.

The superconscious mind or Higher Self is the perfect part of the subconscious mind. The Higher Self comes from the God plane and

---

2 Hosea 6: 1–2, King James Version.

advises us on how to perfect the subconscious. When we do eventually achieve this ideal, our subconscious merges with the Higher Self and ascends to the higher planes (see chapter 5).

"Cleansing" is the technique of introducing the subconscious to the Higher Self so that a connection results. This connection will allow the Higher Self to raise the quality of the subconscious mind's energy (frequency vibrational rate) to a higher and more perfect level. This is the main technique I use with my patients in my Los Angeles office to train them to grow spiritually and to become immune to issues they were previously vulnerable to. I also call this a superconscious mind tap.

This cleansing mechanism is the key to conscious dying. By maintaining this connection between the soul and its Higher Self, the soul can learn to repeat this technique at the moment of death. This will result in the soul avoiding the disorienting forces of the karmic cycle that block out all memories of previous lives and makes it nearly impossible for a soul to adapt to the world in its new body in a spiritually positive and growth-oriented manner.

Cleansing is simply the ability to go through death consciously, through birth consciously, between death and rebirth consciously, and maintain the connection between the soul and Higher Self through these various states to help restore the integrity of the soul. This will, in many cases, eliminate the need to reincarnate. If a future life on the earth or other lower plane is indicated, it will be a far more spiritual and fulfilling one. Thus, the universe, as well as the individual soul, will benefit from conscious dying.

During cleansing, we will be able to recall our previous lives. We will become aware of our soul's true purpose, our karmic purpose. It will mean an end to the cycle of birth and death known as the karmic cycle. Christians call this salvation. The *Tibetan Book of the Dead* names this "clear light." Buddhists call it "nirvana." Hindus use the term "moksha." I simply call it cleansing.

Conscious Dying

At the moment of death, our physical body, including the ego, clinically dies. Our subconscious mind or soul survives. If it can maintain direct contact with its perfect energy counterpart—superconscious mind or Higher Self—at this time, it will literally die consciously. The soul, or subconscious mind, will be liberated and spiritual growth will result.

However, if this contact is not maintained (unconscious death), then our soul will have missed a great opportunity for enlightenment and the most uncomfortable characteristics (the disorienting forces) of the karmic cycle will prevail.

Since the subconscious and superconscious mind (Higher Self) are actually energy, they cannot be destroyed. The first law of thermodynamics in physics clearly states that energy cannot be destroyed, merely altered in its form. For example, light can be transformed into electrical energy or heat, but the total amount of energy we end up with in this new form must equal that at the start of this process.

The subconscious and Higher Self are, in reality, electro-magnetic radiation. In Figure 3 (p. 134), note that the God energy overviews the entire process. The soul plane is where the soul goes between lifetimes, to decide on its next life. From the soul plane, most souls will experience the disorienting forces of the lower planes, and go through an unconscious rebirth into a physical body. All memories of the soul's previous lives and its gestation on the soul plane will, for the most part, be lost. Consciousness is evident throughout physical life. Please note the dotted lines that lead to altered states of consciousness (ASC). One form of ASC is an OBE (out-of-body experience). Note how the soul can leave and return from this experience.

The NDE (near-death experience) requires the body to literally die for a few seconds to several minutes, as I discussed in the previous chapter. The NDE can result in a return to the physical body or to actual death itself.

From clinical death, you will note that the solid line returns to the disorienting forces of the lower planes. Then the Higher Self guides the subconscious back to the soul plane to choose its next lifetime. This is unconscious dying.

The conscious dying process is illustrated by the conscious out-of-body experience (COBE), during which our soul is carried through the death experience and avoids the karmic cycle on its return to the soul plane. When this liberated soul (subconscious mind) is reborn, it again avoids the karmic cycle interference and this conscious rebirth process is complete.

What is doing all of this traveling is the subconscious mind (soul). The Higher Self advises it and is present throughout physical life. The Higher Self is especially pronounced on the soul plane. Please note that the Higher Self is able to go to and from the soul plane, as indicated by the arrows going in both directions.

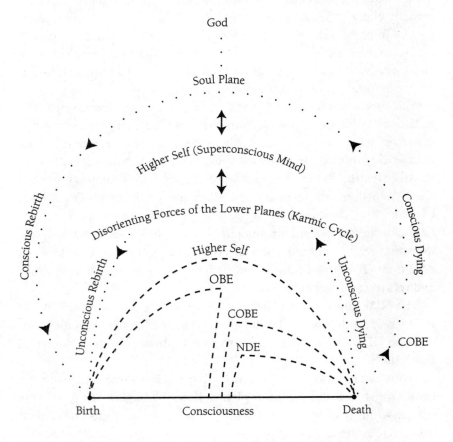

Figure 3. Conscious versus Unconscious Dying

The Soul Plane

This plane is an intermediary or "demilitarized zone" between the lower planes and higher planes. This is where the Higher Self spends most of its time and it is here that a soul chooses its next lifetime. The white light, often described by near-death experiencers, is actually the Higher Self, which escorts the soul to the soul plane. Masters and Guides and departed loved ones may also be in attendance at this location. Telepathy is the mode of communication and there are no secrets. Any entity now can literally read your mind, so truth in its pure form is evident.

You will be shown fragments of your most recent incarnation here, along with several other of your past lives and future life options. Your spirit guides and your Higher Self will often advise, but your next life is always your choice. The soul always has free will. When you have consciously died there are only three possible choices:

◆ You may ascend into the higher planes to join God.

◆ You may remain on the lower five planes as a spiritual guide.

◆ If you haven't quite perfected your soul, you will have to reincarnate. This will be a conscious rebirth and your new life will be a most rewarding one. You will remember your past lives.

Conscious versus Unconscious Dying

Near-death-experiences (NDEs) have been discussed in the previous chapter, but for our current purpose let us refer to it as unconscious dying. The main difference between an NDE and death itself is that in the former, the recipient lives to talk about it. NDEs are an actual form of death, but only for a short time. There is no connection made between the subconscious and Higher Self during this time. This thread of continuity that is so critical for conscious dying is simply missing. We refer to an NDE as unconscious dying for that very reason.

NDEs represent one form of out-of-body experiences (OBEs). The other types of OBE do not require physical death for a brief time. Runner's hypnosis, dreams and reverie states, drug-induced states, and the mind's response to extremely stressful situations are common examples of OBEs. All OBEs are perfectly safe. It is only the NDE that may result in actual physical death. These states are also referred to as altered states of consciousness (ASCs). I will use the term conscious out-of-body experience (COBE) to refer to conscious dying.

Both unconscious dying and conscious dying involve the departing soul entering a white light to escort it to the soul plane. NDEs only report entering the white light. This light is your Higher Self, and only when you merge with it will you consciously die. In either type of transition, *whenever a departed soul enters this white light, the bereavement process ends for the loved ones on the physical plane.*

Summarizing the Moment of Death

At the moment of death, the dying person is aware of a brilliance emanating from a white light. There is no pain. Peace and love are noted immediately. The soul emerges and is transformed to be with its higher and perfect self. This Higher Self is represented by this white light.

The silver cord is severed. This is the main difference between an NDE and the actual death process. Telepathy and other ESP are exhibited and unusual sounds are heard.

The tunnel experience begins, and the presence of other loving entities is felt. There is total awareness of the physical world left behind and the non-physical one just entered.

It is easy to see the many advantages that conscious dying has over the typical unconscious dying. Shortening our karmic cycle is a primary advantage, resulting in fewer and higher quality future lifetimes, or the perfection of the soul and ascension to the higher planes. Most people enjoy an increase in the quality of the remaining lifetimes. There is an instant recall of all past lives. Conscious dying also leads to empowerment and more exposure to spirit guides. Cleansing and its subsequent elimination of habits, phobias, and other self-defeating behavior is experienced, as well as accelerated spiritual growth. There will be an increase in psychic abilities, and the fear of death is eliminated.

Conscious dying shortens the bereavement (grief) period for the loved ones left behind, assisting the guidance of departed loved ones into the Light, and slowing down the aging process. There is a general increase in the quality of the universe as a whole.

Death and the Fate of the Soul

The last thought and utterance at the moment of death, according to Hindus and Buddhists, determines the quality of the soul's next life. By *rightly directing* this thought process of a dying person, conscious dying will result. It is preferable if the dying person has had a lifetime of preparation for this climactic moment. A friend, relative, or guru well versed in conscious dying techniques may assist the voyager.

The Eastern philosophy clearly states that our present thinking determines our future status. Along the same line, our past thinking has significantly influenced our present status. The meditation and self-hypnosis script that follows will assist you in having your own COBE, and in preparing for your own conscious dying.[3]

Conscious Out-of-Body Experience Technique

Now you are about to embark on a very special journey. This is an experience that you have already prepared for many times. Your soul has traveled here many times. This time your preparation is guided by your Higher Self and your Masters and Guides with your complete awareness. You are perfectly safe.

> See the white light around you, protecting you so that there is no need to be concerned. Be one with the white light. You are the white light.
>
> You are able to maintain your connection with your Higher Self at this time. You are able to keep this connection as your soul crosses into spirit and leaves the physical body. You are always safe and protected. You can and will be able to communicate with your Higher Self. It may be by telepathy. You can also hear sounds from the earth plane. You are protected and safe.
>
> Look back at your physical body. Do not be concerned about it. You are spirit. You are soul. You are immortal. Be one with your Higher Self. Be one with your perfect energy. You are your Higher Self.

---

3   A more thorough discussion of conscious dying and several case histories, including a documented case, is presented in my *Peaceful Transition* (St. Paul: Llewellyn Publications, 1997).

Leave behind all earth plane baggage. Leave behind all fears, pain, worries, and insecurities. Immerse yourself in the protective white light coming from your Higher Self. Be one with your Higher Self.

Listen to your Higher Self. It will guide you on a fantastic journey. Be open to its instructions. Have no fear. You are protected. You are perfectly safe.

Do not cling to your old physical body. Do not cling to your Higher Self either. Be empowered. Be confident. You are an evolved soul and are with your Higher Self.

You are now on your way to the soul plane. Feel yourself being drawn up to the soul plane. Feel the presence of your Higher Self advising you, protecting you. Realize that you have consciously died.

Note the changes in colors and sounds as you move toward the soul plane. See how well you have adapted to this trip. See how you avoided the disorienting forces of the lower planes. See how easy it is to do this. Be one with your Higher Self.

As you enter the soul plane, observe how peaceful and organized it is. It is warm, yet efficient in helping you choose your destiny. Note how your Higher Self is with you always.

See how the selection process is done. Note how your Higher Self assists you in this choice. See the presence of your Masters and Guides as you are presented with choices on this, the soul plane.

Let your Higher Self and spirit guides assist you as they teach you about ascension. If you can now ascend to the higher planes, rejoice, for shortly you will be with God. You will no longer need to be assisted by your Higher Self. You will be your Higher Self. You and your Higher Self have merged. You are your Higher Self.

You are your Higher Self. Rejoice. You are one with the universe. You are pure consciousness. You are the white light. You are your Higher Self.

PLAY NEW AGE MUSIC FOR 8 MINUTES

Now it is time to return to your body. Again, concentrate on your breath. Now note the other functions of your body. Slowly open up your eyes and do what you feel is important at this time.

Conscious Out-of-Body Experience (COBE)

Self-Hypnosis Technique

Now listen very carefully. I want you to imagine a bright white light coming down from above and entering the top of your head, filling your entire body. See it, feel it and it becomes reality. Now imagine an aura of pure white light emanating from your heart region. Again surrounding your entire body. Protecting you. See it, feel it, and it becomes reality. Now only your Masters and Guides, Higher Self and highly evolved loving entities who mean you well will be able to influence you during this or any other hypnotic session. You are totally protected by this aura of pure white light.

Now as you focus in on how comfortable and relaxed you are, free of distractions, free from physical and emotional obstacles that prevent you from safely leaving and returning to the physical body, you will perceive and remember all that you encounter during this experience. You will recall in detail when you are physically awake only these matters which will be beneficial to your physical and mental well being and experience. Now begin to sense the vibrations around you, and in your own mind begin to shape and pull them into a ring around your head. Do this for a few moments now.

PLAY NEW AGE MUSIC FOR 2 MINUTES

Now as you begin to attract these vibrations into your inner awareness, they begin to sweep throughout your body making it rigid and immobile. You are always in complete control of this experience. Do this now as you perceive yourself rigid and immobile with these vibrations moving along and throughout your entire body.

PLAY NEW AGE MUSIC FOR 2 MINUTES

You have done very well. Pulse these vibrations. Perceive yourself feeling the pulse of these vibrations throughout your entire awareness. In your own mind's eye, reach out one of your arms and grasp some object which you know is out of normal reach.

Feel the object and let your astral hand pass through it. Your mind is using your astral arm, not your physical arm, to feel the object. As you do this you are becoming lighter and lighter and your astral body is beginning to rise up from your physical body. Do this now.

PLAY NEW AGE MUSIC FOR 2 MINUTES

You've done very well. Now, using other parts of your astral body (your head, feet, chest, and back) repeat this exercise and continue to feel lighter and lighter as your astral body begins to rise up from your physical body. Do this now.

PLAY NEW AGE MUSIC FOR 2 MINUTES

Now think of yourself as becoming lighter and lighter throughout your body. Perceive yourself floating up as your entire astral body lifts up and floats away from your physical body. Concentrate on blackness and remove all fears during this process. Imagine a helium-filled balloon rising and pulling your astral body with it up and away from your physical body. Do this now.

PLAY NEW AGE MUSIC FOR 2 MINUTES

See how easy it is to leave your body while remaining in complete contact with your Higher Self. This is the process of conscious dying. It is that simple. Now ask your Higher Self for any instructions that will assist your spiritual growth. Remember, your Higher Self is all-knowing and has access to your Akashic records.

Now slowly and carefully state your desire for information or an experience, and let your Higher Self work for you. Let it help you raise your soul's energy.

PLAY NEW AGE MUSIC FOR 3 MINUTES

You have done very well. Now I want you to further open up the channels of communication by removing any obstacles and allowing yourself to receive information and experiences that will directly apply to and help better your present lifetime. Allow yourself to receive more advanced and more specific information from your Higher Self and Masters and Guides to raise your frequency and improve your karmic subcycle. Maintain the communication and connection with your Higher Self. You are one with your Higher Self. This connection will always exist, even when the physical body dies. Allow your Higher Self to instruct you. Do this now.

PLAY NEW AGE MUSIC FOR 3 MINUTES

All right now. Sleep now and rest. You did very very well. Listen very carefully. I'm going to count forward now from 1 to 5. When I reach the count of 5 you will be back in your physical body. You will be able to remember everything you experienced and re-experienced. You'll feel very relaxed and refreshed; you'll be able to do whatever you have to planned for the rest of the day or evening. You'll feel very positive about what you've just experienced and very motivated about your confidence and ability to play this tape again to experience conscious dying. All right now. 1, very, very deep; 2, you're getting a little bit lighter; 3, you're getting much, much lighter; 4, very, very light; 5, awaken.

A Thanksgiving Day Conscious Dying

Ashley was a patient of mine who had experienced her share of grief. In June of 1996 her husband died and she came to my office a few months later to learn conscious dying techniques. Even though her husband died unconsciously, it is still possible, using my conscious dying tape training program techniques, to effect conscious dying on the soul in transition. These procedures, including COBEs, were conducted in my office.

Following therapy Ashley left, feeling quite a bit better about herself. Almost immediately after guiding her late husband's soul into a COBE and having it merge with its Higher Self, her grief ended. Whenever a soul enters the white light, even following unconscious dying, the bereavement cycle stops. With a COBE and conscious dying, even after the physical death, this effect is more dramatic.

November 28, 1996 was the first Thanksgiving Ashley spent without her late husband Ron. She did volunteer work at a local hospital hospice program and went to this hospital at 9:00 A.M. that morning.

One of the male patients was not expected to survive the day. His breathing was quite labored and he was nonresponsive. Ashley stayed with him until 1:00 P.M., practicing the conscious dying meditation I had taught her in her own therapy. She told the man that she could sense angels all around him, and that they were waiting to assist him in his transition—to bring him home.

Ashley is a kind and beautiful soul. She thanked this man for the privilege of being there with him on that day, and then left the hospital to spend the afternoon with her friends. At 6:00 P.M., Ashley called the hospital to check on the man's condition. The nurse on duty informed her that he had died at 4:00 P.M. Ashley viewed his body and described what happened next in a letter she wrote me later that day. Here is an excerpt:

> When I got there, he definitely looked at peace, but there was something else I sensed about him. I held my hands above his body and felt the most incredible, pulsating energy radiating from him. I knew he was still in there and I began to tell him all the things I told him before, in addition to telling him to focus on his forehead and move in that direction.
>
> After just a few minutes I could feel a tremendous shift in energy. There was no longer much of anything over his body but I could actually feel his soul rising up out of his forehead, across my hand. Wow!

The following week Ashley attended a business meeting and relayed this story to one of her colleagues, who was synchronistically thinking about entering a hospice training program. During the conversation a raven flew into this room through an open window, flew in a circle above her head and flew out another window. In all of the times she had been in that room, this had never happened before.

To further add to the synchronicity of this case, I received a letter from a woman who read my *Fate* column, "Hypnotic Highways," inquiring about my professional services and tapes. On her envelope was the Raven Dance stamp (available at the U.S. Post Office).

This turned out to be a most memorable Thanksgiving for Ashley. Conscious dying works wonders and enhances the spiritual growth of all that we encounter. Ashley's case illustrates how easy it is to transfer this technique to another soul in need of a peaceful transition.

Lucid Dreaming

All dreaming states are out-of-body traveling. This is a process through which we can accelerate our spiritual growth and experience astral voyages. You might think of out-of-body techniques as a form of conscious dreaming. There are five basic types of dreams.

The sexual dream is the first type and deals with more than just sexual fantasies. It includes any experience that gives us pleasure. This may involve professional accomplishments, eating, drinking, and so on. This dream functions as a release of tension and emotional stimulation.

The various spirit guides and your Higher Self create a second projection dream category. Education and spiritual growth are the purpose of this dream type.

Spiritual dreams are the third type, functioning as an ESP laboratory. Here our soul experiences clairvoyance, precognition, and travel to other dimensions. This space-time continuum exposure is how seers and prophets predict the future. You may also master this method by diligent practice of the techniques presented in this book.

The memory dream is the fourth type, and consists of reviewing past lives. This dream may be combined with the projection dream to assist us in our nightly spiritual education and growth.

When you are aware of dreaming during your dream it is called lucid dreaming. This fifth category is the most significant in that it affords us the ability to determine and direct the outcome of our dream. Another benefit of lucid dreaming is that it gives us conscious memories of our astral voyaging.

American anthropologist Dan Sheils studied astral projection in sixty-seven cultures. He discovered that the most important source of OBEs in about eighty percent of these cultures is the dream state.

I am not trying to explain away OBEs by lucid dreaming or any type of fantasizing. My position is that lucid dreams afford us a sneak preview of where our astral body journeyed while our physical body slept. This is borne out by numerous examples of controlled experiments with remote viewing demonstrating that the projectors actually left their bodies and reported details they could only know if they actually visited sites while out of the body—we will explore this evidence in chapter 14.

Lucid dreaming demonstrates that dreams are neither irrational nor unconscious, as was previously thought. By directing both the plot and its outcome, lucid dreaming presents us with the opportunity and mechanism to facilitate creative problem-solving, promote personal growth and empowerment, and accelerate our spiritual growth.

Whatever we learn during our nightly excursions and lucid dreaming will be retained by our conscious minds. Conversely, we can apply the knowledge and experience from our waking lives on the astral plane through lucid dreaming. The ordinary dreamer cannot do this, since he or she loses any connection between the two dimensions.

The most extensive research in the field of lucid dreaming has been conducted by Stephen LaBerge at the Stanford Medical Center. In his classic book, *Lucid Dreaming*, LaBerge describes some examples of creative lucid dreamers: Robert Louis Stevenson's inspiration for *The Strange Case of Dr. Jekyll and Mr. Hyde*; Kekule's discovery of benzene's chemical structure and development of organic chemistry (the basis of the pharmaceutical industry); Elias Howe's development of the sewing machine; the creative works of William Blake, Mozart, Beethoven, and

Wagner; and the success of Jack Nicklaus, who improved his golf score by ten strokes overnight as the result of a lucid dream.[1]

What makes lucid dreams so unique is their neurophysiology. Basically all dreams occur during the REM (rapid eye movement) stage of our sleep cycle. We experience four of five such cycles every night resulting in about three hours of nightly dreams. These REM cycles alternate with the completely unconscious non-REM stages of sleep.

The unique aspect of lucid dreaming is that, although completely out of sensory contact and fully asleep to the outer world, these individuals are in as complete possession of their mental faculties as when awake. They are fully awake to the inner world (astral plane) of their dreams. This completely revamps previous scientific notions about conscious dreaming and reality.

It is possible for anyone to learn to dream consciously by practicing the exercises in this chapter. The British occultist Hugh Callaway, who wrote under the pen name Oliver Fox, was one of the first chroniclers of astral voyaging. He was well known as a lucid dreamer, and referred to them as "dreams of knowledge." He presented several techniques to induce lucid dreaming in his book *Astral Projection*.[2]

Lucid dreaming has been reported since antiquity. It parallels the discovery of electricity. The ancient Greeks knew about electricity. It wasn't until the nineteenth century that both electricity and lucid dreaming were seriously studied.

LaBerge's research shows that dreams take place in the same amount of time the actions would require in real life. In other words, we dream in real (physical plane) time. This applies only to lucid dreams.

There are no limitations for the lucid dreamer. Anything is possible. You can fly, have an erotic encounter with a movie star, access your Higher Self, converse with a departed loved one, confront someone you have been avoiding, and so on.

Our Brain Waves

Sleep laboratory research has discovered four different brain waves that we all possess. Beta brain waves are characteristic of our normal waking

---

1 Stephen LaBerge, *Lucid Dreaming* (Los Angeles: Jeremy P. Tarcher, 1985).
2 Oliver Fox, *Astral Projection* (London: University Books, 1962).

state. We associate alpha brain-waves with our subconscious and hypnotic (daydreaming) levels, in addition to the REM cycle at night. Slower theta waves relate to superconscious mind taps and the beginning stages of sleep. Finally, the delta level is common during the deepest stages of sleep.

The Stages of Sleep

In discussing lucid dreaming and OBEs, it is important to understand how our brain works during its sleep cycle. This is one aspect of our twenty-four-hour cycle during which we predictably leave our body.

The UCLA Brain Information Service developed a manual for sleep-stage scoring.[3] This manual requires the simultaneous recording of three parameters: brain waves (EEG), eye movements (EOG), and muscle tension (EMG). When you lie in bed awaiting sleep, your EEG usually shows a continuous alpha rhythm. Isolated REMS and occasional blinking may be observed on your EEG, while a moderate degree of muscle tension is noted on your EMG.

This progression from stages one through four takes about one and a half to two hours. Following this, these stages are reversed and REM sleep (dreaming) begins. Rather vivid and detailed dreams occur at this time. Your initial REM phase is short (five to fifteen minutes), and increases throughout the night. The last REM cycle may last forty minutes to an hour. The intervals between these REM periods decrease as the night progresses from approximately ninety minutes to as little as twenty minutes in the late morning.

Will the Real Lucid Dreamer Please Stand?

One of the most confusing concepts is that of who is doing the lucid dreaming. The individual sleeping has two major choices here. Is it the character in the dream whom the sleeper identifies as themselves? Stephen LaBerge calls this the "dream actor" or "dream ego," since it is merely a representation of ourselves.[4]

One argument for this dream actor not being the actual dreamer is presented by the fact that there are many dreams during which we do

---

3   E. Kiesler," Images of the night," *Science*, 80 (1980): 1436–43.
4   LaBerge, op. cit.

not appear, but are merely observing from an outside vantage point. LaBerge labels this a "dream observer."

Some lucid dreams involve varying degrees from the complete detachment of the dream observer to the complete participation of the dream actor. In these cases, the lucid dreamer is more likely a composite of both the dream observer and dream actor.

Lucid dreaming requires a delicate balance between participation and detachment. If we are too obsessively attached to our dream role, or too rigidly detached, we would not realize or care that we are actually dreaming; therefore this particular dream would not be lucid.

We must participate in a dream, according to LaBerge, for it to be correctly identified as a lucid one. In addition, there must also be a certain amount of detachment present, so that we can step back and say, "I know this is a dream." These two different levels of awareness are prerequisites for a dream to be truly labeled a lucid dream.

Problem-Solving with Lucid Dreams

I have briefly discussed the advantage of using lucid dreams to solve various types of problems and arrive at creative ideas for new projects. This is based on the fact that anything is possible during a lucid dream, and the astral plane you go to has no physical laws as far as we know.

Research has demonstrated that dreaming lowers brain excitability and favorably affects our moods. Janet Dallet has researched dream theories and concludes that "contemporary theories tend to focus on the function of environmental mastery, viewed from one of three perspectives: problem solving, information processing, or ego consolidation."[5]

A growth and developmental function to dreams has been stated by psychologist Ernest Rossi:

> *In dreams we witness something more than mere wishes; we experience dramas reflecting our psychological state and the process of change taking place in it. Dreams are a laboratory for experimenting with changes in our psychic life. . . . This*

---

5   Janet Dallet, "Theories of dream function." *Psychological Bulletin* 6 (1973): 408–16.

constructive or synthetic approach to dreams can be clearly stated: Dreaming is an endogenous process of psychological growth, change and transformation.[6]

In *Lucid Dreaming*, LaBerge gives an example of how this method may assist children in overcoming phobias.[7] Seven-year-old Madeleina had a series of nightmares of being threatened by a "little-girl-eating" shark each time she went swimming in Colorado. Madeleina was informed that there were no sharks in Colorado so this had to be a dream. Since a dream shark can't harm her, she was trained to make friends with it. The following week she proudly announced that she "rode on the back of the shark!" Her nightmares abruptly ended.

I have already discussed the observation that during an OBE we create a replication of our physical plane that is imperfect in reference to minor details. Activities conducted while out-of-body on the physical plane by our astral body demonstrate this replicate world hypothesis. An experienced astral projector and lucid dreamer named Keith Harary reported the following lucid dream:

> *One night I awoke in an out-of-body state floating just above my physical body . . . a candle had been left burning. . . . I dove for the candle head-first from a sitting position and gently floated down toward it. . . . I put my "face" up close to the candle and had some difficulty in putting out the flame. I had to blow on it several times before it finally seemed to extinguish. . . . The next morning I awoke and found that the candle had completely burned down. It seemed as if my out-of-the-body efforts had affected only a non-physical candle.*[8]

Lucid Sex

This heading may shock you, but it is noteworthy that two-thirds of author Patricia Garfield's lucid dreams have sexual themes, and about half of them result in orgasm. She states in her book *Pathway to Ecstasy* that these were "profound" in intensity. "With a totality of self that is

---

6   E. L. Rossi, *Dreams and the Growth of Personality* (New York: Pergamon, 1972), p. 142.

7   LaBerge, op. cit.

8   D. Scott Rogo, *Mind Beyond Body* (New York: Penguin, 1978), pp. 248–49.

only sometimes felt in the waking state," she went on, she found herself "bursting into soul and body-shaking explosions."[9]

These reports have been made by many other lucid dreamers and thoroughly studied by LaBerge at Stanford. The flying aspect of a lucid dream coincided with orgasms in women. Men have a lower percent of physical plane orgasms that correspond with their astral sexual encounters. With men it is the actual engagement in astral sex, not flying, that results in orgasm. Lucid dream sex has as significant an effect on the dreamer's body as the real thing.

Hypnosis, Lucid Dreaming and Healing Effects

Using hypnosis to induce lucid dreams has been shown to result in healing of the physical body. By performing a true healing on the astral plane, the lucid dreamer may correspondingly bring about a cure to their psychosomatic ailment on the physical plane.

Hypnotic dreams while in deep trance function much like lucid dreams, and, in fact, are a form of lucid dreaming. In my own Los Angeles practice I have witnessed my patients eliminate pain, stop bleeding, reverse allergic reactions, and increase the T lymphocyte blood count to fight cancer and AIDS. Those effects are even more accomplishable when you are trained in the art of lucid dreaming.

I presented some rather dramatic examples of this effect in my book *Soul Healing* (1996). By consciously creating a perfectly healthy dream body, we can affect a true healing onto our physical body. We will discuss astral healing techniques in chapter 13.

Preparing for Lucid Dreaming

Before looking at several techniques on how to induce your own lucid dreams, there is additional background you should know. Whether you call this state "double consciousness" (as does Dr. Morton Prince of Harvard) or lucid dreaming, remember that this is a natural phenomenon.

It is rather easy to control dreams by simple hypnotic programming. Only a small percentage of the population has lucid dreams on a regular basis. Like other forms of OBEs, the average person reports only one or two of these throughout their life.

---

9 P. Garfield, *Pathway to Ecstasy* (New York: Holt, Rinehart & Winston, 1979).

The most commonly reported lucid dream occurs during a nightmare when the dreamer realizes the experience is so unreal that it must be a dream. They fail to exercise control over the situation and experiment with different "plot twists," as does the experienced lucid dreamer.

Researchers like LaBerge, and Keith Hearne of Hull University in England, have clearly demonstrated the ability to artificially induce lucid dreaming in a laboratory. The techniques that follow do not require such a formal setting. Anyone can induce lucid dreaming by following these methods.

When you have an OBE you are definitely aware that you *are not* dreaming. The lucid dreamer, on the other hand, is quite aware that they *are* dreaming. The difference is that of awareness and not of function. In both types of phenomena, the astral body may travel and document these voyages as is reported in remote viewing experiments. There is little doubt among researchers that information is somehow acquired by the projector/dreamer beyond that attainable by our five senses.

A lucid dream may serve as a building block to the OBE. It may very well be a preliminary step to the full blown OBE. At present we cannot determine the precise moment a lucid dream ends or is transformed into an OBE.

There are methods of determining whether your voyage is a true OBE or a lucid dream. A lucid dream entails occupying a body, whereas OBEs are perceived as disembodied. There is a consistent environment and a feeling of being in a real world for most OBEs. Lucid dreamers more likely find inconsistencies in their environment. Whereas lucid dreaming originates from more traditional dreaming, the OBE most likely occurs in a waking state. Most reports of OBE are ordinary, whereas exotic and impossible events are described by lucid dreamers.

There are other considerations in undertaking lucid dreaming exercises. A "false awakening" may occur, during which you "awake" after a lucid dream but discover you are still asleep. It is rather easy to induce an OBE from this state by simply willing your astral body to separate.

Another effect of inducing lucid dreams is increased awareness. This is a form of spiritual growth and one thing you may notice are symbols appearing in your dreams that instruct you further on more effective OBEs. You will be given several different cues. Experiment with each method to determine the most comfortable and efficient one for you.

To better use these methods, convince yourself that your dreams are meaningful and important. By respecting and learning from your dreams, they will respond in kind and provide you with a natural laboratory for astral voyaging and psychic empowerment.

Keep a dream diary to find the most comfortable position to be in, the time of the day to practice, and so on. Lucid dreams are most likely to occur in the early morning hours following a good nights' rest. Make your initial attempts immediately upon awakening to insure success.

Always try to make the entire dream lucid so that you become an active participant. This simple method will act as a reminder to initiate a full blown OBE when you feel it is appropriate.

When practicing these exercises, convince yourself that they will work. This conviction, combined with an increase in your awareness, increases your chance of having a productive lucid dream and subsequent OBE. Developing a proper attitude towards lucid dreaming is the most important preparatory exercise I can suggest.

Techniques

LaBerge developed a simple method he calls Mnemonic Induction of Lucid Dreams or MILD.[10] His technique can be summarized as follows:

1. In the early morning when you have awakened spontaneously from a dream, quickly go over every detail of the dream in your mind and repeat the process several times until you have completely memorized the dream.

2. Then, while you are still lying in bed, repeat to yourself several times, "Next time I'm dreaming, I want to remember to recognize that I'm dreaming."

3. After repeating this phrase, picture yourself back in the dream, only imagining that this time you realize that you are dreaming.

---

10 LaBerge, op. cit.

4. Keep the visualization in your mind until it is clearly fixed or you fall back asleep.

Patricia Garfield, in her book *Creative Dreaming*,[11] suggests you instruct yourself before going to sleep to specifically dream about a certain situation with actual people you know. She suggests using phrases such as: "Tonight I will dream about my friend so-and-so." Always prepare yourself and script your dreams.

The following are some additional techniques to induce lucid dreams. Suggest a nightmare to yourself, and program yourself to awaken from it during a specific incident. By awaken I mean a false awakening, so that your dream environment will become peaceful and you will continue in this dream, now fully aware that you are dreaming.

Program yourself to have a flying dream. Flying dreams are far more characteristic of lucid dreams than they are of regular dreams. This type of suggestion works rather quickly and well. It is also easier to transform this dream into a true OBE when you view yourself flying.

Another simple method is to simply recognize the discrepancies in your dreams. Prepare yourself by giving your subconscious mind strict instructions on thinking analytically during this excursion. Further direct yourself to identify any irregularity and immediately acknowledge the unreality of this dream.

This last method can be developed by approaches such as the following. Remind yourself throughout the day that your dreams are not real. This form of subtle self-brainwashing will train you to immediately recognize your dream as being unreal and to continue with this experience as a lucid, not ordinary, dreamer.

Fixate your subconscious on the fact that you will observe and participate in your dreams with a highly developed degree of conscious awareness, and maintain this awareness up to the very moment of drifting off to sleep. Admittedly, this is not easy to accomplish. Inducing a lucid dream from the waking (hypnagogic) state, rather than from the dream state itself, requires more practice and patience.

Methods are available to transform a lucid dream to a full blown astral voyage. For instance, when you recognize that you are dreaming,

---

11 P. Garfield, *Creative Dreaming* (New York: Ballantine, 1974).

clear your mind and block out your dream environment. Focus solely on your own thought process and the dream environment will soon disappear and you will find yourself out-of-body.

Whatever the content of your dream is, simply begin flying. As soon as you perceive yourself off the ground, direct yourself to awake out-of-body. Suggest to yourself to return to your physical body when you are lucidly dreaming. However, instruct yourself not to wake up. All you need to do now is suggest that your astral body separate from its physical counterpart. An astral voyage will soon begin.

Another method of using the dream state to induce both lucid dreaming and astral voyaging is to monitor your thoughts before sleep for several weeks. Limit awareness and cognition to yourself. Remember that you are awake, but drifting off to sleep during the hypnagogic state.

When you have mastered the above method, devise a dream in which you play an active role. This scenario must include an OBE and activities that you find pleasing, for example, going up in an elevator or a ferris wheel at a carnival. Concentrate on the sensations of enjoyment as you ride the elevator (ferris wheel, etc.). You will be conscious of these mechanisms and feelings, yet still retain awareness that this is all a dream.

Mentally observe minute details of your environment, including the weather, landscape, and the presence of animals and people. In the elevator dream, see and feel yourself moving upward slowly to the top floor, getting out, and viewing the skyline from the top of the building. Then place yourself back in the elevator and slowly descend, returning to the lobby of the building.

Elevator Visualization Self-Hypnosis Technique

Here is a script for just such an exercise using an elevator visualization:

> The next time you go to sleep you are going to recognize the fact that you are dreaming and recall it in vivid detail. Think about the most recent dream you had and recreate it now. This time see yourself in your dream recognizing that you are dreaming. Do this now.
>
> PLAY NEW AGE MUSIC FOR 2 MINUTES
>
> Now I want you to program yourself to have a most unusual dream tonight. In this dream, you will be flying, and aware that

this is only a dream. You are also to note any discrepancies and irregularities that you find in this dream.

Immediately acknowledge the unreality of this dream and analyze its contents. Maintain your objectivity, but still stay a player in this dream sequence.

Lastly, I want you to repeat these instructions to yourself up to the very moment of drifting off to sleep. Do this now.

PLAY NEW AGE MUSIC FOR 3 MINUTES

You have done very well. Now I want you to program yourself to have the following dream:

You are moving up a building in an elevator. Concentrate on the sensation of enjoyment as you ride the elevator. You will be conscious of these mechanisms and feelings, yet still retain awareness that this is a dream.

See and feel yourself moving upward slowly to the top floor, getting out and viewing the skyline from the top of this building. Now go back into the elevator and slowly descend, returning to the lobby of the building.

All right now. Sleep now and rest. You have done very, very well. Listen very carefully. I'm going to count forward now from 1 to 5. When I reach the count of 5, you will be back in the present. You will be able to remember everything you experienced. You'll feel very relaxed, refreshed, and you'll be able to do whatever you have planned for the rest of the day or evening. You'll feel very positive about what you've just experienced and very motivated about your confidence and ability to play this tape again to experience lucid dreaming and astral voyaging. Alright now. 1, very, very deep. 2, you're getting a little bit lighter. 3, you're getting much, much lighter. 4, very, very light. 5, awaken. Wide awake and refreshed.

Repeat this exact dream over and over again, until you reflexively transport yourself into this dream elevator just as you drift off to sleep. The astral body will now ascend in the elevator, upright itself above your physical body and move outward as you exit the elevator on the top floor.

This process will also work in reverse when your astral body re-enters the elevator after its voyage and descends down to the lobby. As the elevator moves down, the astral body lowers itself until it finally rejoins with the physical body.

Another technique is to recall a recurring dream during the day during which astral voyaging occurred. This may be facilitated by keeping a dream journal. All you need to do now is rehearse the dream action mentally and physically (if possible), and thereby increase the likelihood of waking up in your astral body when you have this dream again.

It is critical to fix the details of this dream in your mind. Instruct yourself, using any of the self hypnosis exercises presented in this book, to awaken in your astral body the next time you come to a certain landmark (a doorway, lake, park, etc.) that is characteristic of this dream scenario. You will now awake in your astral double.

Always remain calm regardless of the dream content. There is no possibility that you may be harmed in any way. Think of rising in the air and floating or flying to facilitate the separation mechanism. Classically, the rising or flying elements of these lucid dreams represent the lifting out of the astral body from the physical shell. Falling components are associated with the return of the astral double to its physical counterpart. The key to successfully utilizing these techniques is practice, determination and perseverance.

Summarizing Lucid Dreaming

We can improve our ability to experience lucid dreaming, and grow spiritually at the same time, by keeping in mind the following methods to improve your lucid dreaming abilities: realize that you are dreaming if you become frightened; recognize incongruities and dream-like qualities in your dreams; develop a critical attitude during your dreams.

Since anything is possible in a lucid dream, this occasion offers us unlimited opportunities for experimentation and growth. You can rehearse solutions to problems, practice skills you wish to improve on the physical plane, experience psychic development, and more.

Lucid dreams are vividly recalled so memory and analytic thought are better in lucid dreams than in ordinary dreams. Specific recent details may be distorted in lucid dreams.

Don't allow yourself to become too emotional in a lucid dream or you will awaken. If you appear to awaken from a dream, test the reality of your experience. If you discover you have had a false awakening, you can precipitate a lucid dream.

You can improve your ability to have lucid dreams by programming yourself to have dreams of flying. As you practice skills in lucid dreams, you increase the probability of their occurrence in waking life.

Lucid dreams are achieved more easily after several hours of sleep—between 5:00 A.M. and 8:00 A.M. for most people.

Brief flashes of lucidity can be extended into prolonged states.

Advanced Astral Voyaging Techniques

I n this chapter, we will look at more sophisticated approaches to soul travel. These approaches will involve visualization, body positioning and the use of apparatus to induce OBEs.

Consciousness Expansion

Intense, expanded, and powerful states of consciousness facilitate our spiritual growth and movement toward self-realization. These exercises are designed to help you to cope with all subjective realities and experiences of deep psychic and spiritual dimensions.

These methods will prepare you to benefit from these voyages to the other planes. In addition, your fears about leaving your body will be removed by a conscientious application of the procedures presented.

Consciousness Expansion Exercise

In this first exercise, use the standard white light protection and self-hypnotic relaxation technique presented earlier.

Remain deeply in this relaxed trance state. Go even deeper and now perceive yourself being transported to a mountainous

157

region that looks as if it might be somewhere in Tibet or India. As you approach a large stone temple you begin to climb up many steps.

You are going deeper into trance, and ascending those steps, and entering into this ancient temple. Inside the temple, you observe that there are monks who have come into the temple to sing and to pray.

And these monks will sing the music developed by their order over thousands and thousands of years, a music that has the function of making an immediate, direct contact with their Higher Self, so that these monks, as that singing rises upward and outward, experience their Higher Self coming to them through the music, and this is a very, very powerful and beautiful music for you to hear. Listen to this music for a few moments to make contact with your own Higher Self.

PLAY NEW AGE MUSIC FOR 2 MINUTES

Very good. You've done well. Now continue in this timeless void where there is only consciousness. Becoming even more deeply relaxed, see yourself dreaming late at night. You get out of bed and walk across the room to a closet. There is a door in the back of this closet that opens up to bring into your line of sight a stone staircase.

It is a very ancient-looking stone staircase, winding down and around, and in the dim light you begin going down the staircase, not afraid, but eager to go down, deeper and deeper, descending on down through the dream, going always deeper, a step at a time, until finally reaching the bottom of the stairway to stand at the edge of what you recognize as dark water, where a small boat is tied.

Now, you are lying on blankets in the bottom of the boat, the boat adrift and floating in blackness, dark all around, but rocking gently from the motion of the water, back and forth and rising and falling, gently rocking as the boat drifts on and on, as the boat drifts down and down, as you feel only that gentle rocking, listening to the lapping of the water, nearing an opening where the boat moves along toward a light at the opening, passing out of the opening and into warm sunlight.

Still floating, downstream, feeling the warm sunlight, and a soft breeze that passes over you, as you drift down and down, and along the bank the birds are singing, and the fish are jumping in the water, and there is the smell of flowers and of the freshly cut grass in fields that have just been mowed. Feeling a great contentment, serenity, drifting drowsily down and down, down and down, with that gentle rocking, and now just let yourself feel it for a while. Be aware of this whole situation, the movements, the warmth, the sounds, the odors, as you keep on drifting down, down and down.

Continuing now to float, to rock, gently, drifting deeper and deeper, until your boat approaches the shore and runs smoothly aground at the edge of a meadow. Leaving the boat now, and walking through the meadow, the grass against your legs, the breezes on your body, the smell of the flowers all around, of birds singing in the trees, of the movements of your body as you walk, approaching a large tree and seating yourself beneath it, in its shade.

But now, for a while, just feel your surroundings, be in a total harmony with all that exists here in this world out of time, this world without separations, this world where all is one, where you are one with All That Is . . . .

Visualization Technique

This next technique is a visualization exercise that trains you to clear your mind and open yourself up for consciousness expansion.

Imagine you are in a motion picture theater all alone. Before you is a giant screen—absolutely blank. See it so in your mind's eye. The screen is illuminated by a great white light so now you are looking at a huge white screen which is completely blank.

Within a fraction of a second other images will start to crowd in, some on the screen, some on the periphery of your vision. With these intruders will come sounds, memories and desire fantasies. These must be pushed back, all of them, the sights, sounds, smells, feelings, everything, so that only the blank white screen remains.

This is not easy and will require concentration, will power, and lots of practice before you will be able to hold the image of the screen, clear and unsullied before your mind's eye for as long as five seconds. Once you are able to exclude everything from your awareness but the brilliantly lit white screen for a solid five seconds, you are then ready for the next step which follows.

Now carry yourself right into the white brightness of the screen so that it is all around you. At this point you may experience a pleasurable tingling on the surface of your skin or some other distraction. For the present, this must be ignored if you are to achieve the results you are striving for. When you are quite sure this scintillating brightness is all around you and you are conscious of nothing else, no stray thoughts, no sensations, no emotional fantasies of any kind, you are then in attunement with your Higher Self and have developed yourself to a point where you can consciously seek out both its flow of information and its guidance toward dimensional travel. Feel the power of enlightenment manifesting in you.

PLAY NEW AGE MUSIC FOR 6 MINUTES

End your trance as usual.

Advanced Out-of-Body Experience Hypnotic Technique

Now listen very carefully. I want you to imagine a bright white light coming down from above and entering the top of your head. Filling your entire body. See it, feel it, and it becomes reality. Now imagine an aura of pure white light emanating from your heart region. Again surrounding your entire body. Protecting you. See it, feel it, and it becomes reality. Now only your Masters and Guides and highly evolved loving entities who mean you well will be able to influence you during this or any other hypnotic session. You are totally protected by this aura of pure white light.

Now as you focus in on how comfortable and relaxed you are, free of distractions, free from physical and emotional obstacles that prevent you from safely leaving and returning to the physical body, you will perceive and remember all that you encounter during this experience. You will recall in detail when you are physically awake only these matters which will be beneficial to your physical and mental being and experience. Now begin to sense the vibrations around you, and in your own mind begin to shape and pull them into a ring around your head. Do this for a few moments now.

PLAY NEW AGE MUSIC FOR 2 MINUTES

Now as you begin to attract these vibrations into your inner awareness, they begin to sweep throughout your body making it rigid and immobile. You are always in complete control of this experience. Do this now as you perceive yourself rigid and immobile, with these vibrations moving along and throughout your entire body.

PLAY NEW AGE MUSIC FOR 3 MINUTES

You have done very well. Pulse these vibrations. Perceive yourself feeling the pulse of these vibrations throughout your entire awareness. In your own mind's eye, reach out one of your arms and grasp some object which you know is out of normal reach. Feel the object and let your astral hand pass through it. Your mind is using your astral arm, not your physical arm, to feel the object. As you do this you are becoming lighter and lighter, and your astral body is beginning to rise up from your physical body.

And now going deeper and deeper and deeper, feeling your mind going deeply into trance, feeling your body going deeply into trance, your whole mind-body going deeper, and deeper, as you know and respond to a mental force that is greater than any you have known or responded to before for this purpose of deepening trance.

And that force will continue to pull and to draw you, deeper and ever deeper, as now you are becoming very aware of your body, of the form and the substance of your body, and finding yourself now surrounded by darkness, and knowing that your body has been somehow transported out into space, far, far out into space, where it floats in the darkness, as you keep going deeper.

Your mind is with your body, drifting out there in space, all alone except for your awareness of my voice, my words, taking you deeper, and deeper into trance, and toward important new experiences, and liberating within you capacities you have, but in the past could not use. And you will go deeper in order that you may become free.

Your body out there drifting in space, and your legs are spread wide apart, and your arms are flung out and extended, as you drift there in that blackness, as you go deeper, and now are aware of your body growing, and growing, and growing, to a size that is immense, a size so vast that you become aware of yourself as a constellation of stars that might be perceived as having human form, so that someone seeing that constellation might create a drawing of you and regard it as an astrological sign or as a figure that may be perceived in the heavens, there by accident or by the intention of some great, superhuman power.

And riding now, riding faster and faster, across the vast reaches of the cosmos, the universe, riding in ever-expanding circles, around and around, going deeper and deeper, and becoming aware of yourself, despite your vast dimensions, as being no more than an infinitely minute cell in some organism gigantic far beyond all your powers of imagining.

But becoming aware now of other cells around you, and your relationship to those cells, growing in awareness by that means, extending the scope of your being with a very fast-increasing knowledge and interrelationship with other parts of this organism, feeling yourself to be in harmonious interaction, growing in understanding, expanding toward knowledge of the total organism of which you felt yourself to be a part, and discovering finally that the organism is yourself, that your awareness for a time had been centered in a single cell of your own body, and that now you have become aware of your whole body and self.

Focus on this entire experience.

Perceive your body as more and more porous, so that the wind could just blow right through you, and now the wind is coming, a gentle breeze, and it does just pass right through you, a wonderful feeling of lightness, a feeling of openness, of freedom, and now you are the wind.

Now you are a breeze, blowing free, skimming freely along, rustling the leaves of the trees, stirring grasses, blowing in a gentle caress over plains and waters and bodies of animals and people, a hot wind passing over desert regions, a cool wind whispering to people on an island.

Now your whole mind-body system is absorbing, assimilating, and understanding as these processes continue.

Focus on this now.

And feel yourself now, as wind, slowly whirling, whirling, and becoming transformed into a human body, your own body, experienced as quite normal once again.

All right now. Sleep now and rest. You did very very well. Listen very carefully. I'm going to count forward now from 1 to 5. When I reach the count of 5 you will be back in your body. You will be able to remember everything you experienced and re-experienced. You'll feel very relaxed and refreshed. You'll be able to do whatever you have planned for the rest of the day or evening. You'll feel very positive about what you've just experienced and very motivated about your confidence and ability to play this tape again to experience leaving your physical body safely. All right now. 1, very very deep; 2, you're getting a little bit lighter; 3, you're getting much much lighter; 4, very very light; 5, awaken. Wide awake and refreshed.

The 37-Degree Technique

The Lascaux Cave drawings, dating from 15,000 B.C., were discovered in 1940 near the French village of Montignac. One drawing is of the stick figure of a shaman lying in front of an aurochs. This shaman was lying at a precise angle of 37 degrees to prepare for an ecstatic astral voyage into the Sky world (upper world). This same 37-degree posture appeared in an Egyptian drawing of Osiris 12,000 years later. Before Osiris' astral voyage, he was placed at a 37-degree angle and his body was dismembered and reassembled by his sister, according to Egyptian legend (see illustrations below).

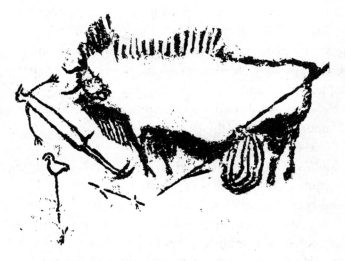

Figure 5. The Lascaux Cave Drawings
(As depicted in Paul Devereaux, *Earth Memory* (St. Paul: Llewellyn Publications, 1992).

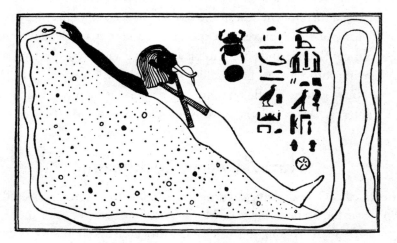

Figure 6. Osiris preparing to leave his body
(As depicted in E. A. W. Budge, *Egyptian Book of the Dead* (London: Methuen and Co., 1904.)

You can use this energy-building technique for embarking on astral voyages with a simple apparatus like the one shown below. The procedure is as follows:

1. Place your body at a 37-degree angle with your feet parallel, slightly apart, and at a 90-degree angle to your legs.

2. With your elbows in a locked position, stretch your left arm beside your body. Keep your left thumb stiff, so a straight line can be drawn from your shoulder, through your elbow and wrist, to the tip of your thumb.

3. Face the palm of your right hand toward your thigh, while resting this arm at a 37-degree angle from your body.

4. Now rest your right thumb on top of your fingers. Your eyes should be closed and your head facing forward. Rest back on the support structure and relax yourself with accompanying white light protection.[1]

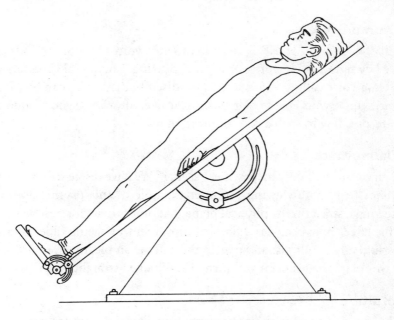

Figure 7. The 37-degree Position

1   Belinda Gore, *Ecstatic Body Postures: An Alternate Reality Workbook* (Santa Fe: Bear & Co., 1995). Reprinted with permission from Bear & Co.

This technique seems to connect with the forces both within the body and the universe. It generates a great deal of energy and creates sexual arousal. If you refer back to the Lascaux Cave drawing, you will note the erection experienced by the shaman. An arousal of the first chakra could very well explain these effects.

Enhanced Psychic Abilities

Accessing your Higher Self will facilitate both astral voyaging and your spiritual growth. Throughout history, from the ancients to modern yogis and shamans, enhanced spiritual growth has been linked with improved psychic abilities. This book has provided you with many ways to grow spiritually. An intensification of your psychic gifts will be an added fringe benefit to your astral voyaging. These psychic abilities include clairaudience, clairvoyance, intuition, precognition, prediction, psychometry, telekinesis, and telepathy.

Clairaudience

This "voice of the spirit" is an ability to hear voices or other sounds that are beyond the range of your normal hearing. The initial experience is often a voice calling your name. This disembodied voice can be from a spirit guide, your Higher Self, or a discarnate. Always use good judgment in responding to such a communication.

Clairvoyance

Clairvoyance literally means "clear seeing." We have discussed this in reference to remote viewing. Another example of this psychic ability is viewing a spirit on the physical plane that others may not be able to see. This effect may occur as a flash of movement or seeing objects in the peripheral of your visual range. In the latter example, the object or spirit would not be visible if you turned and looked straight at it.

Intuition

This form of psychic ability has been described as a "gut feeling," and is emotionally based. When you instantly "know" that something is going to happen, you are expressing your intuitive talent. Interestingly, many people who deny they have psychic abilities often exhibit this gift.

Precognition

We have discussed this ability to see the future on the Earth and Astral Planes. Lucid dreams and other forms of astral voyaging bring this psychic talent into your waking consciousness.

Prediction

Those of you that practice any form of scrying (crystal ball gazing, tarot cards, runes, and so on) will find your abilities quite enhanced. The ability to lay out a future event, called prediction, actually encompasses precognition, clairvoyance, intuition, and other psychic gifts.

Psychometry

When you know the history of an object by merely touching it, you are practicing psychometry. You are particularly sensitive to the vibrations of the object when you exhibit psychometry. Cloth, leather, plastic, and paper do not lend themselves to this technique. You will be more successful with metal objects, stones, and pottery.

Telekinesis

This psychic talent involves the moving of objects without touching them in any way. By using your alpha brain waves, you can cause compass needles, pencils, and other small objects to move about.

Telepathy

When you communicate with another person by sending a thought alone you are exhibiting telepathy. Close family members illustrate this principle. This form of communication is the norm on the other planes.

12

Astral Sex

As soon as you begin astral voyaging, you will begin to meet beings on the "other side." Some of these entities will be spirit guides and compromised souls undergoing NDEs and the transition from physical death on their way to the soul plane to reincarnate.

You will occasionally see "regulars" during your projections. These entities will become astral friends where everybody knows you. The big question is, "Can you engage in sex on the astral plane?"

This chapter will explore astral sex, beginning with an exercise intended to induce an astral voyage following sexual orgasm on the physical plane. You will learn how you can enjoy astral sex, and significantly add to your spiritual growth at the same time.

Astral Sex with Your Partner

Orgasmic projection is a most pleasurable method of experiencing an astral voyage with your partner. This procedure triggers an orgasm and rolls the astral body upward in a sweeping sensation and out through the top of head.

The greater the bonds of trust and emotional (if not spiritual) intimacy, the more successful this approach is. Since two people will be projecting together, this method offers the possibility of one astral partner assisting their partner's astral body to complete its projection, should the latter exhibit only a partial separation.

The initial step is to practice temporary celibacy. This is done to build up sexual tension and increase frustration. Do not avoid sexual stimulation, just the climactic release. The yogic breathing exercises I have presented previously are highly recommended with this technique.

Proper breathing assists greatly in focusing our concentration and in oxygenating our body so both the stamina and quality of the sexual union will be enhanced. Unfortunately, most of us breathe too quickly and too shallowly. Easterners have long preached the connection between breathing and psychic well-being. One only has to consult the very basic books on yoga to confirm this fact, not to mention the Hindu scriptures.

Deep breathing is the key to these exercises, which will help you acquire the technique of proper breathing.

Stand upright, keeping your arms relaxed at your sides and your feet apart. Breathe normally through your nose with your mouth closed.

Place both of your hands, one over the other, on your abdomen just below your navel. Breathe in deeply and distend your stomach muscles by taking in air, not by muscular force.

Breathe out and press both hands gently against your abdomen until all of the air has been released. Repeat this sequence five times to constitute one cycle. Breathe normally four breaths and repeat the entire cycle four additional times. Repeat this sequence, except now breathe mainly from the chest.

When you practice these exercises enough times, your body will become conditioned so that with one smooth in-breath, the air is directed into your fully expanded chest, leaving some room in your abdomen. As you continue breathing in, the abdomen fills up with air.

The reverse occurs upon breathing out. Most of the air in the chest is now released, and subsequently the air from the abdomen. Next, the remaining air in your chest, and finally in your abdomen, is let go.

To summarize, breathing in, or inspiration, is from: abdomen → chest → abdomen → chest. Expiration, or breathing out, is indicated by the following: chest → abdomen → chest → abdomen.

Men typically have more difficulty with breathing from their chest, and favor stomach breathing. Women, on the other hand, find abdominal breathing harder, as they tend to breathe from their chest.

To obtain the maximum benefits from this approach, continual practice is required. Practice will quickly illustrate that this deep-breathing technique is the natural way to breathe.

You can expect the following benefits from deep breathing: increased concentration, relaxation, heightened vitality, calmness, increased confidence, and increased stamina.

One method to project with sex is for the male partner to refrain from orgasm as long as possible. The application of firm pressure on the base of the penis works well in this regard. Women who are capable of multiple orgasms should also delay this response. A simultaneous orgasm is the ideal situation.

During intercourse each partner is to practice any of the visualization techniques presented as they move toward orgasm. A mutual astral voyage will now manifest itself. Another technique is to practice any one of the basic approaches at the precise moment after the orgasm has been experienced. You are much more prone to an OBE following an orgasm than at any moment of your waking life.

Looking for Love in All the Right Places

If you are without a lover or involved in an unsatisfying relationship, consider the option of an astral lover. Your senses are far more intense on the astral plane than on the physical. In addition to being the ultimate "safe sex," this affords you the same tenderness, support, warmth, communication, and satisfaction (if not more) of equivalent encounters on the Earth plane.

Our astral body is referred to as the *emotional* or *desire body* for a very good reason. Always keep your ethics and goals high when you contemplate an astral relationship. This will insure attracting a high-level entity into your universe.

Please do not consider this "cheating" on your current lover. Your astral lover is your companion only on this other dimension, and he or she will not interfere with your physical plane life. In fact, you will find your astral lover far more tolerant of your physical plane life than the other way around.

A true high-level astral lover will exhibit many desirable qualities. They will not be jealous of your present lover. A true astral companion does not want you to be alone on the physical plane.

This astral soul only wants you to be happy, and will assist you in any way possible to help your spiritual growth, health, and other aspects of your physical plane sojourn. Your ability to astrally travel will be improved under their guidance. An astral lover can help you to improve the quality of your current relationship.

Their advice is always for your best interests. They can alert you of future problems and facilitate your healing when you are ill.

When considering acquiring an astral lover, the question arises, "Should I tell my significant other about this relationship?" This is a personal decision, but I strongly advise against this disclosure. For one thing, you will undoubtedly be subject to ridicule or jealousy.

Another problem with informing your mate about this companionship is that he or she will be insulted. Women especially will feel quite intimidated if their partner seeks spiritual (they may also assume emotional and/or physical) satisfaction from someone else.

This is not quite the same as a sexual surrogate. The image of a "ghost" rival will not improve your communication with your physical plane lover. They may very well question your psychological stability. You most certainly would not want this situation being discussed at the office either.

The Experience of Astral Sex

Can you really have sex on the astral plane? The answer is yes, but astral sex is quite different. Your throat chakra will first expand considerably and produce a sexual tingling throughout the astral body. Another benefit of this encounter is an increase in your creativity and psychic gifts.

The next phase is to assume a face to face position with your astral lover, lining up both of your now expanded throat chakras. What results is an exchange of light energy that is quite difficult to describe. As a white light descends over both of you, beams of light enter your chakras one by one. Each of these energy centers opens wide to receive this onrushing energy. All blockages are eliminated and a complete purification of your astral body unfolds. Finally, your root chakra creates a sudden surge of Kundalini energy that rises like an oil well, gushing through your crown chakra.

Some have compared this effect to a nuclear explosion or a light show at Disneyland. Bursts of energy fill the room, and your entire body quivers in response to this energy surge.

Your astral lover now moves closer to you, until both of your bodies are touching. Next, a whirlpool of light energy emanating from both of your crown chakras swirls around your bodies, which now function as one unit. You have never experienced such ecstasy in your physical plane life.

Slowly, your astral lover moves away from you and decreases this energy flow. Soon you regain your previous vibratory rate. He or she will most likely gently kiss you and disappear. Shortly after this you return to your physical body.

One side effect of this form of astral union is a corresponding reaction in the physical body. You may awake feeling completely energized and very stimulated to engage in physical plane sex with your mate.[1]

---

1   D. J. Conway, *Perfect Love: Find Intimacy on the Astral Plane* (St. Paul: Llewellyn Publications, 1996).

The Astral First Date

There are certain principles about astral encounters you should know before embarking on an exercise to meet an astral lover. When you contemplate your initial meeting with this entity, it is best that you remove as much tension, fear, and negative programming as possible.

The easiest way to accomplish this is to practice the higher chakras link technique presented in chapter 6. This method will balance your chakras and increase your frequency vibrational rate.

By properly preparing yourself in the manner just described, you are more likely to attract a higher level astral being into your consciousness. When you leave the body to initiate this astral encounter, I strongly recommend exiting through the sixth or seventh chakra. Never leave through the first, second, or third chakra as this will attract lower-level entities.

Other preparations for this astral date include grooming, wearing a sexy nightgown or silk pajamas when going to bed, and programming your thoughts to those of love, spirituality, and companionship.

You might want to formalize this preparation by listing four categories in your life that need work. These are physical, emotional, mental, and spiritual components. When your list is complete, begin working on your deficiencies in each category.

Limit your therapy to one category at a time. Physical issues may include health problems of all sorts. Insecurities, anger, outbursts, resentments, "baggage," and other such factors can be in your emotional column. When you exercise too many defense mechanisms (rationalization, intellectualization, poor concentration, etc.), you are now dealing with mental issues. Spiritual deficiencies can involve not taking time for your own spiritual enhancement and ignoring psychic communication (intuition, precognition, and so on).

Visualization Technique for Removing Issues

Here is a simple technique to assist you in removing these issues:

1. Practice a self-hypnosis exercises using white light protection.
2. Create a room on the astral plane that is empty and bare. This is your sanctuary.

3. Add furniture, flowers, statues, paintings, and anything else you desire to reflect your spiritual side. There should be a pool of some sort in this large and beautiful room. Remember, the astral plane is much more expansive than our physical plane.

4. Mentally focus on your list of physical problems. Memorize this list and state to yourself how you can resolve each issue.

5. Remove whatever clothes you are wearing and enter this pool. As you immerse yourself in the sacred and cleansing waters of this pool, you are releasing your problems to the healing energy of this water.

6. Finally leave the pool and allow the warmth of the sun to dry you and revitalize your body, resulting in the physical changes you desire.

Repeat this visualization technique with the emotional, mental and spiritual categories on your list. Every six months or so you may want to repeat this cleansing.

Another consideration you could be thinking about are the characteristics you want in your astral lover. Here are some possibilities: integrity, patience, decisiveness, gentleness, intelligence, physical beauty, spiritual growth, truthfulness, supportiveness, high self-image, compassion, and concern.

Locating Your Astral Lover

I have already mentioned that it is preferable to leave your physical body through your crown chakra in order to enhance the possibility of you meeting a high-level astral entity. Once you have arrived on this astral dimension, all that is required is sending out the thought and desire to meet a kindred spirit. It is not unusual to find this spirit waiting for you upon your arrival.

Another method is to go to the special room with the sacred pool you created earlier. Simply meditate there and your lover will soon arrive.

When he or she finally does arrive, take a few minutes to introduce yourself and discuss your mutual goals. This entity may have shared a past life with you. If this is the case, they will most likely be dressed in the attire of that era and resemble their persona from that lifetime.

Ask them their name, hold hands and embrace this astral being. Feel free to ask lots of questions, such as: why does he or she want to be with you? If you sense any impatience or anger at any of these questions, dismiss this being and meditate for another.

You should always feel comfortable in the presence of your astral companion. Refrain from sexual activity right away. It is usually the low-level entities who immediately want to "hop into your astral bed." Their astral body will most likely reflect yellow or green, indicating joy and sexual desire respectively.

Begin a courtship and make it last as long as necessary before engaging in astral sex. When you do finally share intimacies with this entity, begin with the brow chakra, but no lower. Under no circumstances should you initiate sex from the lower three chakras.

Your new astral companion may take you to a temple to access your Akashic records (kept on the causal plane). Any lifetimes you two may have shared together will be explored at this time. You may also explore other lifetimes of yours in which this entity did not participate. This is a wonderful opportunity for spiritual understanding and growth.

This astral being may take you on journeys to interesting places within that vast dimension. You may view scenes back or forward in time, contact a departed loved one or solve a current problem you may be having on the physical plane.

Although your astral lover is unlikely to ask for anything in return for his or her kindness, I recommend you repay them by fulfilling a request of theirs. This might take the form of relaying a message to someone on the physical plane or some other such desire. Exercise good judgment in these matters. Your lover should never suggest anything that is harmful or violates your code of ethics. Only a low-level being would do that.

One thing you do not want to do is become obsessed with your astral lover or your astral voyaging. Never forget about your physical plane life and responsibilities. Doing so will result in emotional, financial, and other problems. In addition, you will retard your spiritual growth and create problems in your aura by becoming too involved with these experiences.

Evaluating Your Astral Lover

The first impressions you receive from any being (physical or astral) are very valuable in judging the quality of an encounter. Be very wary if your companion is quick to suggest that you trust them. If they ask you to make dramatic changes in your life or you catch them lying, you are dealing with a low-level entity. Simply dismiss them if this is the case.

Benefits from Astral Lovers

There are many healthy and spiritually empowering reasons to acquire an astral lover. Among these are:

- ◆ This contact can assist you in improving your life emotionally, physically, materialistically, and spiritually.

- ◆ You will be shown your Akashic records and can use this information to facilitate your own karmic cycle and spiritual growth.

- ◆ The resulting empowerment is very difficult to duplicate through conventional means on the physical plane.

- ◆ Your astral lover can assist you in finding a high quality mate in your earth life.

- ◆ Your ability to end a current dysfunctional relationship without the usual procrastination and guilt aspects will be facilitated.

- ◆ An astral lover can keep you fulfilled during occasions when your earth mate is out of town, ill, or otherwise unavailable. This astral entity can teach you how to unite with your physical lover during their absence too. Your physical lover must agree to this to keep within the bounds of spiritual ethics.

- ◆ The sharing of limitless travels, deep insights, and spiritual bliss enhances life as nothing else on the physical plane can.

- ◆ Since anything is possible on the astral plane, it is easy to use this experience to remove doubts and inhibitions, and build your self-image.

- ◆ For those of you that are sexually frustrated, astral sex provides you with a healthy outlet and helps reduce the anxieties, obligations and pressures incurred from our Earth plane sojourn.

Another benefit is the lack of physical exertion required to engage in astral sex. This is attractive to the elderly and those recovering from a life-threatening illness such as a heart attack. You can have your proverbial cake, eat it too, and not gain weight or incur dental problems.

In summary, let me state that the astral lover can function as a teacher, advisor, friend, protector, and lover, all rolled into one. Your association with this being can eliminate despondency, loneliness, and frustration. The wisdom of ancient knowledge will now be at your disposal, thanks to your companion on the other side.

Your astral lover is only a thought away, and awaits your presence. This true friend and companion has probably been with you before, and will be there for you when you cross into spirit once again. Keep your thoughts pure, and happy hunting.

Astral Healing

O ne of the great advantages of voyaging to the astral plane is that our thoughts instantly materialize into reality and create an object or person. We can use this principle to initiate our own healing or the healing of others.

If you are going to apply these techniques to others, you must first obtain their consent. Even though you may mean well, karmic ethics requires this permission. Individuals choose to be ill for reasons unique to their karmic subcycle. You do not have the right to interfere with this system.

The notion of healing centers on the astral planes (and the other dimensions also) is not new. We have folklore records of the Fortunate Isle of the Celts, the Upperworld (upper astral plane) and Underworld (lower astral plane) of the shamans, and the Greek healing temples of Aesculapius and Hygeia. The Aesculapius center was based on the Temple of Askleposis in the capital city of Sahasradal Kansal on the Astral Plane.

Do not be surprised if you experience flashing colored lights and hear ethereal music as you travel to these healing centers. The easiest

way to establish your astral healing center is to use the room you created in the previous chapter in which to meet your astral lover.

You may find it useful to glance at your Akashic records to see if the
origin of your difficulty originates from a past or future life.

The basic principle in this astral healing technique is to create an
examining table in your room and project onto it a perfect representation of your physical body. To heal another person you may apply these
methods to a representation of their body.

We will be using chakra healing approaches to effect positive changes
in your physical body, or that of your patient. You may wonder why I am
suggesting that you voyage to the astral plane to effect chakra healing
techniques. Can't you simply apply these methods on the physical plane?

These methods may be used in our present physical world, but the
results are less dramatic. Since every thought materializes an object on
the astral plane, it is far easier to obtain energy balancing using the laws
of that dimension.

As a retired dentist, another analogy comes to mind. Using the astral
plane to effect chakra healing is equivalent to doing a filling on a tooth
in your hand, rather than having to work on the same tooth back in the
mouth, with the tongue in the way, and saliva all around it.

The Relationship of Color to Healing

Western society seems to overlook the healing powers of color. We may
dress in various color combinations and decorate our homes and
offices a certain way, but the healing effects are generally ignored by
health professionals.

Color affects us on many levels. Some colors stimulate us, others
soothe our state of being. Certain pigments are considered warm and
others cool. These colors actually have the ability to bring about a physical, mental, emotional, and spiritual change in us.

When you study color, you must always remember that it is a proper-
ty of light. Light is composed of frequencies, or wave lengths. Each frequency vibrates at a different rate, producing a certain color that is seen
by our eyes.

Every frequency of light, in the form of color, has its own way of affecting our aura and ultimately our physical, mental, emotional and spiritual states. Certain colors exert a greater affect on the physical body, while others influence our mind. For a list of color relationships to our various states of existence, see pages 32–33.

To use color appropriately in healing, you must understand the properties of each color and apply techniques to absorb and project color.

The Healing Significance of Colors

These principles are only to be used as guidelines in your approach to chakra healing. Your own experience will orient you more toward certain shades of colors that will be more effective in your hands. Nothing is etched in stone. Since each individual's energy field is unique, certain hues may not work with them, while others that seem to bear no relation to their condition do.

Experimentation is always the key to being a good astral chakra healer. This requires an open mind and a willingness to try something new. Always follow your own intuition, as your higher self will assist you with these endeavors.

The use of colors in chakra healing techniques must constantly be adapted to the individual. The aura changes, as does the status of chakra imbalances. The principles I present here are simply models for you to start your approach. You will undoubtedly develop your own color combinations that work best for the techniques you employ.

The chart that follows shows the positive and negative effects of the seven colors of the rainbow.

CHAKRA	COLOR	POSITIVE EFFECT	NEGATIVE EFFECT
7	Violet	Inner Wisdom	Ignorance
6	Indigo	Balance	Chaos
5	Blue	Freedom	Self-indulgence
4	Green	Discipline	Procrastination
3	Yellow	Self-expression	Conceit
2	Orange	Cooperation	Self-pity
1	Red	Individuality	Selfishness

Figure 8. Chakra Color Effects

The body's chakras need all colors. They may require a predomi-
nance of a certain color, but each color is needed by the major chakras
periodically. This is why a certain chakra may function better with a
color not normally associated with it.

Chakra energy healing uses colors to heal. An imbalance of a certain
color can be treated and enhanced with its complementary color. For
example a primary color (red, blue, or yellow) imbalance is treated with
its opposite secondary color (orange, green, or violet), and vice-verse.

The following chart illustrates these recommended color sequences:

COLOR DEFICIENCY	COLOR TO RESTORE BALANCE
Red	Green
Blue	Orange
Yellow	Violet

Figure 9. Chakra Color Sequences

Some examples will help make this system easier to understand. An
individual's auric field will be predominantly blue if he or she has difficulty in expressing emotions. The healer would focus on this aura with
an orange ray into the second chakra. If another person was suffering
from an emotional trauma, they would have an excess of orange in their
aura. The treatment here would consist of sending blue light into the
second chakra.

Another instance could present a client with an excess of mental chat-
ter resulting in an overabundance of yellow in their aura. By projecting
violet to the individual's crown chakra, the healer would help the client
cure this imbalance.

Our physical body's organs react to certain colors, based on their
location. An organ responds to the color of the chakra in which it is
found and to the color of the complementary or opposing chakra. The
pancreas, for example, resides in the third chakra. This organ will
respond to yellow or violet. The chakra healer would use both colors to
restore the energy balance of the pancreas and to initiate its healing.

Each chakra complements the other. All seven major chakras must act
together in balance so that we may function as a complete sentient
being. As the energy moves up the chakras, each chakra sorts out the

particular color frequency required in that part of the physical body. This is particularly accentuated when you direct this healing from the astral plane to a body you have materialized there.

In this section we will discuss the metaphysical meaning and clinical applications of various colors to chakra healing[1]:

Violet

This color signifies practical spirituality and purification. It may be applied to conditions of the veins, the nervous system, and skeletal system. The crown chakra is directly affected by this color. Violet helps in the balancing of both spiritual and physical energies. The bluer shades of this color help with arthritis.

Violet assists the body in the assimilation of minerals and nutrients. It stimulates dreaming, humility, and our inspirations. Using this color can open up the mind to receive past life data. Since violet is half red and half blue, it assists in restoring a proper balance of the physical and spiritual components in our lives, keeping them practical and in alignment.

Indigo

Altered states of consciousness, purification, and integration are represented by indigo. This is the color of the third eye chakra and has applications to the reproductive and endocrine systems, conditions of the face and head, and infections in general. Indigo functions to strengthen the immune system, the glands, and the body's ability to purify the bloody and detoxify.

This color has a sedative-like effect and helps to balance the left and right brain. It facilitates our intuition and the attainment of deeper levels of consciousness. Obsessions and problems with the lungs can be treated with indigo. Depression may be the result of too much indigo, and this can be balanced by using soft shades of orange.

Blue

Blue denotes aspiration, faith, creative expression, and a feeling of peace. It has a relaxing and cooling effect on the body. The ears, eyes, throat, nose, veins, and respiratory system can be treated with this color.

---

1 Ted Andrews, *The Healer's Manual* (St. Paul: Llewellyn Publications, 1993), pp. 128–130.

This color is associated with the throat chakra, and is beneficial in dealing with high blood pressure, rheumatism, jaundice, childhood diseases, and asthma. Blue can activate artistic talents, help with loneliness, and it works well in combination with red and orange.

Green

This hue is associated with growth, balance, and tranquility. Emotional problems, and difficulties with the sympathetic nervous system and circulatory system can be treated with this color. Never use green to heal tumors, as the color stimulates growth.

Green can be used to increase compassion and sensitivity. It soothes us and aids in most forms of healing. This color is recharging and it helps awaken our hope, faith, and friendliness. The heart chakra is controlled by green. You can apply this color to ulcers, high blood pressure, exhaustion, and conditions of the heart.

Yellow

This color deals with all types of intellectual functions. It is applied to left-brain activities, the adrenal glands, and our digestive system. The solar plexus chakra is associated with yellow.

You may correctly apply this color to treat headaches, to facilitate learning capabilities, or to awaken an enthusiasm for life and depression. It is suggested that blue be used to balance an excess of yellow. Mental tension and anxiety can result from an overabundance of yellow in an individual's aura.

Orange

Orange assists with our energy reserves and optimism. The excretory system, muscular system, and emotions can be helped by this color. This is the hue of the spleen or second chakra. Creativity, wisdom, joy, and gregariousness are stimulated by orange. Use this color to assist with the healing of the stomach, spleen, intestines, pancreas, and adrenal glands. The shades of blue and greens can help balance too much orange.

The peach shades of orange are ideal in dealing with emotional paralysis. This combination assists in recharging the body and is recommended after an illness and to help the excretory system of the body at any time.

Red

Our sexuality, willpower, and life force itself are affected by this color. Use red to heal the circulatory system, the lower extremities and to stimulate metabolism. The first chakra is associated with this color. Our deeper passions, such as revenge, hatred, love, sex, and courage are activated by red.

You can use red to elevate the temperature of the body and energize the blood. Too much red can cause high blood pressure. We use green to balance red.

Black

This color is used for grounding, strengthening, and protection. Black activates and strengthens the feminine energies of the body.

Depression may result from too much black. It is best applied in combination with white, as it activates the subconscious and assists in putting life in a proper perspective. Never use black by itself.

White

Purity and amplification are symbolic of this color. The entire color spectrum is found in white. It may be used with all systems of the body. Use white if you are unsure of what color to apply to any condition you are treating.

White cleanses and purifies all forms of energy. It amplifies the effects of any other color, and should be used to begin and end a color therapy session.

Silver

Intuitive clarification and amplification are associated with silver. This color is effective in meditation, and in ascertaining the metaphysical origin of an illness. This color balances and stimulates the feminine energies and creative imagination, and amplifies the effects of other colors.

Turquoise and Light Blue-Greens

We use this color to strengthen metabolism, ease fevers and inflammation, and treat skin problems (especially when combined with pink), throat conditions, respiratory system illness, earaches and acute pain. Turquoise is purifying, and vitalizes all systems of the body.

Gold

This color amplifies and strengthens. Use this hue to strengthen the heart and the immune system. It can renew enthusiasm and activate the individual's own healing powers. Gold is also a protective color.

Purple

This color has always symbolized intense purification. It detoxifies the body and is useful in healing precancerous and cancerous conditions. Use this color sparingly, as too much of it can cause depression.

Purple is used to treat headaches, and the red-purple range assists in balancing the polarities of the body. You can apply the blue-purple range to ease inflammations, cool the body, and shrink tumors.

Brown

Stabilizing and grounding functions are associated with this color. This hue calms and grounds emotions and stabilizes overexcited states. It assists in the awakening of discrimination and common sense. Brown has been used to treat hyperactivity in children (especially rust to deep brown shades) and dissociated mental states.

Royal Blue

This is a purifying color. It assists the body in oxygenation, both internally and externally. Use this shade to ease depression and clear a confused mind.

Pink

This color is always soothing. It can awaken love and compassion, and facilitates meditation. Use this hue to treat the immune system, inflammation, and skin disorders (especially when combined with turquoise).

Lemon

This color enhances our mental functioning. Lemon is stimulating to the digestive system and left side of the brain. It can detoxify the body, is good for bones and tissues, assists the body in assimilation of nutrients, and is used to treat senility and Alzheimer's Disease.

To sum up this section, begin and end all color healing with white. Blues are cooling and cleansing and are applied to our spiritual energies. Reds are warming and stimulate the physical body. Yellow acts as a bridge between these two and exerts its influence on mental energies.

Therapeutic Applications of Color and Chakra Healing

To sharpen your abilities in dealing with color, the following visualization exercise will help you:

1. Relax, sit comfortably, and take a deep breath. Hold this breath for a count of eight and exhale. Repeat this and hold this breath to a count of ten.

2. Close your eyes and breathe normally. Visualize a band of energy from the earth rising up and entering both of your feet. Feel this energy vibrate and tingle as it moves past your knees and into your hips.

3. Imagine a red color for this energy as it enters the first chakra in your sacrum (lower back). Take another deep breath as you perceive this color. Let this breath out slowly.

4. Now inhale and imagine this energy turning orange as it enters the second chakra. Exhale slowly. Inhale again and see this color become yellow as it moves into the 3ird chakra. Gently let your breath out.

5. Inhale again and follow this energy as it enters the heart chakra, where it turns green. Slowly exhale.

6. Breathe in deeply and visualize the energy moving up to your throat chakra, as it now appears blue. Exhale slowly.

7. Continue with your deep breathing as the energy enters into the third eye or 6th chakra, and is seen as indigo.

8. Now inhale again and see this energy leave from the top of your head or crown chakra, where it now appears as violet. Exhale gently and perceive this violet aura surrounding your entire body. Notice how this violet color changes to white and pulsates around your entire physical body, creating a wonderful relaxing and protective feeling.

9. Stay with this image and feeling for five minutes. Open your eyes.

Another visualization and balancing exercise applied on the astral plane will assist you in strengthening your physical and other bodies:

1. Sit comfortably, apply protection, and breathe deeply. Imagine a rainbow that has formed in the sky above. Visualize a red ball of light coming out of the rainbow and entering the top of your head. See it descend through your body, spinning and radiating intense red energy that heals each and every part of your body.

2. Focus all of your attention on this red energy and see it spinning down to your feet, filing you with this healing energy. The moment it reaches your feet this red energy dissipates, but not its healing effects on your body. Meditate on this for two minutes.

3. Take another deep breath and visualize an orange ball of light being emitted from the rainbow and entering the top of your head. See it descend through your body, spinning and radiating intense orange energy that heals each and every part of your body.

4. Focus all of your attention on this orange energy and see it spinning to your feet, filling you with this healing energy. The moment it reaches your feet this orange energy dissipates, but not its healing effects on your body. Meditate on this for two minutes.

5. Take another deep breath and visualize a yellow ball of light being emitted from the rainbow and entering the top of your head. See it descend through your body, spinning and radiating intense yellow energy that heals each and every part of your body.

6. Focus all of your attention on this yellow energy and see it spinning to your feet, filling you with this healing energy. The moment it reaches your feet this yellow energy dissipates, but not its healing effects on your body. Meditate on this for two minutes.

7. Take another deep breath and visualize a green ball of light being emitted from the rainbow and entering the top of your head. See it descend through your body, spinning and radiating intense green energy that heals each and every part of your body.

8. Focus your attention on this green energy and see it spinning to your feet, filling you with this healing energy. The moment it reaches your feet this green energy dissipates, but not its healing effects on your body. Meditate on this for two minutes.

9. Take another deep breath and visualize a blue ball of light being emitted from the rainbow and entering the top of your head. See it descend through your body, spinning and radiating intense blue energy that heals each and every part of your body.

10. Focus all of your attention on this blue energy and see it spinning to your feet, filling you with this healing energy. The moment it reaches your feet this blue energy dissipates, but not its healing effects on your body. Meditate on this for two minutes.

11. Take another deep breath and visualize an indigo ball of light being emitted from the rainbow and entering the top of your head. See it descend through your body, spinning and radiating intense indigo energy that heals each and every part of your body.

12. Focus all of your attention on this indigo energy and see it spinning to your feet, filling you with this healing energy. The moment it reaches your feet this indigo energy dissipates, but not its healing effects on your body. Meditate on this for two minutes.

13. Take another deep breath and visualize a violet ball of light being emitted from the rainbow and entering the top of your head. See it descend through your body, spinning and radiating intense violet energy that heals each and every part of your body.

14. Focus all of your attention on this violet energy and see it spinning to your feet, filling you with this healing energy. The moment it reaches your feet this violet energy dissipates, but not its healing effects on your body. Meditate on this for two minutes.

15. Now overview your entire body and note how it radiates with a vibrant vitality. Perceive yourself being healed and balanced. Visualize the rainbow moving down from the sky and centering

itself directly over your crown chakra. It is permanently located here and every time you practice this exercise this rainbow and its healing effects will grow stronger within and around your energy field.

Color Breathing

Color breathing is a powerful healing method. Our body converts air into energy, and our thoughts determine the strength and frequency of that energy. We can facilitate the healing of many imbalances by breathing different colors. On the astral plane, an actual color will materialize as you practice color breathing.

Selecting Colors

To assist you in selecting an appropriate color, the following summary may be of help[2]:

Purple Breath: This is indicated for detoxifying the body. It is most effective when used with white. Use this color to treat flu symptoms, negative emotions, obsessions, and infections.

Red Breath: This color breath also helps with flu symptoms and colds, and assists in raising the body's physical energy.

Orange Breath: Respiratory problems, muscle conditions, and creativity blocks are treated by this breath. It also restores a joy for life.

Yellow Breath: This shade helps us to learn more quickly and aids in digestion.

Green Breath: Use this color to activate a sense of prosperity, ease nervous conditions, and cool and soothe most systems of the body. The pale green breath is ideal for treating bad habits and improving vision.

Blue Breath: This shade eases respiratory problems, activates artistic talents, and has a generally soothing and calming effect. It is ideal for use with children.

Dark Blue Breath: Use this color to increase intuition, strengthen the endocrine system, and facilitate healing after surgery. When you combine

---

2   Ibid., pp. 129–130. Used with permission of publisher.

this with a small amount of green (producing a teal blue color), it helps in healing bone ailments.

Turquoise Breath: This is great for arthritis and respiratory problems. When you combine this with pink, you facilitate weight loss.

Violet Breath: Purifying and detoxifying the body, activation of spiritual attunement, and aligning the mental and physical aspects of our body are the effect of this breath. It also helps the nervous and skeletal systems.

Pink Breath: This color of breath is good for puffiness, skin conditions, loneliness, and anger.

Color Breathing Exercise

The following exercise will help you to practice these principles:

1. Sit comfortably, apply protection, and breathe deeply. Slowly inhale through your nose and hold that breath for a count of seven.

2. Exhale and inhale again through your nose, holding your breath for a count of eleven. Exhale slowly through your mouth for a count of seven.

3. As you inhale, see and feel the air as a particular color. Visualize this color of air filling up your entire body. Each breath soon begins to glow and vibrate within your body.

4. Imagine this colored breath healing and balancing whatever is needed by the body at this time. Continue this process for ten minutes.

Scanning the Physical Body Created on the Astral Plane

Before beginning any chakra energy work, it is necessary to scan the body with your hands. This will alert you to damaged chakras, blocks in energy flows, weak aura areas, and so on. The technique is rather simple.

1. Relax, apply protection and breathe deeply. Ask your Higher Self for guidance.

2. Hold your hands six inches above the body. First establish contact with the aura, which will feel like a slight pushing sensation or a buoyancy against the hand.

3. Move your hands slowly along the edge of the aura of this body, starting with the feet. Pay attention to any unusual sensation (hot spots, cold spots, etc.) at the outer edge or within its auric field. Normally there is a liquid-like sensation beneath your hands, and a sense of flow.

4. Note any gaps, bulges, holes, and hot or cold spots. Complete this process at the top of the body's head.

Laser Healing

When you concentrate your psychic energy into an intense beam of light, we refer to it as laser healing. This should be used for short periods only, as it is rather intense.

The procedure is as follows:

1. Have the person you wish to heal stand in front of you. Lift his or her hand for a minute or two to tune in to its energy.

2. Begin transmitting a fine blue light and another green light of energy from your third eye area. Hold the two beams of light until you feel a tingling, cold, or warm sensation on your forehead.

3. When this is felt, add to these beams the appropriate color that reflects the problem. Mauve is added for communication, yellow for fear, green for creativity, and blue for depression.

4. Now move these three laser beams of light down from the subject's forehead to the affected area. Hold them in one position for ten seconds, and then fan them out over this area.

5. Move these three beams about twelve inches over the subject's head and combine them with his or her aura. Fan these light beams down the person to his or her feet.

6. Meditate for three minutes and do not touch the subject's body. Place his or her hands together, move away from them, and brush your hands against your thighs.

This technique activates healing energy while revitalizing both the sender and receiver.

At this time, feel free to apply the principles of color healing to any of the damaged areas you noted as you scanned the body (yours or someone else's) that you materialized on the astral plane.

Hypnosis and meditative practices aid in restoring a sense of control to an individual's life, and can generally induce a more positive life outlook. More recently, Eastern techniques of chakra healing, meditation, and visualization have been applied directly to disease, and it appears that this process of psychophysiological integration can have a dramatic effect on the disease process and initiate soul healing, especially when directed from another dimension.

Scientific Studies
on Astral Voyaging

Throughout this book I have alluded occasionally to scientific literature to support the validity of the other planes and our other bodies. This chapter contains a more thorough survey of the scientific data on this intriguing discipline. The focus of this material will be on breakthrough research and major contributors to this field.

Throughout this century scientists have sought ways to prove the existence of the soul. Dr. Duncan McDougall of Haverhill, Massachusetts conducted a series of experiments in the 1920s, during which he weighed patients dying of tuberculosis to ascertain the precise weight of the soul. His method consisted of placing these patients—bed and all—on a specially designed scale. He noted the before and after death weights and discovered a difference of between two and two-and-a-half ounces. This was the deduced weight of our consciousness.[1]

---

1 Muldoon & Carrington, op. cit.

According to Dr. Karlis Osis, the only meaningful "proof" of the astral body would be for it to be both seen and photographed during controlled laboratory experiments.[2]

That the OBE phenomenon is a widespread human potential that anyone is capable of achieving has been demonstrated by several research centers, among which are the Menninger Foundation in Topeka, Kansas, through the work of Dr. Glen Gabbard; the Topeka V.A. Medical Center through the research of Dr. Stewart Twemlow; and the University of Kansas Medical Center, under the auspices of Dr. Fowler Jones.[3]

The results of these Kansas teams have shown that OBE ability is common throughout the general American population. The experience is pleasurable and appears to benefit the recipient psychologically. It is a normal human phenomenon, but there is no special type of individual that is especially prone to astral voyaging.

The Society for Psychical Research (SPR)

The SPR was founded at Cambridge University in England in 1882 "to investigate that large body of debatable phenomena designated by such terms as mesmeric (refers to hypnosis), psychical, and spiritualistic, without prejudice or prepossession of any kind, and in the same spirit of exact and unimpassioned enquiry which has enabled science to solve so many problems." In 1886, SPR members Edmund Gurney, Frederick Myers, and Frank Podmore published *Phantasms of the Living*, a two-volume work on their findings. Many cases of astral voyaging were included among the 702 cases cited.

One member of the SPR reported an astral voyage to the bedroom of two women he knew who resided three miles away. They later reported to him that they were shocked by the sight of him standing at their bedside in evening dress.

Frederick Myers presented overwhelming evidence for soul travel, which he termed "self-projection," in his classic book *Human Personality*

---

2   Dr. Karlis Osis is retired and functions as research director emeritus for the American Society of Psychical Research.

3   Osis and Haraldsson, Op. cit.

and Its Survival of Bodily Death.[4] This work ironically was published after his own transition in 1903. He concluded that "self-projection is the one definite act which it seems as though a man might perform equally well before and after bodily death."

Another example of astral plane workings was that Davis actually saw into his own future! He described a house in great detail that he was not residing in at the time. This structure was reported by Davis as having "a funny, dark tunnel." Later on Soal visited Davis when he had moved to a house that possessed a long dark passageway that clearly resembled a tunnel. Other details of this house corroborated what Davis told Soal during the seance.

The only explanation I can come up with to explain why Davis actually thought he was dead when he attended the seance is that of role playing. Since Soal and everyone else present at the seance presumed Davis to be a discarnate, Davis' astral body picked up on those feelings and thoughts and acted accordingly.

American Society for Psychic Research (ASPR)

The ASPR, headquartered in New York City was directed by Karlis Osis during the 1970s. This scientific organization investigates OBEs and looks for the following types of evidence: introspective awareness of the projector, observations by witnesses, physiological changes in the subject as noted by recordings of mechanical devices, and changes in the energy patterns of the target area.

One objective of the ASPR was to separate a clairvoyant vision from a true OBE. Osis and his associate Janet Mitchell began a fourteen-month study in 1972 with an artist named Ingo Swann.

The "Fly-in" Experiments

A test was designed by Dr. Osis in which psychics by way of their astral body would visit his office on the fourth floor of the ASPR building, and report on various objects in the room.[5] Fifteen of the one hundred

---

4   Frederick Myers, *Human Personality and Its Survival of Bodily Death* (London: Longman's Green, 1903).

5   K. Osis and E. Haraldsson, *At the Hour of Death* (New York: Avon, 1977).

psychics participating in this experiment were successful in accurately describing the objects.

Dr. Charles Tart

When Dr. Tart was teaching at the University of Virginia School of Medicine in 1965 and 1966, he conducted some classic OBE research with Robert Monroe. Monroe's bodily functions were measured by machines during his OBEs.

Tart instructed Monroe to project to an adjoining room and read a randomly selected five-digit number printed on a high shelf—too high to be seen by normal vision. Monroe did project to this room, but could not read these numbers (these details are the hardest for an astral body to see). He did, however, accurately report a conversation that one of the technicians had with her husband in the corridor outside of this room. Monroe went on to write a classic book, *Journeys Out of the Body*, and two sequels on his astral journeys. He founded the Monroe Institute in southern Virginia to continue this research.[6]

Later, another subject, Miss Z., participated in a similar experiment with Dr. Tart at the University of California-Davis where he was then Professor of Psychology. Miss Z. correctly identified the digits. This occurring by pure chance can be ruled out, as the odds against this happening were 100,000 to 1.

Miss Z.'s pulse and brain-wave patterns did not slow down as they would in deep sleep, and REMs were completely absent, showing that she was not dreaming. Her EEG showed a lowered voltage during her OBE. Monroe's EEG pattern also exhibited this trait. This observation, as I mentioned earlier, was also noted in Osis' data.[7]

---

6   Robert Monroe, *Journeys Out of the Body* (Garden City, NY: Doubleday, 1971), pp. 11–12. Also Charles Tart, "A second psychophysiological study of out-of-the-body experiences in a gifted subject," *International Journal of Parapsychology* (1967), pp. 251–58.

7   Monroe, ibid.

The Psychical Research Foundation (PRF)

In the early 1970s, Dr. Robert Morris was director of research at an independent research center in North Carolina, the Psychical Research Foundation, where he worked with Duke University student, Keith (Blue) Harary, who proved to be an excellent astral voyager.

Harary was able to project to a separate building, read some cards, and report back to Dr. Morris on what he read. They found that his astral body could take one of three forms: a glowing ball of light that was either blue, white, or gold; a pinpoint in space with circular vision; or an astral body, an exact duplicate of his physical body. The blue light perception may explain why he liked to be called "Blue."[8]

Harary stated that the world of the astral double is not identical to that of the physical body. I have discussed this concept of the astral body creating a parallel, but artificial and somewhat inaccurate, physical world. Harary would see the target area in "full color," often more vivid than normal. His astral body would hear sounds from the physical plane and often beyond it, which he would describe as "incredibly beautiful and harmonious."

Stanford Research Institute (SRI)

Stanford Research Institute is located in Menlo Park, California. During the 1970s and the early part of the 1980s, physicists Russell Targ and Harold Puthoff conducted classical studies in "remote viewing."[9] They defined remote viewing as a form of clairvoyance, rather than a true OBE. They felt that remote viewing and OBEs lie on a type of continuum of psi experiences. They described remote viewing as like "seeing a remote scene, as though it were a movie."

Their experimental design consisted of an *outbound experimenter* or *beacon*, who would be sent to a distant outside location or *target site*, chosen randomly while the beacon was in transit. An *interviewer* back at

---

8   John Palmer and C. Vasser. "ESP and Out-of-Body Experiences: An Exploratory Study," *Journal of the American Society for Psychical Research*, 1974, pp. 68, 257–80.

9   R. Targ and Harold Puthoff. "Remote Viewing of Natural Targets." In L. Oteri (Ed.)., *Quantum Physics and Parapsychology* (New York: Parapsychology Foundations, 1975).

the laboratory asked the projector to focus his or her psychic abilities on the target site and describe it verbally and/or draw it. The interviewer was unaware of this randomly chosen target site.

SRI used outdoor areas as targets. One trial consisted of giving Ingo Swann the latitude and longitude of a target area and instructing him to go there in his astral body. Swann projected to an island in the Indian Ocean, so small that it is not located on most maps.

Out of the nearly one hundred remote viewing trials Swann participated in, he was successful seventy-five times, missed on fourteen attempts, and six other descriptions could not be evaluated. Swann's experiences were truly OBEs, as demonstrated by his summary of what he encountered. He described his other body actually traveling to the target site during certain trials. He also described seeing "ionized particles" in the form of specific objects during some of his astral voyaging.

The late Pat Price, former mayor and police commissioner of Burbank, California, was another astral voyager who was studied at SRI. Price was to leave his body and follow SRI staff members to locations around the San Francisco Bay area that were randomly chosen.

Price would relax, free his mind, and suggest his astral body locate and observe the outbound experimenter. He then sketched what his astral body saw. These sketches and transcripts of his statements were given to outside judges in random order, and the judges matched the sketches and transcripts to a particular location. Price correctly identified six of nine locations, both in sketches and verbally. He at times guessed what the target location was even before it was randomly selected. Was Pat Price exhibiting precognition while out of his body?

Evaluating OBE Research

The late Dr. Robert Crookall was an eminent scientist in Great Britain who devoted his retirement years to evaluating reports of OBE studies. Crookall's critical analysis of a large number of cases (nearly one thousand), earned him an international reputation as an objective and competent researcher. Crookall's twelve books are listed in the bibliography.

Crookall used four categories of analysis for these OBE cases. Among these is what is known as "Whatley's Law of Evidence." This principle states that if enough independent witnesses confirm the details of an observation, and it is impossible for them to have collaborated together, then the likelihood is high that the observations made are genuine.[10]

Our understanding of OBEs has been greatly facilitated by Dr. Crookall's painstaking work. Crookall has shown that man possesses another body that survives death. His work also demonstrates that the multitude of OBE reports can be subjected to scientific assessment.

Research Problems with OBEs

The relationship and emotional bond a projector develops with the researchers affects and sometimes interferes with the experiment. It is hard for the astral body to identify with an inanimate object. Many projectors wandered off in search of the staff rather than directing their doubles to the designated target areas.

Both PRF and ASPR subjects had difficulty in clearly seeing letters and numbers, especially if they were small. The astral body was also more sensitive to color and light, which are spiritual attributes. SRI tests fared better by using daylight and natural outdoor settings.

The cooling-down period used by Harary may be necessary for all future trials in order to reduce the subjective feelings created from the conscious effort dictated by the experimental parameters. SRI researchers suggested that mental noise (composed of memory and imagination) was responsible for some of the difficulties of the projectors.[11]

The distortion registered by Harary when in the form of a ball of light, and the ionized particles described by Swann, suggest a perception problem when compared to the eyes of the physical body. Let us not forget the voltage drops in Swann's EEGs, Harary, and Monroe as contributing to these distortions.

There is finally a definition problem with SRI's use of the term: "remote viewing." Although they closely defined it as a form of

---

10   Robert Crookall, *Casebook of Astral Projection*, op. cit.

11   D. Scott Rogo, *Mind Beyond the Body* (New York: Penguin, 1978).

clairvoyance rather than a true OBE, their experimental results strongly demonstrate that these remote viewers were actually astral voyaging.

The sixty-six percent success rate reported by SRI, as evaluated by a panel of independent judges, has been duplicated by other research institutions in the United States. Mundelein College in Chicago, the Institute for Parapsychology in Durham, North Carolina, and Princeton University have all reported similar results.

This would appear to be, and certainly is, quite positive. The problem with SRI is in the source of its funding, which is the Department of Defense (DOD). The DOD is responding to the Russian interest in using remote viewing as a means for mental influence from a distance.[12]

Russian academician Yuri Kobzarev listed the following institutions conducting psychic research for the purpose of influencing psychological behavior: the Division of Cybernetics at the Leningrad Polytechnical Institute; the Scientific-Industrial Unit, "Quantum," in Krasnodar; the Tbilisi State University in Georgia; the Kazakh State University in Alma-Ata (Dr. Victor Inyushin's laboratory); the Ukrainian Institute of Cybernetics in Kiev; Bauman Higher Technology School in Moscow (Dr. Vagner's laboratory); Moscow Energetics Institute (Dr. Sokolov's laboratory); Research Institute of General and Pedagogical Psychology at the U.S.S.R. Academy of Pedagogical Sciences, Moscow; the Division of Cybernetics of the Research Institute of Biophysics, U.S.S.R. Academy of Sciences, in Pushchino; and Leningrad State University (Prof. Pavel Gulyaev's Aurametry Laboratory).

On August 13, 1977, the *Chicago Tribune* reported that CIA director Stanfield Turner: "confirmed reports that the Russians are studying persons who claim to be able to read minds and 'teleport' themselves into secret meetings and into the future. Turner confirmed that U.S. intelligence operatives have discovered that the Soviet Union is spending money and time researching whether occult and psychic methods could be used for spying on other nations."

The DOD considers Russian psychic research efforts designed primarily to use psychic abilities to influence and control human behavior.

---

12   John D. LaMothe, "Controlled Offensive Behavior—U.S.S.R., U.S. Defense Intelligence Agency (*Unclassified)," prepared by the U.S. Army, Office of the Surgeon General, Medical Intelligence Office (Washington D.C., July 1972) (#CT–CS–01–169–72), and other government publications.

SRI's attention was directed toward counter-espionage, which is the main reason why Targ, Puthoff, and others left this institution. This negative use of astral voyaging is offensive both personally and professionally to this hypnotherapist and parapsychologist.

The good news from the U.S. Federal Government is that it confirms the validity of OBEs. *Omni* magazine reported, in July, 1979, a statement made by Congressman Charles Rose:

> *What these persons "saw" was confirmed by aerial photography. There's no way it could have been faked . . . intelligence people I've talked to know that remote viewing works . . . not yet as good as satellite photography. But it seems to me that it would be a hell of a cheap radar system. And if the Russians have it and we don't, we are in serious trouble.*

Putting It All
Together

T his chapter brings together the various concepts we have discussed to illustrate some practical applications of astral voyaging. As a baby boomer, I can remember the term "tripping out" receiving much publicity back in the 1960s.

This expression was applied to psychedelic drug excursions, but the term itself is of great interest to our discussion. Those that experimented with hallucinogenic substances (LSD, PCP, etc.) actually generated a drug-induced astral voyage.

I do not recommend this approach. The "bad trips" reported by many of these people undoubtedly represented excursions to the lower astral plane. This is the worst possible example of a forced projection. Do yourself and the universe a favor and keep it natural.

No matter how simple and time-tested astral voyaging techniques may be, there are always people who fail to obtain results in their initial or subsequent trials. This may be due to one or a combination of four factors that can impede success: fear, health problems, timing, and the weather.

Fear is the number one reason why a projector will not allow their astral double to separate from its physical counterpart, yet no one has ever been harmed as a result of these experiences. The only way to convince yourself of the safety of these techniques is to try them. I wouldn't be writing this book if there were any danger involved. Considering the many hundreds of times I personally have voyaged to other dimensions, obviously if this were harmful my location would currently be on the soul plane rather than in Los Angeles.

You will facilitate your chances of succeeding with the recommended techniques if you are in better physical, mental, emotional, and spiritual health. Although illness can bring on an OBE, it is far more desirable to have a firm foundation to benefit from these excursions. I recommend using superconscious mind and chakra healing tapes, or my pain and healing cassettes to assist you in your energy balancing.

Timing in life is everything. I strongly recommend that you practice astral voyaging during periods when you are relaxed and the physical environment around you is quiet. Other factors to consider are making these attempts at night, during full moons, and when there is nothing distracting your mind or attention.

Weather is the final factor. It may sound far-fetched, but thunderstorms definitely inhibit one from leaving the body. As I explained earlier, thunder is the sound associated with the physical plane. The electrical fields created by storms act as a hindrance to the electromagnetic energy represented by your soul as it attempts to separate from the physical body. Ideally you should select a clear night when the weather is warm, if not humid. You can create a similar atmosphere in your practice room, as I have already suggested.

The Origin of Folklore

We have all been exposed to stories of leprechauns and their pot of gold. Other "little people" such as elves, pixies, gnomes, and natural spirits of all sorts abound throughout history. I believe they actually do exist, but on the astral plane.

Can these creatures manifest on the physical plane without the added factor of too much alcohol or other drugs? Yes, that is theoretically possible. Thought-forms may be created, as I have discussed. Just as I described the origin of the term "trip," these tales appear to be remnants of astral voyages.

Why Do We Have a Lower Astral Plane?

This question is a logical one and one that has boggled the mind of man for thousands of years. Fear, obstinacy, indifference, low levels of spiritual growth, and other factors appear to account for many souls choosing to reside on the lower astral plane where there is no possibility of growth.

An ancient Hermetic expression states, "When the student is ready, the teacher will appear." It is only when a lower astral plane soul specifically requests guidance from their Higher Self and/or guides and enters the white light that they ascend to the higher astral plane, and eventually end up on the soul plane.

We need to consider that many souls feel comfortable being surrounded by the negativity of this lower astral plane. Their life on Earth often was quite dysfunctional, and they become conditioned to an environment of cynicism, depression, and evil acts. In addition, from this dimension a soul can observe their loved ones from their physical plane life. The inability to break this astral form of co-dependency keeps them stuck on this dimension as an earthbound spirit.

Another factor relates to the brainwashing we are all exposed to by religion. The lower astral plane is equivalent to the Purgatory of Christianity and the bardo state of the Tibetans. If a soul feels they are a sinner and haven't earned the right to enter heaven or nirvana, they will remain right where they are and continue to suffer.

The pleasures of astral sex also keep some souls from moving on. Sex with low-level astral entities is not the same as that discussed in chapter 13, but it does feel good nonetheless. A sexaholic on the physical plane, or an immediate gratification personality profile in general, will retain this trait on the astral plane. This clouds their judgment and makes them much less receptive to entering the Light.

If a soul had a particularly poor or frustrating sex life while in the physical body, this only adds to the incentive for them to make up for lost time now. An astral body does not engage in the typical games people play on Earth. Melding with an astral lover is easy, and sex is readily available.

Time Travel on the Astral Plane

It is relatively simple to traverse time while on the astral plane. All one need do is focus on a specific period of time in the "past" or "future," and he or she will be instantly transported there. However, even on the astral plane it is not easy to arrive at the precise date you desire.

One technique is to imagine a clock face with its hands rapidly turning forward or backward. This technique is useful for shorter time travel journeys. For longer trips, images of a calendar with pages being torn off or flipping back or forward in time seems to give excellent results.

Reports from my patients, along with my own personal voyages, bring to the surface certain limitations to astral time travel. First, you have the option of going only to certain time locations. If the knowledge of this time era would significantly interfere with your spiritual growth or that of others you will not be allowed access to this data. There are certain areas of "forbidden knowledge" that apply.

Secondly, you may not be able to travel to a time three hours ahead of you, but a scene two days in the future might be relatively easy to attain. Some voyagers failed to venture ten days into the future, but found going ahead by one month child's play.

The further you attempt to travel either backward or forward in time, the more disjointed these "windows in time" appear. For example, you may easily travel one year ahead in time, but find excursions two, three, or five years forward impossible. On the other hand, a trip five hundred years into your future may come easily.

Many theories have been proposed to explain this phenomena. They range from the forbidden knowledge hypothesis previously cited to the fact that our reality intersects the realities of other time zones (and parallel universes) at continuously changing locations. A rigorous discussion of this quantum physics paradigm is presented in my book *Soul Healing* (1996).

Another oddity about astral time travel is the amount of time that elapses on the physical plane during your trip. For instance, you might very well spend several days or weeks in the twenty-eighth century, while only a few minutes have elapsed on the physical plane.

The opposite occurs as you travel back in time. An astral trip to the French Revolution that required only a few seconds of real time, may have actually involved several minutes on the physical plane.

Other observations concern color perception. Remote viewing studies show that color is easily perceived on the astral plane when these experiments occur in the present or near future. The farther you travel back in time, the duller the colors appear, taking the appearance of a black-on-white monochrome as you venture very far back in history.

Moving into the future results in a sharpening of color perception. This can have an almost psychedelic effect, as colors appear quite brilliant the farther ahead you go. This principle applies equally to the other senses of sound, touch, taste, and feeling.

Controlling Your Own Destiny

By using these principles of astral time travel, you can exert a significant influence on your own destiny and spiritual growth. You may preview your own future on the physical plane and effect changes to result in a different outcome to the circumstances you are facing now.

A very practical application of this technique is to use this information to make or change decisions relevant to your life at this time. You can also influence the actions of others. For example, if you have an important business meeting and are unsure of whether this person will work with you, visit them astrally.

Prior to the conference, visit this individual on the astral plane and get to know them without the restrictions of the physical plane. Chances are when you do have a face to face meeting with them they will feel that they have somehow known you before, and you will more than likely be treated as an old friend.

I am not suggesting you unduly manipulate other Earth souls or attempt to brainwash people by using this approach. In a way this is no different then complimenting a business associate on their clothes, or discussing some common interest. As the Beatles so nicely put it, "I get by with a little help from my friends." Anything is possible on the Astral Plane.

An Astral Voyage Saves a Life by Seeing into the Future

Many people who are not particularly interested in metaphysics in any form ask me why my patients want to leave their body. Their initial concern is danger.

In over twenty-five years of experience astral voyaging, and working with thousands of patients to train them to leave their body, I have never experienced or heard of any type of harm resulting from these techniques. Just the opposite occurs. The elimination of the fear of death and the resolution of physical, mental, emotional, and spiritual issues are what I observe daily as a result of these OBEs. To this I must add the many thousands of people who astrally voyaged by simply purchasing my tapes and informed me of their results.

The following case illustrates one of the most dramatic advantages of this experience. This patient named Tami actually saved her physical plane life by astral voyaging.

Tami had just graduated from college in June of 1996. She lived in New York and came to my Los Angeles office to learn how to leave her body. I completed her training by the second week in June, and she returned to New York.

One issue Tami had was what to do during the summer before entering graduate school that September. She did not tell me about this until much later that year. After a few days of contemplation, Tami decided to travel to Europe and spend the last half of the summer there.

She practiced the techniques we worked on during her stay in Los Angeles, and became a fairly experienced voyager by the month of July. At that time she decided to fly to Paris first, as some of her friends were there and wanted her to join them on their European trip.

Tami visited the Learning Temple of Askleposis on the astral plane and viewed her Akashic records. She was able to report glimpses of her future. One thing that shocked her was the foreknowledge that she was destined to die on her way to Paris.

This at first bothered Tami. She became excited about going to Europe, but her astral voyages had already demonstrated their accuracy in a few earlier trips, during which she was able to see into the future and effect minor changes in her life.

Her solution was to not leave for Europe until the end of July. Tami's original plans called for her leaving New York on July 17th on TWA flight 800. I'm sure this flight will be familiar to you. It crashed, killing all 230 passengers and crew.

Had Tami ignored the information she obtained from her OBE, she would be there now, only she wouldn't be returning to the physical plane as Tami. She would have died and crossed into spirit with a severed silver cord.

I didn't hear from Tami until late September when she called my office to inform me of these events. She was very thankful to me, although I reiterated to her that it was her abilities and spiritual growth that saved her life, not me. I merely trained her.

Quantum physics demonstrates that we live in a space-time continuum in which all events occur simultaneously. The Astral Plane has no time concept as we know it on Earth. Perhaps the physical plane's time perception is merely an illusion.

Astral Voyaging Ethics

The behavior you exhibit and attitude you manifest is critical to your spiritual growth. If you act in a negative fashion, you will attract negativity into your life. The reverse is also true. This principle is even more exaggerated on the astral plane, where very thought and desire materializes instantly.

Here are some simple principles of ethics that will keep you from getting into astral trouble:

- ◆ Keep your motives pure. If your "heart of hearts" is stimulated by greed, vengeance, insecurity, or any other negative reason, think twice about acting on this impulse. "What goes around comes around" is applicable here, so look upon this as a "do unto others…" approach.

- ◆ The universe presents lessons for us to learn. Do not feel that you are being punished when things don't go as you would like. Furthermore, it is not your purpose to play God and try to harm others or manipulate them. Part of our spiritual growth is to overcome the tendency to retaliate against the actions of others. "An eye for an eye" does not work on any dimension, least of all the astral plane.

- ◆ Material benefits. There is nothing wrong with accumulating wealth and other physical plane rewards as a result of your astral voyaging. As long as you don't try to harm anyone or violate any universal law, your attempts at "karmic capitalism" will be successful and add to your growth in general.

Motivation and actions are what count the most in exercising astral empowerment techniques. You may use these methods to improve your life in many areas, including money, a better job, psychic development, finding a soul mate, establishing peace of mind, developing friendships, and improving your health.

Never attempt to use these methods to control others. You cannot change the past, but the future is mutable. Seeing a certain desirable future doesn't assure that it will become a reality. Resting on your laurels is not why these laws were established, nor the universe created.

You have to earn your wings every day. This entails discipline, goal orientation, and a willingness to work within the parameters of the universe's design. Being selfish and ruthless will only lead to hardship and frustration, and result in a low level of spiritual growth.

Take some time to inspect your life. Socrates informed us that an unexamined life is not worth living. Do not use astral voyaging as an excuse for laziness or procrastination. The universe does not exist for your pleasure alone.

Learn from Ancient Wisdom

As a scientist, clinician, and scholar, I place a great deal of credibility on the track record of any discipline or source of information. If I note a repeated pattern of accuracy and scholarship, my general rule is to look favorably on the other emanations from this source.

The ancient Egyptians illustrate such a principle. The Rhind Papyrus has inscribed on it all the degrees of latitude from the Equator to the North Pole. The pyramid at Giza is a most remarkable architectural achievement. The northern face was aligned, almost perfectly, to true north, the eastern face almost perfectly to true east, the southern to true south, and the western face to true west. The average error was only around three minutes of arc. This accuracy would be considered incredible for any era of time and was an inexplicable feat for Egypt of 4,500 years ago.[1]

My conclusion from this truly amazing example of technology is that the ancient Egyptians used astral voyages to assist them in their pyramid construction. I have already discussed how all inventions originate from the astral plane in chapter 5. The ancient Egyptians indicate much knowledge of astral travel in their writings. In chapter 11, I discussed the 37-degree astral voyaging technique and cited ancient Egypt as one of its sources. These ancients also used OBEs in their healing approaches, especially when considerable physical pain was involved.

The Egyptian cosmology is a most interesting study in itself. Here is a sample of some of their major components[2]:

KA—The etheric body that continues to be connected to the physical body after death. This is one reason they carved a tomb in the shape of a statue which was the exact replica of the departed person's body.

BA—This is the astral body that, although housed within the Ka, was completely separable. It is immortal and represented as a human-headed hawk capable of visiting the Ka after its physical death.

---

1 P. Smyth, *The Great Pyramid: Its Secrets and Mysteries Revealed* (New York: Dell Pub., 1990).
2 Gerald and Betty Schueler, *Egyptian Magick* (St. Paul, Llewellyn Publications, 1989).

KHU—A celestial being that is formed when the Ba is purified is called Khu. It retains the shape of the physical body and lives with the gods.

SEKHEM—This was the life force that initiated life itself. Another aspect of this category was that it also represented the power generated when one had mastery over something.

KHAIBIT—The dark side of our being was represented by a shadow or khaibit.

REN—The secret name of power that each person has that allows you to control that person. Another unusual practice of the ancients was to eliminate an individual's very existence by removing that person's name from all records.

The TUAT or DUART—The lower astral plane, approached either at night on moonlight beams, or by land in the daytime.

SOKHET AARU—The land of reeds is equivalent to the upper astral planes. It is described as a perfect farm, devoid of animals, but well-kept, large, and located in close proximity to the "mother of life," the Nile. Entities who reside here are very large, being "seven cubits high."

The MAAT—Our concept of the soul plane is represented by this realm. Here a soul is judged by Osiris. Whether you ascended into the higher planes or reincarnated was based solely on Osiris' evaluation.

The Temples of Wisdom of the ancient Egyptians, built on the model of the Askleposis Temple on the astral plane, taught that the astral body (the "double") was the animating principle of its physical counterpart. If the physical body was damaged, it affected the double and likewise if the double was injured in any way, the body of flesh suffered accordingly. The double is possessed of the same senses as the body of flesh, but it possesses additional senses and abilities not normally evidenced by the physical body.

The double uses five senses that correspond to the five physical senses but are keener and more intense. It also employs two additional senses or abilities. One of these is the ability when stimulated to recall any event, any action, that has ever taken place on this planet, no matter how far back in the remote past this may have been. This has been described by some as the ability to "read the Akashic records," but it is not like reading anything. It is more like being there.

The second of these psychic talents is the ability to focus on any event taking place anywhere in the world. This is a highly developed form of clairvoyance. To avoid overloading, the astral body screens out most of this data, and functions like the telephoto lens of a camera to isolate and observe one particular occurrence.

In order for us to receive this psychic data (remember all psychic abilities originate on the astral plane) the Egyptians deduced that we must quiet the mind by hypnosis, meditation, or contemplation techniques.

Other cultures also described the astral realms. Russian translations of Mayan codices reveal many aspects of knowledge of the astral plane. Lao Tse, the Chinese philosopher, taught contemplation techniques for leaving the body.

Celtic lore describes shape-changing, "the land under the hill," and other references that point directly to the astral plane. The Celts' religion was based in part on the Druid priests' powers of extrasensory perception. Their Bardic literature preserved many of the truths known to the ancients. For instance, the size and round shape of the earth was recorded, although two thousand years later most of the civilized world still considered it flat. Many ancient writers declare that Pythagoras gained much of his learning from the Druids and, according to Pliny the Persian, esoteric knowledge was also Druidic in origin.

The Druid priests' ability to employ their astral doubles' powers made them true seers. This is where the term "second sight" comes from; the seer is aware of what is appearing before their eyes and at the same time "see" what is taking place in a distant spot.

We can also find in the Norse tales of Valhalla and the spiritual realm of the Aesir allusions to the astral plane. African folklore presents further evidence of astral travel in the continent that we assume gave birth to Western civilization.

The Neoplatonists further illustrate the ancients experience with astral voyaging. Plotinus describes in his *Enneads* an eternal world: "boiling with life," full of movement, light, and color, in which everything is one with everything else. Does this not sound like plane travel? He, like many other Neoplatonists, emphasizes *theurgy*. Theurgy consists of magical rites whose purpose was to conjure up positive spirits to effect changes on the physical plane. This technique persisted all the way down through history, culminating in the Spiritualist movement of the nineteenth century and early twentieth century, in addition to the practice of magic today.

Most saints and holy men talked about leaving their physical bodies at will, and transcending to higher planes where they received their wisdom. A careful study of the history of music, myth, astrology, and numbers adds to our historical approach to information about the astral plane.

Astral Voyagers Who Read the Akashic Records

Seers have existed in all places and in all ages as far back as memory and history recall. Ancient kings, rulers, and powerful tyrants employed seers, usually as personal guides and members of their court. This seeking for paranormal information and guidance persists to the present day. Abraham Lincoln, Franklin Roosevelt, Ronald Reagan, and many other leaders were known to have consulted various types of diviners and forecasters.

All proficient seers, diviners and prophets have the ability to "read" the Akashic records. Everything that has occurred on this earth from the day of its formation has left its mark or imprint on what is called the "Astral Light." The mechanics of this are not known, but these imprints remain and are called the Akashic records, and are kept on the causal plane.

When you astrally voyage, mechanisms on the Astral Plane (mostly through the Learning Temple of Askleposis) are available to you to access the Akashic records and return to physical awareness with an account of what you "read" there. The experience is like tuning in to a three-dimensional color movie where you are right in the center of the action, but not part of it.

All of us tune in on the Akashic records at one time or another, but only when our physical awareness is distracted and we enter into relaxed alpha state, such as hypnosis, meditation, or another daydream level.

We are most likely to make an Akashic contact when we are asleep, in a trance, or in a borderline state between sleeping and waking, but at such times we do not have good directive control of our attention, so the recollection we bring back is usually confused and often meaningless. It is only when, upon retiring, we have instructed our inner self to bring to waking consciousness a specific bit of information that we can prove to ourselves that such a contact actually takes place.

Merlin

The facts concerning Merlin's birth are not clear. Many authorities feel he was born in a nunnery in A.D. 417. We are not sure whether his mother was a nun or the daughter of King Demetia, who sought refuge there.

Merlin was trained by the Druids and brought to the court of King Vortigern. He mastered a thorough knowledge of astrology, numerology, divination, and magic. As a young child, he foretold the coming of King Arthur, saying "the Boar of Cornwall will rise in might and defeat the White Dragon" (the Saxon King). He foresaw the downfall of Vortigern, his protector, and after warning him, prudently left the court before the sons of Constantine, Vortigern's predecessor, arrived to avenge their father's murder.

He made many prophecies, some ranging ahead hundreds of years. One foretold a great famine in the reign of Cadwallader some 200 years in advance of its actual occurrence. Another spoke of the Danish invasion and the weakness of Ethelred in the face of it. Merlin accurately saw the disappearance under the sea of the coastline in Kent, leaving only what is now called Godwin Sands. He told of William the Conqueror and also of Richard I, the Lionheart, who was not born until 1157, some seven hundred years later.

We don't know Merlin's precise technique, but it is reported that he employed self-hypnosis and practiced astral voyaging. Reports have stated that he "heard" his prophecies. This clairaudience manifested as a small voice within him that he could detect at certain times while in trance.[3]

---

3 Herbert B. Greenhouse, *The Book of Psychic Knowledge* (New York: Taplinger Publishing Co., 1973).

Nostradamus

Nostradamus (Michel de Notredame) was one of the best known seers in history. This sixteenth century Frenchman wrote his predictions in the form of quatrains or four-line poems. One thousand of them were published in 1568, in ten groups of 100 each, a form known as centuries. The topics he covered ranged from contemporary events of his century to the year A.D. 7000!

Some of Nostradamus' quatrains were extraordinarily accurate. For example, one quatrain, roughly translated, says: "The young Lion shall overcome the old one in a duel on the field of battle. Through the golden cage he will put out the eye of the old one who upon receiving two wounds from one thrust will die a cruel death." This prophecy was borne out when a young Scottish knight competing in a tournament with King Henry II of France, the Old Lion, accidentally ran his lance into the cage-like opening in the front of Henry's golden helmet. The lance broke, and a splinter pierced Henry's eye and entered his brain, causing his death.

Nostradamus described his method of forecasting in the first and second quatrains in *Century I* as follows: "When I am seated alone at night in my secret study, musing over the brass bowl which rests on a tripod, a slender flame comes forth from nothing and signals the time for me to utter the sacred mantram. With divining branch in hand its wet tip points to limb and foot. Then my hand trembles and, overcome by awe, I await. Heavenly Splendor! The Divine Genius is present!"

Roger Bacon

One of the reasons the prophets and seers of the Middle Ages usually wrote in obscure language was the suspicious nature of their contemporaries. All such gifts were superstitiously regarded as the work of the devil or evil spirits. The plight of Roger Bacon is an example of this type of ignorant persecution.

Roger Bacon (not to be confused with Francis Bacon), a Franciscan monk in thirteenth-century England, was a noted scholar. He mastered several languages, chemistry, astronomy, and other sciences. Bacon designed lenses that paved the way for the invention of the modern telescope. He made many prophetic statements of scientific development similar to the following:

Chariots will be made so as to move with incalculable speed without any beast drawing them. . . . Engines of navigation will be constructed so that the greatest ships with only one man to steer them will sail swifter than if they were fully manned. . . . The most beautiful music will come from the very walls themselves.[4]

Mother Shipton

Mother Shipton made many prophetic forecasts in England during the sixteenth century. Like those of Nostradamus, hers were set in verse.

A book of her prophecies was issued in 1641 and another, edited and published by the astrologer William Lilly, was printed in 1645. Most of her predictions were for contemporary or near future events, but some were for the distant future. Like many other seers of the Middle Ages, she saw and described both automotive and air travel, so their development must have been clearly marked in the Akasha for at least 700 years before they came into actual physical being. Let us not ignore the drawings of Leonardo da Vinci during the Renaissance, and the fact that he wrote all of his notes backward to avoid persecution.

Edward Bellamy

Looking Backward, written in 1888 by Edward Bellamy, was one of the most influential American books on social reform prior to the twentieth century. He wrote this masterpiece from the perspective of the year 2000, and it was an attempt to detail an ideal path of social development from 1888 to the beginning of the twenty-first century.

Bellamy described a music room in the home that contained three or four skillfully placed audioamplifiers concealed in the walls. Adjacent to one are several knobs which when turned will bring in any one of four different musical programs at the volume desired. A listing of the programs available at each hour is delivered daily to every home which subscribes to this service. All programs are supplied throughout the twenty-four-hour day and are sent also into the bedrooms where a

---

4   Robert Crookall, *The Interpretation of Cosmic & Mystical Experiences* (London: James Clarke & Co., 1969).

smaller speaker or even headphones are provided. This may seem commonplace today, but we must remember it was written in 1888!

The houses in Bellamy's description had electricity and a central heating system. Public laundries, equivalent to modern day laundromats, were delineated, as were the common usage of restaurants. Restaurants were a relative rarity in his day.

Electric alarm clocks and credit cards that are accepted throughout the world were also components of Bellamy's depiction of the year 2000. One interesting prophecy he made was that of weather control. This has yet to be realized. The eventual harnessing of weather during the twenty-third century is discussed in my first book.[5]

Jules Verne

This nineteenth century French novelist authored several novels about the future. In 1865 he wrote his classic, *From the Earth to the Moon*, in which he described intimate details that paralleled those of America's first flight to the moon by Apollo 11 in July of 1969. For example:

The initial breakaway velocity of Jules Verne's craft was 36,000 feet per second while Apollo 11's third stage velocity was 35,533 feet per second.

The huge cannon which fired Verne's capsule into space was called the Columbiad, while Apollo 11 was named Columbia. Both capsules orbited the moon several times, occasionally at the same altitude. Both teams took photographs, and the Verne capsule crew even charted the Sea of Tranquility, where the Apollo 11 crew landed.

The launch sites were almost identical. Verne chose a spot in Florida about 140 miles due west of Cape Kennedy. In Verne's story, Texas fought for the honor. Today Mission Control is in Houston, Texas.

Verne's capsule reached the moon in 97 hours and 13 minutes while Apollo's time was 103 hours, 30 minutes. In Verne's ship there were three men: two Americans and a Frenchman. Apollo 11 had a crew of three also. Verne's "space capsule" was 15 feet high by 9 feet in diameter; the Apollo command module was 10-1/2 feet high and 12 feet, 10 inches in diameter.

Both capsules splashed down in the Pacific and both crews were picked up by American Navy ships.

---

5 Bruce Goldberg, *Past Lives—Future Lives* (New York: Ballantine, 1988).

The Sinking of the Titanic

Morgan Robertson wrote a novel in 1898 titled *Futility*, in which a supposedly unsinkable ocean liner struck an iceberg on its maiden voyage and sank, carrying the elite society of two continents to their deaths.

Fourteen years later, in 1912, a similar "unsinkable" liner sailed from England with 3,000 passengers aboard. Like Robertson's craft, it was 800 feet long and weighed 70,000 tons but with far too few lifeboats. The real boat, like Robertson's, struck an iceberg and sank with the loss of more than a thousand lives. Robertson had named his boat *The Titan*. The real ship was the *Titanic*.

Edgar Cayce

The most highly respected and best known American psychic was Edgar Cayce. This dedicated and sincere soul devoted the majority of his life to applying his psychic gifts to help others. Cayce's visions of the future were made during one of his psychic readings given to an individual suffering from some ailment and who had requested Cayce's services.

Cayce stretched out on a couch and went into a deep hypnotic trance in order to initiate his accessing of the Akashic records of the person requesting the reading. Cayce gave over 14,000 "readings," or consultations. Most of these were stenographically recorded at the time and are today retained in the archives of the ARE, the Association for Research and Enlightenment, in Virginia Beach (ARE, Inc., P.O. Box 656, Virginia Beach, VA 23451), where any serious student may examine them. About sixty percent of these are physical diagnoses and recommended treatments for people who were injured, ill, or mentally disturbed. Roughly twenty percent are "life readings," reports on previous lives of people who sought advice on marital, social, and economic problems. The remaining twenty percent include readings on business topics, mental and spiritual themes, dream interpretations, and a variety of other subjects. Included in the latter are some prophetic statements given in answer to direct questions. But most of Cayce's forecasts came in the course of counsel to inquirers who were asking for help on personal problems.

The greatest of American psychics, Cayce could tune in on an individual's Akashic records anywhere in the world instantly. He then went on to accurately diagnose the illness or disturbance by which that person might be troubled.

Amazingly, there is no record of an incorrect diagnosis in all of the more than 7,000 readings Cayce gave on physical problems! Cayce's computer-like readings were an unlikely result from a man with little formal education. His treatment recommendations preceded the discovery of psychosomatic medicine, the delineation of the difference between benign and malignant tumors, blood transfusions, and many other medical regimens. It seemed that Cayce's therapy design represented a glimpse into the future of medicine—just what we would expect by accessing the Akasha.

Although Cayce predicted many destructive geophysical changes throughout the world by the year 2000, I will not dwell on them here. We are all well aware of the gloom and doom forecasted by Nostradamus and the Bible.

The Akashic records of the past are set and immutable, but the future, while in the blueprint stage, is always subject to change (even at the last moment).

Prophecies affecting large numbers of people seldom occur in the way and to the degree seen by the astral voyager. It seems that the very announcement of the impending event serves to dilute its effect. On the whole, it is the thoughts of men and women on the physical plane that makes the future. We can create our reality.

An Exercise to Access the Akashic Records

While psychic ability may appear to occur spontaneously in certain people without any great effort on their part, this development was actually acquired over several lives in the past by hard work and great perseverance. You, too, can start right now to develop your psychic abilities and achieve recognizable results in a reasonable length of time. Like any other skill, the better you understand what you are doing and the more you practice, the more proficient you will become.

As mentioned before, certain events, as with locations on the astral plane, are fixed and unchangeable. Accessing your Akashic records, or the Akashic records of anyone else (or the Akasha of the universe in general) will allow accurate forecasts to be made on these events.

Others do not fit into this "etched in stone" variety and may change several times before their final manifestation. The less spiritually evolved the person, the greater the accuracy your prophesy will be. More advanced souls and those of greater intelligence, discrimination, and originality are much more difficult to predict because they repeatedly break out of their established patterns. These are the ones who have it in their power to alter the destiny of the world.

The experience of drawing upon the Akashic records often presents itself to your waking awareness in visual form accompanied by the more essential sounds. Occasionally it will be entirely auditory, as though someone were standing close behind you, telling you what has taken place or will occur in the future. The information you receive is actually vibratory in nature, somewhat like the impressions on a magnetic tape. The images you see or hear are all from your own mind and have been stirred into activity by the Akashic vibrations you have contacted. This accounts to some degree for the variations in the forecast of the same event by two different people. Each makes the same vibratory contact but realizes it according to the experiences in his own image storehouse.

Drawing on Akashic Records Exercise

With this added background, try the following exercise:

1. Use any of the previous self-hypnosis or other exercises to relax and apply white light protection. Lie down or sit in an easy chair, and when you are relaxed turn your attention inward and center it on the area of the third eye. See it glow with a golden white radiance and feel it pulsate with energy. As you do this, your realization of the sounds, colors, and temperature in the room around you should gradually fade, and as they do so the subtle psychic stirrings will become more noticeable.

2. At first, this may be only an impression of inner light or of brilliantly illuminated geometrical figures, or of stars shooting by in ordered procession, or some other visual appearance which will probably be meaningless. Or your first impression may be of sound, as I have previously described.

3. Focus your mind, not on the Akashic records themselves, but on a specific historical event for your initial trials. For example, I suggest you study first the discovery of radium by Marie Curie or the signing of the Declaration of Independence in 1776.

4. Your next step is to go to that historical event and ask yourself: "What happened that afternoon?" If you have properly prepared yourself, you will find yourself drifting into a scenario-like dream.

   In the earlier stages of your development you will not get clearly defined contacts that you can recognize as such, so don't expect them. Accept the dream-like sequence that passes before your consciousness as you sit in reverie. Remember what you observe and write it down as soon as possible thereafter.

5. During these practice sessions you should "feel" this connection between your waking consciousness and the Akasha. When this has been accomplished and you can recall an incident from the past as simply as you can look up an account in the encyclopedia, you are then ready to move on to the next step.

6. The next step is to repeat the previous steps, omitting the preparation phase consisting of reading about the historical event.

7. Next, check your data with specialty books written about that event in detail, not merely an encyclopedia summary.

8. After successful completion of this step, move on to your own future. Begin with a short range, say one week to a month. Log all of your observations into a journal and occasionally verify the accuracy of your prophecies.

9. With a proven track record, you are now ready to venture much further ahead in time in your current life. Try five years, ten years, fifty years, and so on.

10. You may move several hundred years into the future and explore future lives. My books *Past Lives—Future Lives* (1988) and *Soul Healing* (1996) describe nearly twenty such cases as far forward as the thirty-eighth century!

11. Lastly, tap into the general Akasha and allow your consciousness to tune into future world events, inventions, lifestyle changes, and so on.

Remember, the key to successful application of these techniques is proper motivation and attitude and practice. Once you have developed a working connection between your brain and your astral body, it is not too difficult to contact the Akasha. But since these embrace in detail every event since this world began and many events still to come, your first attempts are almost sure to result in confusion.

For instance, you may receive data from events 75,000 years ago, 150 years back, ten years in the future, and 500 years hence, all in rapid succession. This often results in a haphazard overlapping and indistinguishable mess. By directing your mind with specific goals, you can significantly reduce this effect.

In your own life you most likely have inadvertently received data from the Akasha. Often the scene or event observed is not recognized for what it is, and if recalled at all is classified as a trick of the memory or imagination. Even when the vision is so clear that the perceiver is impressed, there is usually no clue as to when in the future it may occur. A conscientious application of this exercise will sharpen your psychic abilities and result in far more accuracy and spiritual empowerment.

Astral Empowerment

One of many advantages of astral voyaging is an extension of the scope of your life. You may be a king, a sheik with a harem, a Florence Nightingale, a Teddy Roosevelt, and so on. Regardless of your socioeconomic class, you can travel in space and time and voyage to the past or future.

New ideas and sources of inspiration may be attained by concentrating your mind for long periods along certain specific lines of thought. The executive seeking the solution of a business problem, the composer desiring inspiration, the sculptor or painter in search of a more profound and stirring subject, all may tap this reservoir and find there a reply to their specific question. There also exist on this level the plans each human soul has made for its own future as well as the far greater plans made by the guides of the human race for our well-being and further development.

Spiritual growth is more attainable by using the techniques I have presented. You are only limited by the desires and imagination of your mind. The knowledge you gain will assist you in understanding your karmic purpose. There is no question that when you practice astral voyaging, you will significantly expand your awareness, knowledge, and mastery of the other dimensions in which all that constitutes the true universe exists.

Conclusion

Astral voyaging is a unique experience that can teach us more about the nature of the universe than anything the physical plane has to offer. All of the techniques presented in this book will work.

Since we are all unique, some methods will be more efficient and effective than others for you. If you have difficulty with mental imagery, the visualization techniques may be too difficult for you. A good dream recall favors the lucid dreaming approaches. Those of you who like to meditate will find the self-hypnosis exercises quickly rewarding.

It is your own individual makeup that determines which technique will work best for you. By all means, feel free to experiment. That is one purpose of this book. Remember, your attitude and desire to soul travel is far more important than any one technique to be successful in astral voyaging.

Many people have had their initial OBEs when they least expected it. Your belief in your ability to leave your body is a critical prerequisite to purposeful astral projection.

Most projectors leave their body for one of two reasons: they desire guidance, or they want to assist others in their hour of need. These motivations may be practical, personal, or humanitarian. In reality they are all spiritually based.

OBEs are induced by the extremes of states of relaxation and stress. Occasionally a simple mood may bring on this dimensional travel. Drifting off to sleep or daydreaming are other common ways that people have spontaneous OBEs.

I prefer not to rely on stress for soul travel. We have discussed NDEs and people who are debilitated, not dying, who seem to be prone to this psychic phenomenon. Good health (mental, physical, and emotional) is always my recommendation for controlled astral voyaging. This is also how we can all facilitate our spiritual growth.

Many parapsychologists feel that the several planes I have described throughout this book are simply inner worlds created by and contained within the mind. I wholeheartedly disagree. My personal and clinical experience has demonstrated that these planes of existence coexist with our physical plane, and can be contacted only while out-of-body.

As the Greek philosopher Posidonius stated over two thousand years ago:

> The souls of men, when released from the body in sleep or in ecstasy . . . behold things that they cannot see when bound to the body—they remember the past, see the present, and can contemplate the future. The body of the sleeper is as one dead, but the soul lives on in the fullness of its power.[1]

As a demonstration of how much our physical world is an illusion, consider a famous quantum physics experiment. An electron was fired at a screen and went through two holes at the same time. It acted as though it were two different subatomic particles.

This electron acted sometimes as a wave, while in other instances it behaved as a particle. Was this the astral double of the electron? Quantum physicists have discovered a particle that is identical to the negatively charged electron, except that it is positively charged and called a positron.

---

1 Plutarch, *On the Delay of Divine Justice*, A. P. Peabody, trans. (Boston: Little Brown & Co., 1885).

Is the positron an electron moving forward in time, or vice versa? The world of subatomic particles bears a strong resemblance to the paranormal world of different planes. That is why our astral body is so much at home in that environment, and looks for excuses to leave the physical plane.

Throughout history people of all nationalities, from primitive cultures to technologically advanced societies, have claimed to voyage out-of-body. The fact that we have thousands of independent, yet similar accounts, gives strong evidence that OBEs are actual experiences. This is especially significant when you factor in the results of scientific studies on remote viewing, lucid dreaming, NDE and other forms of OBE.

Over eighty percent of astral voyages occur to individuals who are normal and well. Leaving the physical body is a normal and natural phenomenon, and not a delusion or sign of pathology. The spiritual growth possible by accessing our Higher Self and spirit guides has become a demonstrated fact. I do this daily with my patients in my Los Angeles office.

The word *entelechy* connotes the perfect realization of what is latent. This corresponds to the Hindu concept of *dharma*, wherein each of us have only one road leading to enlightenment—our way. It is a confirmation of a principle that I train all of my patients to master: psychic empowerment.

If I had to state one advantage to astral voyaging it would be the elimination of the fear of death. I have presented the work of various researchers illustrating that this form of psychic empowerment is common among those who venture beyond the physical body.

Many individuals have used their OBEs to help reaffirm their religious beliefs, view life as meaningful, and give themselves a sense of personal value in an otherwise dehumanizing world. The OBE can profoundly alter our state of consciousness and allow us to peer into the very nature of reality itself.

Let us ascend from the cave of ignorance and societal brainwashing to voyage to the ends of the various planes (if, indeed, they do end); to go where no one has previously ventured. Do not fall into the trap that characterizes many scientists. Phenomena such as astral projection, telepathy, precognition, clairvoyance, and so on are impossible in terms of the current physical world view. Since they can't happen, most scientists do not bother to read the evidence indicating that they do happen; nor are they familiar with the principles of quantum physics. Not having read the evidence, their belief in the impossibility of such phenomena is reinforced. This kind of circular reasoning in support of one's comfortable belief system only retards one's spiritual growth, in addition to being technically inaccurate.

Have you ever wondered about man's obsession with magical wishes throughout history? From the Mystery Schools and on to the Dark and Middle Ages, and finally to current thought, we have all heard stories about wishes being granted.

Whether it be the three wishes of the genie from Aladdin's lamp, or depressing stories of selling one's soul to the Devil in exchange for wish fulfillment, these tales abound. My theory is that they originate from astral voyaging memories.

On the astral plane your very thought becomes an instant reality. Lucid dreaming and other OBE techniques have been known for thousands of years, as I have documented in this book. Isn't it possible (if not likely) that these wishes that we all desire represent our experiences on the astral dimension? Wouldn't you be spoiled if you were on a dimension in which your every thought materialized, and suddenly you found yourself on the physical plane where it doesn't become a reality?

Also, consider the comic book heroes that we are exposed to as children and adults. Superman, who can fly, the Flash's ability to move at great speeds, Wonder Woman, and others. Do these characters not exhibit traits that we associate with the astral plane?

Most of my patients live their lives wishing they hadn't done this or that. Some wish an action or option was taken that wound up being ignored or rejected. Practice the techniques presented in this book and turn your wishes into realities—a form of "Heaven on Earth."

I have always been a great believer in self-hypnosis. All of my patients are trained to use this marvelous technique by the simple use of cassette tapes. My office carries a complete line of hypnosis tapes which you can order if interested.

The following case summary was written by one of my patients describing her own superconscious mind tap:

Prior to going to bed that night, I listened to Dr. Goldberg's self-hypnosis tape "The Superconscious Mind." While in hypnosis I asked for a special message from my higher guides. I asked them to show me what my first day at my new job the next day would be like. That night I was given a vision of what my day would be like. It went like this: Carlos, my new boss, met me in the lobby; however, it was not like the one I saw when I had gone for the interview. Anyway, we talked for a few minutes and Al, his boss, came up and started talking to us. Then Carlos started to show me around and introduce me to some people. We don't get too far and he gets called away. I see a few ladies, I believe they work there also, but they take no initiative to introduce themselves. I go up and shake hands with them and tell them my name. Carlos is back again and he begins to show me how to operate the computer system. I recall looking at and listening to his detailed instructions about Reservations. Then I notice that it's rather dark in the office. I think to myself that this place can't be dark, I am no longer at my other job which used to be in the basement. Also, I see through the windows that it's bright outside. I asked Carlos why it was dark and he said something about the lights. I then woke up.

My actual day was very similar to the vision I had been given. I did end up taking the initiative to introduce myself to two ladies who seemed at first to ignore me. Carlos went over the computer system and showed me how several software programs operated. At about 3:00 in the afternoon, we had a power failure which lasted about 10 minutes. Carlos made a joke about waiting for the lights to come on.

The second experience happened in that state between sleeping to waking. I was laying down, I thought I was awake, but there was also a feeling of sleep-like quality. Suddenly, but slowly, I felt a vibration—kind of like when something is vibrating and you touch it—you can feel the vibrations in your hands. The feeling began from the top of my head and proceeded down the rest of my body. I am thinking that I am being contacted by my higher guides. I began to hear voices. It sounded like a group at first, but one voice was more distinct than the rest. It was a male energy. He began to tell me things and simultaneously showed me animated movie-like pictures on a large screen. At the time this was happening, I understood the messages; however, upon awakening, I could not recall a thing, except that it had something to do with my life.

Note the OBE characteristics during this second experience. This former patient has now become more psychic and has made strides in custom designing her own destiny through the combination of super-conscious mind taps and astral voyaging.

Fran, another of my patients, grieved over the death of her favorite aunt for nearly eight years. She purchased my out-of-body experience tape through the mail, and visited her late aunt astrally. Her aunt instructed Fran to stop mourning her and get on with her life. I met Fran at a workshop several years later and she informed me that she diligently took the advice of her aunt. Fran no longer fears death and is far more spiritually evolved as a result of her continued astral voyaging.

We live in a time during which devotion to spiritual growth will be abundantly rewarded. Astral voyaging affords us the opportunity to reach new levels of awareness and perfect our soul. The ability to explore the self as it exists in other dimensions is more possible than ever before. More people than ever possess the ability to soul travel and explore alternate and probable futures, move into new understandings and concepts of time, control the subconscious, and tap into the powers of their Higher Self.

Sylvan Muldoon said it best when he declared:

For my part, had a book on immortality never been written, had a lecture on "survival" never been uttered, had I never witnessed a seance or visited a medium; in fact, had no one else in the world ever suspected "life after death," I should still believe implicitly that I am immortal—for I have experienced the projection of the astral body.[1]

---

1 Sylvan Muldoon, *The Case for Astral Projection* (Chicago: Aries Press, 1936).

Glossary

Akashic records: The record of a soul's past, present, and future lives stored on the causal plane. The soul may tap into these records on any plane, but it is easier to do this when the soul resides on the soul plane.

All That Is: The highest consciousness of all; the Light; the Source; the creator; God.

Alpha waves: The borderline brain activity between conscious and subconscious; the creative cycle; 8–13 cycles per second.

Altered State of Consciousness (ASC): A term describing the alpha brain wave level that is characteristic of hypnosis, meditation, daydreams, and all out-of-body experiences.

Angels: Entities of pure spirit who assist humans in times of great stress. Many equate these beings with Masters and Guides. Angels are a component of most religions of the world.

Askleposis: A Temple of Wisdom on the astral plane.

Astral body: The form humans use to travel through the astral planes; a duplicate of the physical body, but made of finer vibrations.

Astral dreams: Many humans call their astral travels "dreams," rather than acknowledge them as actual experiences.

Astral entity: Any being or creature that resides on the astral planes and has only an astral form.

Astral lover: An astral being that has close ties and a relationship with a physical person.

Astral planes or levels: The world that interpenetrates and reflects our physical world, but operates on a much higher vibrational level.

Astral voyaging: Projecting the astral body out of its usual position by the physical body and using this form to move about the astral plane or to other physical locations.

Aura: The field of energy around the physical and astral bodies. Bioplasma is another term for this.

Ba: Ancient Egyptian term for astral body.

Bardo: The intermediate experiences between physical death and rebirth, according to Westerners. The Eastern definition implies that it refers to any of six transitory and illusory states of consciousness: waking, dreaming, profound meditation, dying, the reality between lives, and rebirth.

Beta waves: Problem-solving, normal state of conscious brain activity; 14–30 cycles per second.

Bilocation: To be in two locations at one time; when the astral body is seen or felt in one place, while the physical body is busy in another.

Bioplasma: The aura.

Bodhisattva: One who is on the way to attaining perfect knowledge and still has a number of births to undergo before becoming the perfect master.

Causal: The causal body of man is known as the seed body. The causal plane is just above the astral plane. The place where memories and karmic patterns are stored. The reader of the future or past lives looks to this plane for information, or accesses it from other dimensions.

Chakras: The seven major light centers in the astral body.

Clairaudience: The ability to psychically hear what lies beyond physical sound.

Clairvoyance: The ability to psychically see what lies beyond normal sight.

Cleansing: The technique of introducing the subconscious mind and soul to the Higher Self (superconscious mind) so that a connection results. This is also called a superconscious mind tap and Clear Light.

Conscious dying: The process of maintaining a connection between the soul and the Higher Self at the moment of physical death in order to assure the soul's arrival at the soul plane without the interference of the disorienting forces of the karmic cycle. This technique may result in the immediate liberation of the soul from the need to reincarnate.

Conscious mind proper: The analytical, critical, and left brain of our mind. Our ego defense mechanisms constitute this part of our consciousness.

Conscious Out-of-Body Experience (COBE): The state of awareness exhibited by the soul when it dies consciously.

Conscious rebirth: The mechanism of reincarnation characterized by the soul entering a newborn's body without having to experience the disorienting forces of the karmic cycle.

Controlled projection: Willing oneself to project the astral body away from the physical body; done on command. Also called a forced projection.

Delta waves: Deep, slow brain activity found in deep sleep; 0.5–3.5 cycles per second.

Demon: A creature of evil nature from the lower astral plane.

Discarnate: A spirit who is trapped in the physical world, i.e., not the higher planes, without his or her physical body. Used synonymously in this book with "spirit" and "entity."

Doppelganger: The astral double.

Earthbound: A condition of remaining in the physical world as a spirit after the death of the body because of not having made a successful transition into the higher realms. According to esoteric theory, an earthbound entity is actually trapped in the lower astral plane.

Ectoplasm: An albumen substance related to the sexual fluids within the body and secreted by certain glands. It is present during materialization seances and in thinner form also when apparitions occur, as well as in poltergeist phenomena when ectoplasm is formed to move physical objects about.

Electro-encephalogram or EEG: A machine hooked to the head by little electrodes which record brain wave activity.

Entity: The immortal essence of a person. It is used synonymously in this book with "spirit" and "discarnate."

Extrasensory perception (ESP): The knowledge of facts, happenings, or presences through means other than the five senses of the physical body.

Higher Self: This is another term describing the superconscious mind or perfect energy component of the soul. The Higher Self is a remnant of the God energy.

Hypnosis: A state of mind that is highly responsive to suggestion, used to redirect and influence mental activity, and induce OBEs.

Hypnotic regression: A hypnotic technique that produces the remembering and reliving of a past experience from the current life or a previous one, the memory of which is buried in the subconscious.

Hypnotic suggestion: Idea presented to the subconscious mind while in the hypnotic state.

Incarnate: A spirit with a physical body.

Induction: A process for creating the state of hypnosis; usually it is a verbal technique producing deep relaxation and responsiveness to suggestions.

Intuition: The ability to gain knowledge without logical thinking or access.

Karma: The moral law of cause-and-effect that states that the individual's present state of being is determined by the soul's past thoughts and actions. These, in turn, influence future lessons to learn.

Kirlian photography: Special photography which shows the aura surrounding the human body, animals, and plants.

Left brain: The side of the brain controlling logic, language, and mathematics.

Liberation: The ability of the soul to free itself from the karmic cycle or cycle of birth and death. Enlightenment is also used to describe this process.

Lords of Karma: There are four or seven of these entities who function as cosmic administrators, registering all actions and experiences of the soul in the Akashic records. These beings, known as *Lipika*, then parcel out karmic tests to the soul.

Lucid dreaming: A type of dream during which the dreamer is aware of being in the dream state. Lucid dreamers are often able to direct the outcome of the dream. This is a type of out-of-body experience.

Masters and Guides: These perfect entities have long since completed their karmic cycle and have chosen to remain on the lower five planes to assist initiated souls in their quest for perfection. Some refer to these beings as angels.

Meditation: The quieting of the body and mind in order to establish contact with the astral; used to produce an altered state of consciousness.

Medium: A person who is sensitive psychically and able to communicate with spirits and produce manifestations.

Metaphysics: That which lies beyond the realm of physics (physical experience); sometimes considered the occult. Some areas of general interest in metaphysics are reincarnation, possession, levels of existence, auras, spirit guides, mediumship, astral travel, astrology, etc.

Mystery Schools: The religion practiced by the ancients during which initiates were trained in the art of conscious dying and astral voyaging. Mystery Schools have survived throughout history in the form of Freemasonry, the Rosicrucians, Theosophy, and other practices.

Near-Death Experience (NDE): A form of out-of-body experience during which the physical actually dies for a few moments to several minutes before returning back to life. This term was coined by Dr. Raymond Moody.

Nirvana: The Buddhist heaven.

Om: The sound symbol of the mental plane that is often used as a mediation mantra.

Osiris: The Egyptian god and judge of the dead. He is also their symbol of resurrection. Osiris is the arbiter of the future destiny of humanity, according to the *Egyptian Book of the Dead*.

Out-of-body Experience (OBE): An altered state of consciousness that a soul exhibits whenever it leaves the physical body. Dreams, hypnosis, meditation, times of extreme duress, and NDEs are examples of this phenomenon.

Plane concept: The paradigm that the universe is divided into two major types of planes. The lower five planes make up the karmic cycle. The sixth, or soul, plane is where a soul chooses its next life. Finally, there are seven higher planes, with the God, or nameless, plane representing the 13th plane. A soul must be liberated from its karmic cycle to be able to travel through the higher planes to God.

Precognition: Knowing something will happen before it does.

Psychic: A person who is sensitive to perceptions other than those received through the five physical senses.

Psychic centers: The chakras.

Psychometry: Reading the vibrations of an object in order to discover things about the owner and/or the object's history.

Reincarnation: The return to physical existence by the soul in repeated existences.

Right brain: The side of the brain dealing with intuition, imagination, and creativity.

Seance: A special meeting for spirit communication or demonstration of psychic phenomena over which a medium usually presides.

Scrying: To see into the past or future.

Shaman: Commonly known as a "medicine man" or a "witch doctor." One who uses ancient techniques to astrally voyage, and maintain well-being and healing for himself and for members of his community.

Silver cord: A pulsating energy form that connects the spirit to the physical body. It is clairvoyantly perceived as a silver-colored cord that is attached to the spirit when it travels out of the physical body.

Soul: The electromagnetic energy (alpha brain wave) that constitutes our very being. This is also called the subconscious mind and it is what reincarnates into a new body when the previous physical body dies.

Soul travel: Used to describe events similar to OBE and astral projection.

Spirit: The immortal essence of a person. The term generally is used in this book interchangeably with "discarnate" and "entity."

Spirit guides: Highly evolved souls from the spirit world who have elected to help living people. They can also be deceased loved ones who have made successful transitions to the afterlife, and then return to give aid and guidance from time to time. They are often referred to as angels.

Spontaneous or involuntary projection: Uncontrolled projection of the astral body; usually during an accident, surgery, childbirth, or near-death experience.

Subconscious mind: The right brain; the creative, non-logical side of the mind.

Subcycles: These are smaller sets of lessons that the soul must learn as part of its total karmic cycle in order to perfect itself. Group karma is exhibited during a subcycle in which the soul reincarnates with the same collection of souls for several lifetimes.

Superconscious mind: This is the same as the Higher Self.

Telekinesis: The moving of an object without physically touching it; this is accomplished with the power of the mind and the astral body.

Telepathy: The psychic transmission and reception of thoughts.

Thanatology: The science of death and dying, established by the psychiatrist Elizabeth Kübler-Ross.

Theta waves: Drowsy state of brain activity; 4–7 cycles per second.

Third eye: The astral "eye"; connected with the brow center in the center of the forehead. It is a sometimes dormant ability to see multi-dimensional realities or substances.

Thought-forms: Astral forms created by intentional and unintentional thoughts, or by strong emotions.

Trance: A sleep-like state in which there is a lessening of consciousness. It can vary from slight to extremely deep. It can be hypnotic or non-hypnotic.

Trance mediums: Sensitives who lose consciousness and are temporarily and willingly possessed by spirits wishing to communicate or heal.

Unconscious dying: The process by which a soul fails to maintain a connection with its Higher Self at the moment of death and is now exposed to the disorienting forces of the karmic cycle. NDEs are also examples of unconscious dying. Most forms of transitions experienced by souls are unfortunately of this type.

Unconscious rebirth: The process of a soul entering into a newborn after being exposed to the disorienting forces of the karmic cycle because of its failure to maintain a connection with its Higher Self when it died in its previous life. The great majority of rebirths occurring throughout our society's history have been of this type.

Vibration: Used to describe a rapid oscillation or shaking that appears to be physical but is not; tremors that are usually felt during altered states of consciousness, generally after a significant period of meditation or hypnosis.

White light: A tool used to protect oneself from negative encounters with one or more non-physical beings; a type of visualization; a spiritual shield created by the imagination.

Bibliography

Ackerberg, John, and John Weldon. *The Facts on Spirit Guides.* New York: Harvest House Publishing, 1988.

Andrews, Ted. *The Healer's Manual.* St. Paul: Llewellyn Publications, 1993.

_____. *How to Meet and Work with Spirit Guides.* St. Paul: Llewellyn Publications, 1992.

Baird, A. T. *A Casebook for Survival.* London: Psychic Press, 1948.

Bardens, Dennis. *Mysterious Worlds.* New York: Cowles Book Co., 1970.

Battersby, H. F. Prevost. *Man Outside Himself.* London: Rider and Co., 1940.

Baxter, Richard. *Certainty of the World of Spirits.* London: Joseph Smith, 1834.

Bayless, Raymond. *The Other Side of Death.* New Hyde Park, New York: University Books, 1971.

Besant, Annie, and C. W. Leadbeater, *Thought-Forms.* Adyar, Madras, India: Theosophical Publishing House, 1978.

Black, David. *Ekstacy: Out-of-the-Body Experiences.* New York: Bobbs-Merrill, 1975.

Bozzano, Ernesto. *Discarnate Influences in Human Life.* London: John N. Watkins, 1938.

Brennan, J. H. *The Astral Projection Workbook: How to Achieve Out-of-Body Experiences.* New York: Sterling Publishing Co., Inc., 1990.

Budge, E. A. W. *The Egyptian Book of the Dead.* New York: Dover, 1967.

Burr, Harold. *Blueprint for Immortality.* London: Neville Spearman, 1972.

Carrington, Hereward. *The Invisible World.* New York: Beechhurst Press, 1946.

_____. *Modern Psychical Phenomena.* New York: American Universities Publishing Co., 1920.

Chevreuil, L. *Proofs of the Spirit World.* New York: E. P. Dutton & Co., 1920.

Conway, D. J. *Perfect Love: Find Intimacy on the Astral Plane.* St. Paul: Llewellyn Publications, 1996.

Cornillier, Pierre-Emile. *The Survival of the Soul.* London: Kegan Paul, Trench, Trubner & Co., 1921.

Crookall, Robert. *Casebook of Astral Projection.* New Hyde Park, NY: University Books, 1972.

_____. *During Sleep.* London: Theosophical Publishing House, 1964.

_____. *The Interpretation of Cosmic & Mystical Experiences.* London: James Clarke & Co., 1969.

_____. *Intimations of Immortality.* London: James Clarke & Co., 1965.

_____. *The Jung-Jaffe View of Out-of-the-Body Experiences.* World Fellowship Press, 1970.

_____. *The Mechanisms of Astral Projection.* Moradabad, India: Darshana International, 1968.

_____. *More Astral Projections.* London: Aquarian Press, 1964.

_____. *The Next World—and the Next.* London: Theosophical Publishing House, 1966.

_____. *Out-of-the-Body Experiences: A Fourth Analysis.* New Hyde Park, NY: University Books, 1970.

_____. *The Study and Practice of Astral Projection.* London: Aquarian Press, 1961.

_____. *The Supreme Adventure.* London: James Clarke & Co., 1961.

_____. *The Techniques of Astral Projection.* London: Aquarian Press, 1964.

Dallet, Janet. "Theories of dream function." *Psychological Bulletin,* 1973, 6: 408–16.

David-Neel, A. *Magic and Mystery in Tibet.* New York: Claude Kendall, 1932.

Devereaux, Paul. *Earth Memory.* St. Paul: Llewellyn Publications, 1992.

Ducasse, C. J. *The Belief in a Life After Death.* Springfield, IL: Charles C. Thomas, 1961.

Eliade, Mircea. *Shamanism, Archaic Techniques of Ecstasy.* New York: Pantheon Books, 1963.

Evans-Wentz, W. Y. *Tibetan Book of the Dead*. New York: Causeway Books, 1973.

Fodor, Nandor. *Between Two Worlds*. Englewood Cliffs, NJ: Parker Publishing Co., 1964.

_____. *Encyclopedia of Psychic Science*. Detroit: Gale Research Group, 1978

Fox, Oliver. *Astral Projection*. London: University Books, 1962.

_____. "The pineal doorway—a record of research," *Occult Review*, April, 1920, Vol. 31, No. 4.

Garfield, P. *Pathway to Ecstasy*. New York: Holt, Rinehart & Winston, 1979.

_____. *Creative Dreaming*. New York: Random House, 1974.

Garrett, Eileen. *Adventures in the Supernormal*. New York: Creative Age Press, 1949.

_____. Ed. *Beyond the Five Senses*. Philadelphia: J. B. Lippencott Co., 1957.

Glaskin, G. M. *Windows of the Mind: The Christos Experience*. London: Wildwood, 1974.

Goldberg, Bruce. *New Age Hypnosis,*. St. Paul: Llewellyn Publications, 1998.

_____. *Peaceful Transition: The Art of Conscious Dying & the Liberation of the Soul*. St. Paul: Llewellyn Publications, 1997.

_____. *Soul Healing*. St. Paul: Llewellyn Publications, 1996.

_____. *The Search For Grace: The True Story of Murder and Reincarnation*. St. Paul: Llewellyn Publications, 1997.

_____. *Past Lives—Future Lives*. New York: Ballantine Books, 1988.

_____. "Slowing down the aging process through the use of altered states of consciousness: a review of the medical literature." *Psychology—A Journal of Human Behavior*, 1995, 32(2): 19–22.

_____. "Regression and progression in past life therapy." *National Guild of Hypnotists Newsletter*, 1994, Jan/Feb, 1, 10.

_____. "Quantum physics and its application to past life regression and future life progression hypnotherapy." *Journal of Regression Therapy*, 1993, 7(1): 89–93.

_____. "The treatment of cancer through hypnosis." *Psychology— A Journal of Human Behavior*, 1985,3(4): 36–39.

_____. "Depression: a past life cause." *National Guild of Hypnotists Newsletter*, 1993, Oct/Nov, 7, 14.

_____. "The clinical use of hypnotic regression and progression in hypnotherapy." *Psychology—A Journal of Human Behavior*, 1990, 27 (1), 43–48.

_____. "Your problem may come from your future: a case study." *Journal of Regression Therapy*, 1990, 4(2): 21–29.

Gore, Belinda. *Ecstatic Body Postures: An Alternate Reality Workbook.* Santa Fe: Bear & Co., 1995.

Green, Celia. *Out-of-the-Body Experiences.* Oxford, England: Institute of Psychophysical Research, 1968.

Greenhouse, Herbert B. *The Book of Psychic Knowledge.* New York: Taplinger Publishing Co., 1973.

_____. *In Defense of Ghosts.* New York: Simon and Schuster, 1970.

Gurney, Edmund, F. W. H. Myers, and Frank Podmore. *Phantasms of the Living.* London: Trubner and Co., 1886.

Hall, Prescott. "Digest of spirit teachings received through Mrs. Minnie E. Keeler," *Journal of the American Society for Psychical Research*, 1916, 10: 632–60, 679–708.

_____. "Experiments in Astral Projection," *Journal of the American Society for Psychical Research*, 1918, 12: 39–60.

Hartwell, John, Joseph Janis, and Blue Harary. "A study of the physiological variables associated with OBE's," paper prepared for the 1974 convention of the Parapsychological Association, Jamaica, NY.

Heim, A. "Notizen ober den tod durch Absturz. Jahrbuch des schewizerischen," *Alpclub*, 1892, 27: 327–337. Translated, *Omega* 1972, 3: 45–52.

Hemingway, Ernest. *A Farewell to Arms.* New York: Charles Scribner's Sons, 1929.

Hocking, William E. *The Meaning of Immortality in Human Experience.* New York: Harper and Bros., 1957.

Honorton, C. "Psi and internal attention states," *Handbook of Parapsychology,* ed. B. Wolman. New York: Van Nostrand, 1977.

Jaffe, Aniela. *Apparitions and Precognition.* New Hyde Park, NY: University Books, 1963.

Johnson, R. *Watcher on the Hills.* London: Hodder & Stoughton, 1959.

Kiesler, E. "Images of the night," *Science* (1980), 80, 1436–43.

Kübler-Ross, Elisabeth. *On Death and Dying.* New York: Macmillan, 1969.

Kuthumi. *Studies of the Human Aura.* Colorado Springs: Summit Lighthouse, 1975.

LaBerge, Stephen. *Lucid Dreaming.* Los Angeles: Jeremy P. Tarcher, 1985.

LaMothe, John D. "Controlled Offensive Behavior—U.S.S.R., U.S. Defense Intelligence Agency (*Unclassified)," prepared by the U.S. Army, Office of the Surgeon General, Medical Intelligence Office. Washington D.C., July 1972 (#CT–CS–01–169–72).

Larsen, Caroline. *My Travels in the Spirit World.* Rutland, VT: Charles E. Tuttle Co., 1927.

Leadbeater, Charles W. *Dreams: What They Are and How They Are Caused.* London: Theosophical Society, 1903.

Lindbergh, Charles. *Autobiography of Values.* New York: Harcourt Brace Jovanovich, 1978.

Mishlove, J. *The Roots of Consciousness.* New York: Random House, 1975.

Mitchell, Janet. "Out of the body vision," *Psychic,* April 1973.

Monahan, Evelyn, with Terry Bakken. *Put Your Psychic Power to Work.* Chicago: Nelson-Hall Co., 1973.

Monroe, Robert. *Journeys Out of the Body.* Garden City, NY: Doubleday & Company, 1971.

Moody, Raymond. *Life After Life.* New York: Bantam, 1975.

Morrell, Ed. *The Twenty-fifth Man.* Montclair, NJ: New Era Publishing Co., 1924.

Morris, Robert. Paper prepared for the 1973 convention of the Paraphychological Association, Durham, NC.

_____. "Survival research at the psychical research foundation," *Newsletter,* ASPR, Summer 1973, No. 18.

Muldoon, Sylvan. *The Case for Astral Projection.* Chicago: Aries Press, 1936.

Muldoon, Sylvan, and Hereward Carrington. *The Phenomena of Astral Projection.* London: Rider and Co., 1951.

Mumford, Jonn. *A Chakra & Kundalini Workbook.* St. Paul: Llewellyn Publications, 1994.

_____. *Magical Tattwa Cards: A Complete System for Self-Development.* St. Paul: Llewellyn Publications, 1996.

Myers, F. W. H. *Human Personality and Its Survival of Bodily Death.* London: Longmans, Green, 1903.

Osis, K. and E. Haraldsson. *At the Hour of Death.* New York: Avon, 1977.

Ostrom, Joseph. *You and Your Aura.* Northamptonshire, England: The Aquarian Press, 1987.

Owen, Robert Dale. *Footfalls on the Boundary of Another World.* Philadelphia: J. B. Lippincott Co., 1860.

Palmer, John. "ESP and out-of-body experiences: EEG correlates," *Research in Parapsychology–1978.* Metuchen, NJ: Scarecrow Press, 1979.

Palmer, John, and R. Lieberman. "The influence of psychological set on ESP and out-of-body experiences." *Journal of the American Society for Psychical Research,* 1975, 69, 193–213.

_____. "ESP and out-of-body experiences: a further study in research," *Parapsychology–1975*. Metuchen, NJ: Scarecrow Press, 1976.

Palmer, John, and C. Vasser. "ESP and out-of-body experiences: An exploratory study," *Journal of the American Society for Psychical Research*, 1974, 68: 257–80.

Plato. *Phaedo*. Trans. R. Hackforth. London: Cambridge University Press, 1955.

_____. *The Republic*. Trans. Richard W. Sterling. New York: Norton, 1996.

Plutarch. *On the Delay of Divine Justice*. Trans. Andrew P. Peabody. Boston: Little Brown & Co., 1885.

Powell, A. E. *The Etheric Double*. Wheaton: The Theosophical Publishing House, 1925.

_____. *The Astral Body*. Wheaton: The Theosophical Publishing House, 1927.

Ramacharaka, Y. *Fourteen Lessons in Yogi Philosophy*. Chicago: The Yoga Publication Society, 1903.

Ring, Kenneth. *Life at Death*. New York: Quill, 1982.

Roberts, H. C. *The Complete Prophecies of Nostradamus*. Jericho, NY: Nostradamus, Inc., 1947.

Rogo, D. Scott, "Astral projection in Tibetan Buddhist literature," *International Journal of Parapsychology*, Vol. 10, No. 3, Autumn 1968: 27–84.

_____, Ed. "Experiments with Blue Harary." *Mind Beyond the Body*. New York: Penguin, 1978.

_____. *Mind Beyond the Body*. New York: Penguin, 1978.

Roos, A. M. *The Possibility of Miracles*. London: Faber and Faber, 1930.

Rossi, E. L. *Dreams and the Growth of Personality*. New York: Pergamon, 1972.

Sabom, Michael. *Recollections of Death*. New York: Harper & Row, 1981.

Schueler, Gerald, and Betty Schueler. *Egyptian Magick: Enter the Body of Light & Travel the Magical Universe*. St. Paul: Llewellyn Publications, 1989.

Schwarz, Jack. *Human Energy Systems*. New York: Dutton, 1980.

Sculthorp, Frederick C. *Excursions to the Spirit World*. London: Greater World Association, 1961.

Sherrington, Sir Charles. *Man on His Nature*. London: Cambridge University Press, 1940.

Shirley, Ralph. *The Mystery of the Human Double*. London: Rider and Co., 1938.

Smith, Mark. *In A New Light*. Bethesda, MD: Aurora Pub., 1995.

Smith, Susy. *The Enigma of Out-of-Body Travel*. New York: Garrett-Helix, 1965.

_____. *Out-of-Body Experiences for the Millions*. Los Angeles: Sherbourne Press, 1968.

Smyth, P. *The Great Pyramid: Its Secrets and Mysteries Revealed*. New York: Dell Publishing, 1990.

Spraggett, Allen. *The Unexplained*. New York: New American Library, 1967.

Stead, W. T. *Borderland*. New Hyde Park, NY: University Books, 1970.

_____. *Real Ghost Stories*. London: Carlyle Press, 1897.

Swann, Ingo. *To Kiss Earth Good-Bye*. New York: Hawthorne, 1975.

Targ, R., and Harold Puthoff. "Remote Viewing of Natural Targets." In L. Oteri (Ed.)., *Quantum Physics and Parapsychology* (New York: Parapsychology Foundations, 1975.

Tart, Charles. "A second psychophysiological study of out-of-the-body experiences in a gifted subject," *International Journal of Parapsychology*, 1967, 9: 251–58.

Ten Dam, Hans. *Exploring Reincarnation*. Middlesex, England: Penguin Books, 1990.

Twitchell, Paul. *Eckankar: The Key to Secret Worlds*. San Diego: Illuminated Way Press, 1969.

Tylor, E. *Primitive Culture*. London: J. Murray, 1871.

Tyrell, G. N. M. *Apparitions*. Society for Psychical Research, 1953.

Wereide, Thorstein. "Norway's human doubles," *Tomorrow*, Winter 1995, Vol. 3, No. 2: 23–29.

Whiteman, J. H. M. *The Mystical Life*. London: Faber and Faber, 1961.

Wills, Arthur J. *Life, Now and Forever*. London: Rider and Co., 1942.

Yogananda, Paramahansa. *Autobiography of a Yoga*. Los Angeles: Self-Realization Pub., 1974.

Yram. *Practical Astral Projection*. London: Rider and Co., 1935.

Index

Llewellyn publishes hundreds of books
on your favorite subjects.

LOOK FOR THE CRESCENT MOON

to find the one you've been searching for!

To find the book you've been searching for, just call or write for a FREE copy of our full-color catalog, *New Worlds of Mind & Spirit. New Worlds* is brimming with books and other resources to help you develop your magical and spiritual potential to the fullest! Explore over eighty exciting pages that include:

- **Exclusive interviews, articles and "how-to's" by Llewellyn's expert authors**

- **Features on classic Llewellyn books**

- **Tasty previews of Llewellyn's latest books on astrology, Tarot, Wicca, shamanism, magick, the paranormal, spirituality, mythology, alternative health and healing, and more**

- **Monthly horoscopes by Gloria Star**

- **Plus special offers available only to *New Worlds* readers**

To get your free *New Worlds* catalog, call 1-800-THE MOON

or send your name and address to

Llewellyn, P.O. Box 64383, St. Paul, MN 55164–0383

Many bookstores carry *New Worlds*— ask for it! Visit our web site at www.llewellyn.com.

LLEWELLYN
New Worlds of Mind and Spirit